GOD
in
PUBLIC

William R. Coats

Political Theology Beyond Niebuhr

WILLIAM B. EERDMANS
PUBLISHING COMPANY
Grand Rapids, Michigan

Library of Congress Cataloging in Publication Data

Coats, William R   1936-
  God in public: political theology beyond Niebuhr.

  Bibliography: p. 201.
  1. Christianity and politics. 2. United States—
Economic conditions—1945- 3. Socialism, Christian.
I. Title.
BR115.P7C58   261.7   74-632
ISBN 0-8028-3440-X

The publisher gratefully acknowledges permission to quote from the following
sources:
Hannah Arendt, *The Human Condition,* © 1958 by the University of Chicago;
used by permission of the publisher, Doubleday & Company, Inc. Hannah
Arendt, *On Violence,* © 1969, 1970 by Hannah Arendt; used by permission of the
publisher, Harcourt Brace Jovanovich, Inc. Peter Berger, *The Sacred Canopy,* ©
1967 by Peter L. Berger; used by permission of the publisher, Doubleday &
Company, Inc. Ernst Bloch, *Man on His Own,* © 1970 by Herder and Herder,
Inc., and used by permission of the publisher, The Seabury Press, New York. E.
Lampert, *The Apocalypse of History,* 1948; used by permission of Faber and
Faber Ltd. C. B. Macpherson, *The Real World of Democracy,* © 1966 by Oxford
University Press. Herbert Marcuse, *Essay on Liberation,* © 1969 by Herbert
Marcuse; used by permission of the publisher, Beacon Press. Wolfhart Pannen-
berg, *Jesus, God and Man,* Copyright MCMLXVIII by The Westminster
Press. Charles A. Reich, *The Greening of America,* © 1970 by Charles A. Reich;
used by permission of the publisher, Random House, Inc. Joan Robinson,
Freedom and Necessity, © 1970 by George Allen and Unwin Ltd.; used by
permission of Pantheon Books, a Division of Random House, Inc. Scripture
quotations are from the Revised Standard Version of the Bible, copyrighted 1946,
1952 and © 1971, by the Division of Christian Education of the National Council
of the Churches of Christ in the U.S.A. and used by permission.

CONTENTS

FOREWORD

If you belong to that company of people who, in spite of the evidence to the contrary, still look to the Christian heritage for power to break open a closed-in world, to push men and women to new perceptions of reality, to transform radically their values and open up new possibilities of meaning and purpose for their lives—*read this book*. If you have given up any such hope, but are still haunted by a Christian memory that will not go away—give this book a chance to address you.

William Coats is convinced that a particular Christian approach to life and the world has something very significant to contribute to our situation in America today. He knows full well that what he presents flies directly in the face of the dominant trends in our religious life. And he dares to speak out in hope that his words will stimulate us to make new connections with elements in our Christian history which have long been ignored, but which have a strange power to grasp us in times of personal and social disintegration.

Many of us have reached a point where we are tired of history, tempted to settle for survival or seek a new experience of "Life" in some realm detached from history. Over against this, Coats calls us back to the burden of historical involvement as an inescapable Christian stance. He contends that our heritage compels us to recognize that man's destiny is an historical one; that God wills the transformation of all earthly hopes; and that human freedom is inextricably bound up with the shaping of the *polis*. He also reminds us that, in choosing this road, we are not destined to be overwhelmed by an impossible burden but rather to be surprised again and again by grace.

At a time when an increasing number of men and women are latching onto religion to provide a shelter from the threat of personal and social disintegration, and to give new credibility to the American dream when it has become, for many, not a promise but a nightmare, Coats challenges us to move in a quite different direction. He presents, in a compelling way, the main lines of a well-established tradition offering a new vision of personal vocation and national destiny, available on the other side of the breakdown of the present order of things.

He is able to do this as he explores—and re-interprets—the peculiar perspective on *life in time* provided by Biblical eschatology. It is this perspective which creates a special sensitivity to closed-in situations, and provides antennae for perceiving qualitatively new possibilities breaking into the present out of the future. Anyone who perceives his or her world in this way gives special attention to the contradictions built into the present order of things, and dares to press those contradictions until a new social vision emerges and begins to set the terms for political action.

For most of us, life in time is a movement toward sclerosis and death. In the perspective of Christian eschatology, death is brought into the center of life again and again; as we pass through it we experience resurrection, the possibility of a new start. This frees human intentionality to expand and grow as we move toward a future of promise. "Time," in the words of the author, "is duration pointing toward meaning." A break with the conditions imposed by the given order of things, which implies discontinuity, offers us a way to re-connect with our past and discover, in it, power for creation.

For William Coats, eschatology becomes the central element in social ethics, especially in a time of crisis. It frees us from the necessity to seek solutions to our problems within the given parameters. Deriving its norms from "the end of time," such an ethical stance exposes the limitations of the options open to us within the established order, stirs our imagination, and forces us into the struggle to give shape to new forms of social, economic, and political organization which move in the direction of greater freedom, equality, and justice. It also turns our attention toward the poor and the dispossessed, the victims of the present order, as those who witness to God's judgment on our society and are the bearers of a new social vision as well as of the power for transformation. As Coats puts it, the new age appears in and from the outcasts.

In recent years, a number of theologians in America and Europe have been captivated by this eschatological approach and have written a great deal about it. What William Coats does in this book is unique because he relates it directly to our historical experience. By dealing specifically with the character of the American experience and American politics, he follows in the steps of Reinhold Niebuhr, at the same time that he attempts to spring free from the boundaries and solutions established by Niebuhr. By looking at our history from an eschatological perspective he is able, not only to provide us with a new interpretation of how and where we went wrong, but also to distinguish sharply between the liberal and radical vision. As he sees it, the liberals, including Niebuhr, stayed within the parameters set by bourgeois society, thus affirming too strongly our American individualism, and counting on the state to solve our political problems.

Coats challenges us to probe more deeply into the problem. For him the democracy we have affirmed implies equality, but our capitalistic system, based upon the idea of the free market and depending upon motivation coming from an hierarchical type of remuneration, creates increasing inequality. Consequently, democracy has been replaced by the myth of *social* equality coupled with the hope of future affluence for all; property and wealth are concentrated in fewer hands, leading to the extension of class privilege; and this same system operates in our relations with the countries of the third world, leading to the internationalization of gross inequality.

As America was not burdened with the remnants of the feudal system nor by powerful traditions, this new world, wide open to growth and initiative, offered tremendous possibilities for the realization of freedom. But the ethos of capitalism provided few resources for a rich vision or experience of freedom. Freedom was reduced to economic individualism; those persons caught up in that pursuit gradually lost control of more and more of life. Today, this poverty is legitimized by technology, which makes the present process appear inevitable no matter how far it goes in dehumanizing us.

Our early industrial development occurred in the context of an attitude of confidence in the world, a product of the Christian view of life and history. As our bourgeois society developed, however, reality was identified with fact and appearance, and the basis of human confidence in the world shifted to success or failure in economic advancement; worth was determined by outward signs.

William Coats perceives these as fundamental contradictions in our present society, contradictions which, if not overcome, will prove increasingly destructive to our existence as human beings, to our American society, and to the rest of the world. To follow this path is to head toward social death. For America to have a future means we must break out of the circle of contradictions in which we are caught, face and go through the breakdown of the present order, and create a more just and human society on the other side. Christian faith offers such a vision and calls us to work for, and expect, a new day of greater freedom and equality for ourselves and others along this road. This is the only road open to us if we hope to move toward the fulfillment of the "promise of American life."

Coats is well aware that preaching and moral persuasion will not bring about such a change of perception or of politics. This can come only as we are confronted by groups and movements which are bearers of God's judgment and offer us signs of promise for the future, and if we have eyes to see them. For him, the poor in our own society have that vocation. They are the ones who bear witness, in and through their suffering, that the present order is moving toward death. They possess the secret of the kingdom as bearers of judgment and signs of the promise of change. In a dramatic reversal of their fate, shattering the forms of the present age, lies the dawn of a new freedom.

Likewise, the Vietcong have fulfilled that vocation for us in regard to our relations with the third world. Confronted by them, we can discover that no powerful nation has, in itself, the resources to overcome its own failings or to perceive a radically new possibility for itself or for the world. Confronted by the Vietcong we can also realize that our future as a nation depends upon a fundamental change in power relationships. As the new nations find their place in the world and share in the exercise of power, they may lead the way to the development of new structures of economic, social, and political life which, in the long run, will benefit all of us.

In the midst of an apocalyptic situation such as is ours in America today, Christians who experience the present as the occasion for perceiving and giving form to a new future have a unique opportunity and responsibility. They can discern—and identify themselves with—those movements which reveal something of God's ultimate purpose for all people; they can contribute to a re-interpretation of our American experience which frees us from the limitations of our present system, and pushes us toward more creative responses to the new challenges facing us.

William Coats is quite specific about the shape of that new social order: an egalitarian society, one in which a vision of human equality is implemented throughout our social, economic, and political institutions. And the name for that new order is socialism. Not socialism as it now exists in any of the communist countries, where it has been distorted by scarcity in the early stages of industrial development and by the perversion of bureaucratic party control. But socialism as it can come into being in America as society is re-structured in the direction of economic equality, the eradication of classes, the abolition of the wage system, the end of privilege and exploitation, the participation of an increasing number of people in determining their economic and political destiny, and the establishment of more authentic egalitarian human relationships. A society in which personal identity is defined in terms of service to the common good, in which personality develops in sharing with others rather than in competition, and in which the social ownership of the means of production allows the energies of the self to be associated primarily with other people rather than with things.

In other words, socialism gives shape to Christian hope as the resolution of the specific contradictions of American capitalism at this stage in history. And for Coats, vital Christian faith will contribute significantly to the shaping of that vision, to the struggle to make it a reality, and to the maintenance of concern for social justice all along the way. This does not lead him to propose some type of Christian socialism over against Marxism or to emphasize the importance of Christian-Marxist dialogue. If I read him correctly, what is important for him *theologically* is his conviction that a serious confrontation with Marx and Marxism is essential for Christian self-understanding. Marx gave concrete secular form to central elements of a Christian eschatological perspective which most of us have long since forgotten: the drive to overcome the contradictions in a given social order by radical transformation of structures; the connection of the future of history with the fate of the oppressed and despised classes; and the combination of confidence in human history and human effort which gives power to the proletariat in their long and arduous struggle.

I confess that I am fascinated by this book and by what I believe it can contribute to our efforts to find our way in Christian social thought at this time. Rubem Alves and others have spoken of the power of theological language as language of protest and utopia. Coats has demonstrated this power in relation to the contemporary American scene. He has also demonstrated, once again, the power of the Christian tradition to provide resources for transcending the boundaries in which it has become enclosed, thus raising new issues, pushing toward changes in perception, and contributing to new social vision as well as new forms of political action. I hope this book will be widely read and discussed.

For me, the important thing is not whether we agree with all that the author has to say, or even whether we buy the solution he offers at the end. What is important is that we are shaken out of our lethargy, that we are confronted by perspectives and insights that get us moving beyond where we now are, and that we take a fresh look at our Christian history and allow it to speak to us. As we do this, it is just possible that we will experience, in our reflection on society, something akin to the early Barth's discovery of "the strange new world of the Bible"—an encounter with historical events and their interpretation which radically challenges and transforms our perception.

As one step along this road of revitalization of our theological reflection on society, I suggest that we not only read what Coats has to say but that we engage in a critical dialogue with him. If we do that, we will learn a great deal from him; we will be stimulated to work harder at finding our way; and, in the process, we may also be compelled to carry the discussion beyond where he, at least in this volume, leaves us. Let me suggest very briefly a few points at which this might happen:

1. In my own reading of where we are in America today, I would give much more attention to *process* than to proposals for alternative structures. I find myself surrounded by men and women who have been brought up on the American dream, with all the internalization of values and of expectations that goes with it. Now they see that the dream is largely unrealizable and that

the achievement of the goals it sets brings not fulfillment but tremendous frustration and despair. To offer these people an alternative model for American society does not prove very helpful. What they need is to discover resources in themselves and in their relations with other people which will enable them to question radically their own expectations and values, to get a new sense of what is important and fulfilling for them, and to find energy and courage to follow out their new intuitions. A revolution is not just the transfer of power from one group to another in society, with the consequent re-structuring of the social order that goes with it. A revolution is essentially the creation of a new human type, and the re-structuring of relationships and of institutions which gives expression to this new human reality. If that is what we want for America, then the major question we must face is this: By what process of transformation do we begin to move from here to there—in our personal lives and in the communities to which we belong?

2. I am appalled by the irrationality and the destructiveness of American capitalism and I find Coats' proposed alternative to it a very attractive one. I would rejoice to see us moving toward the sort of egalitarian society he outlines. But I am not at all sure that Marxism and socialism will be as useful as he imagines, either to provide us with adequate categories for the analysis and critique of the established order, or to offer us the tools we need for the creation of alternatives and for experimentation with them. I too would like to have some trustworthy categories for thought and models for social re-organization. But I am not at all sure I can settle for any of those now available. And part of my reason for not doing so is that I am compelled to apply the same eschatological perspective presented in this book to the development of socialism as well. Marxism was an eschatological response to the problems arising as Western capitalism set the terms for the early stages of the process of industrialization. But we, at least in America, are today facing the realities of a "post-industrial" era. Our prophetic task is to perceive how and where the eschatological future is breaking into *these* structures. Is our major problem who owns the means of production or the productive process itself? Should we be primarily concerned about who controls the tools or the structure of the tools themselves? Why has bureaucracy become such a dehumanizing and conservative force in socialist as well as capitalist societies? These and other questions do not invalidate what Coats is working for. But they do suggest, for me at least, that the much needed interaction with Marxism which he calls for should push us to define a new set of questions. It is in formulating and working on those questions that the power of socialism, as well as of other ideologies, will be tested.

3. When I was in a revolutionary situation in Brazil a number of years ago, I tried to offer Christian students the sort of theological undergirding Coats presents in this book. Eventually I discovered that many of those involved in

the revolutionary struggle lost interest in what I had to say. In trying to understand what was happening, I concluded that participation in revolutionary politics accentuated our experience of the radical historicizing of life which a number of philosophers and theologians described at the turn of the century. In this political involvement it soon became clear that our traditional theological categories belong to a quite different world, as does also our way of thinking about life and the world. For me, this in no way invalidates the theological stance Coats presents in this book. That theology had a power to shape thought and transform life which we desperately need today. But, if I am correct about the change in human consciousness that is now occurring, then our theological work must begin with our experience in the struggle for personal and social liberation and develop as we engage in an ongoing dialogue with a broken-down tradition. In other words, our theological heritage will have power for us only as we attempt to re-invent it, only as it is articulated in a new language which names and interprets the future that is breaking open our present order and transforming it.

That task may claim the rest of our lives, so we should not be critical of William Coats if he does not do it for us. If we take him seriously, we will find ourselves in a context in which we will be forced to tackle this problem. We will also, I believe, be working on the right issues and be focusing our attention on those elements of the tradition that are of most value to us at this time. If this book can do that much for us, it will make a decisive contribution.

—Richard Shaull

INTRODUCTION

Knowledge has no light save that which shines upon the world from the standpoint of redemption: all else exhausts itself in imitation and remains a piece of technique. Perspectives must be created in which the world looks changed and alien and reveals its cracks and flaws in much the way as it will one day be destitute and disfigured in Messiah's light. To attain such perspective without arbitrariness or force, entirely out of sensitiveness towards things—that alone is the aim of thought.   —T. W. Adorno

Behold he is coming with the clouds and every eye will see him.
                                                    —The Revelation of John

1

Political theology, properly speaking, is theological meditation on the work of God in the public arena. It refers to the *polis,* that is, to the arena of visible, corporate action, in the scheme of God's grace. Further, since it assumes that the full development of man involves activity beyond the personal or private sphere, political theology points to the efficacy of grace which extends beyond the life of the family or the private affairs of the individual. Political theology focuses on the juncture where historical conditions, in their political, economic, and social form, affect human life and where human destiny assumes a public, as opposed to a merely private, character. In order to conduct this meditation, political theology should draw upon the Old Testament conviction that man's true destiny is an historical one, the New Testament apocalyptic hope that God wills the transformation of all earthly affairs, and the classical view that human freedom is inextricably bound up with the role of the citizen, not in the affairs of the household—which for the Greeks was the realm of necessity—but in the shaping of the *polis.*[1]

15

Christianity has not generally included the political dimension in its theological scheme. This is not so much because of the so-called otherworldliness of Christian theology, but because during its crucially formative years in the Hellenistic world Christianity emerged as a religion of the household. The majority of the earliest converts to Christianity were slaves, or else drawn from the urban proletariat. They came, that is, from those whom the ancient world believed to be a part of the realm of necessity, the dimension of labor which was concerned not with freedom but with matters of basic human need. In this realm both household duties and familial virtues represented the highest ideals.* As a result public virtues were practically ignored, and early Christian ethics remained the ethics of the household and not the ethics of the city or the empire.

In these circumstances it was extremely difficult for the explicit political nature of the Old Testament or the social nature of New Testament apocalypticism to come to expression. It is true that from time to time Christians prayed for public officials,[2] dealt with political authorities, and even resisted constituted authority; but these activities had only the most incidental impact on the general course of theology. Indeed, even in the case of early Christian martyrs, it is hard to characterize their actions as political in the fullest sense of the word, inasmuch as they drew their strength, not from an intention to seize or affect political power, but from a strong desire to be left alone. In any case, the political sphere, properly understood, was closed to the early Christians, and theology was separate from political matters. Thus, Tertullian was correct when he proclaimed with his accustomed frankness: "no matter is more alien to us than what matters publicly."[3]

The alliance of Christianity with organized political authority in the fourth century brought to an end the division between theology and politics. Henceforth, both the wider constituency of the Catholic Church and the Church's increasing role in political affairs dictated a shift in theological understanding. For over a millennium theology wrestled with the problems of power, authority and economic form. Thus, however much one may speak of the otherworldliness of traditional medieval theology, one should not overlook the degree to which that theology also recognized a political dimension.[4]

It is only in the modern period that we are, once again, faced with a radical separation between theological thought and political life. While this separation can be ultimately traced back to the early days of Christian

---

*The recitation of ethical virtues in Romans, I Corinthians, and the Pastoral Epistles gives clear testimony to the private nature of Christianity. Even when public virtues are mentioned—as in Romans 13 or I Peter 2—the tone is clearly passive, with docility and obedience encouraged above all else. The only public work of the early Christians is that of the Divine Liturgy. However, even here it is quite distinct from the affairs of the city or empire.

expansion in the Roman empire when the public and private spheres were sharply divided, it is most properly understood in terms of major developments within contemporary Western society.

The astute observations of G. W. F. Hegel and Karl Marx on the tumultuous effects of the growth of bourgeois society are pertinent here. Both men reported that bourgeois society brought about the emancipation of the individual from the substantive ties of the medieval order. They correctly foresaw that modern society would rest on the notion of the self-subsistent individual pursuing selfish ends without reference to any societal interest. They noted that individualism was the product of the laws of movement of the emerging civil society. Marx summed up these developments in his classic description of the Rights of Man, one of the great products of the French Revolution:

> None of the so-called rights of man goes . . . beyond the egoistic man, who as a member of civil society, withdraws into himself, his private interest and his private arbitrary will and is an individual separated from the community. . . . Society . . . appears as a framework external to the individual, as a restriction on his original independence. The only bond that holds men together is natural necessity, need and private interest, and the preservation of their property and their egoistic persons.[5]

Both Hegel and Marx understood the development of bourgeois society to be the result of the rise of capitalism. They gave clear expression to the primary significance of economic activity: to the amassing of wealth made possible by the sanctity accorded property and capital. Both individualism and class antagonism were the products of capitalist development. "When civil society," Hegel noted, "operates without impediment . . . the amassing of wealth increases . . . on the one hand; whereas, on the other hand, there is an intensification of the subdivision and restriction of labor of a specific kind, and consequently an intensification of the dependence and need of the class tied to this kind of work."[6]

While Marx and Hegel outlined the contours of bourgeois society similarly, they offered significantly different solutions to the contradictions of that society. Hegel proposed to end the separation between individualism and substantive morality, as well as the antagonism inherent in the growing class conflict, through loyalty to the state. For Hegel, the state would serve to check blind egoism and provide a center of unity which transcended particular class interests. He offered a "fusion of the substantial and particular" in which "my obligation to the State becomes at one and the same time the existence of my particular freedom." "The principle of modern states," he asserted, "has immense strength and depth inasmuch as it allows the principle of subjectivity to realize itself in the self-sufficient extreme of personal particularity, at the same time bringing it back to the substantive unity and thus maintaining substantial unity in the principle of subjectivity itself."[7] For Hegel public morality and private interests came together at the level of the state.

Hegel's solution, however, failed to resolve the dilemmas of bourgeois society. His statism posited a mystical, but not a real; solution to societal problems, because he left untouched the question whether the state was more than a mystical ideal. He overlooked the possibility that under historical conditions the state would operate as a political apparatus and reinforce, rather than resolve, the contradictions of bourgeois society. As an ideal the state may very well promote an intense loyalty which appears, at least psychologically, to reconcile individual and societal interests; but on a more profound level it does not successfully deal with individualism and class frustration. These are material matters, securely rooted in socio-economic life. As such, they demand more than mystical or psychological solutions.

For these reasons Marx felt that Hegel had inadequately dealt with the conflicting dynamics of bourgeois society. Marx did not see the state as an answer to the dilemmas of civil society, but rather as another form of civil society. In his turn, Marx located the central problem in human labor* and the capitalist mode of production, and posited, contrary to Hegel, not the glorification of the state (which, at any rate, Marx took to be a new vehicle for the establishment of bourgeois power) but the growth of the proletariat, a revolutionary class which portended a new historical epoch entirely. Thus, Marx did not propose a political solution but rather an historical transcendence—the complete transformation of the basic goals, assumptions and power relations of the bourgeois epoch itself.[8] In the predicted victory of the revolutionary proletariat was to be found the historical step *beyond* the bourgeois society, economic capitalism, and the ideology of individualism. The coming classless society would end the separation between the public and private realms and introduce an era free of the human alienation perpetrated by the capitalist class. The Marxist solution, therefore, moved beyond any notion that politics was formal participation at the level of the state or involved loyalty to a central administrative apparatus. Instead, it looked toward the democratization of society itself in which public matters were as easily open to collective decision-making as private enjoyments were available to individuals. By making political matters the business of all people at the level of society, Marx intended to create the first, true, human democracy.

---

*The Lutheran doctrine of Calling in which secular work is given exalted status appears in transformed fashion in the Marxist concept that labor is not only a social activity but, in fact, the crux of the issue of human dignity. Since Marx's time it has been impossible to relegate labor to the private realm. All subsequent political theory and practice have been forced to deal with it as a central social concern.

2

With rare exceptions Christian political thought either has allied itself with the individualism and egoism that were a product of early capitalist development, or it has joined with one or another form of state activity as a means of solving political problems. Political theology has, in short, remained within the parameters set by bourgeois civil society. It has followed Adam Smith or Hegel, but it has not followed Marx.

The explanation for this is that the history of the modern era has involved the ever increasing identification of Christianity—particularly Protestant Christianity—with the bourgeois class. Indeed, so close has this alliance become, it is difficult to describe the one without reference to the other. As a result, for the last three centuries Christianity has generally been articulated in terms of the egoism, individualism and privatism Marx and Hegel saw as the prominent marks of bourgeois society. On the one hand Christianity provided a system of personal comfort for those unsettled by the economic and social upheavals of capitalist development; on the other, it offered a systematic justification for the primary economic activities of the system itself, i.e., the sanctity of private property, the prerogatives of capital, personal egoism, and economic aggrandizement. Further, it joined the commercial classes to destroy the substantive unity of the feudal age, suggesting that the goal of history was not the collective destiny of all people, but rather the achievement of the individual. As a result it exalted private actions and personal self-interest. Moreover, Christianity insisted that the exercise of private and personal virtues (those classical thought deemed inferior) was tantamount to social health. Thus, under laissez faire capitalism, Christianity persistently echoed the bourgeois contention that self-interest and individual aggrandizement were, in fact, corporate and public necessities.

This provided the basis for the political theology of both the so-called Gospel of Wealth in the late nineteenth century, and the contemporary evangelical movement associated with Billy Graham. In these schemes it is assumed that the practice of private virtues is the totality of public responsibility. In fact, it is precisely by means of a delineation of the private sphere—its duties and rights—that one arrives at an understanding of social reality. This is reflected in the ethic of Mark Hopkins: " ... the general well-being and progress of society has been in proportion to the freedom of every man to gain property. ... The acquisition of property is required by love, because it is a powerful means of benefiting others. ..."[9] It is further imbedded in the claim of Billy Graham that the substance of Christian social responsibility is the Golden Rule.[10]

But both systems, closely wedded to the individualism and fragmentation Marx and Hegel had pointed to in the new bourgeois civil society, suffer from the fact that private virtues cannot be exalted into public virtues, and that communal responsibility and destiny cannot be assured by the intensification of private effort or by the extension of private morality. Top bourgeois theologians have confused the public and private spheres, a mistake all the more regrettable in times of complex industrial growth when such confusion makes it impossible to analyze public problems.

As we saw, Hegel was aware of this difficulty and suggested its resolution in loyalty to the state; this has been the course generally adopted by Christian political thought when it has moved beyond the individualism of early capitalism. Hence, when the egoism and privatism of laissez faire capitalism became unserviceable during the American industrial age, political attention was directed toward increased state activity, and progressive theologians turned to a theological justification for the state as an instrument of human justice.

In the late nineteenth and early twentieth centuries, for example, American social Christianity relied chiefly on the state to ensure social justice.* But even as it looked toward the state to play a greater economic and political role, social Christianity defined the ultimate goal of such activity in decidedly bourgeois terms. For social Christians the purpose of extended government remained the furthering of individual interests. Thus, while they were prepared to forego the principle of the ultimate sanctity of private property, they were not prepared to call for the complete transformation of property and capital relationships which would lead to a truly historical transcendence. Their basic commitment was to formal democracy and general conceptions of moral equity. In the face of the growth of monopoly capital, they asked the state to reduce corruption, extend welfare, limit profits, guarantee fair wages and working conditions, extend the franchise, and regulate the economy. Bold moves to be sure, but none altered basic notions about property, capital, or the doctrine of individualism, or challenged privatistic and moralistic conceptions of social reality. Social Christianity held, Ralph Gabriel observes, "that man can be the master of his fate, that his only reliance is reason, that the State is his instrument and that the planned society is the solution for social ills."[11] The theology of social Christianity was able, therefore, to direct attention to matters of the public sphere, but its ultimate commitment was still to individualistic notions of freedom, and it still had ultimate confidence in the power of moral suasion and personal good will. In the final analysis, social Christianity asked the state to help restore those private virtues and opportunities which were, in fact, both products of and responsi-

*This was true of the Christian liberals and the Christian socialists whatever their other differences.

ble for the perpetuation of bourgeois civil society.* As a result, the classic goals of bourgeois liberalism were preserved.

The political theology of Reinhold Niebuhr offers another example of reliance on the instrumentality of state power. Niebuhr possessed a deeper understanding of American history and offered a more sophisticated defense of bourgeois democracy. Unlike the social Christians, Niebuhr was under no illusion about the power of moral suasion or the serviceability of liberal rationalism or individualism. His major concern was to undergird democracy with a more realistic understanding of man and history. Democracy, he argued, was a system of proximate justice which took into account both man's capacities and man's corruptions. "Democracy must be regarded . . . as a system of government which men's rational and moral capacities make possible, and . . . as a system of checks and balances which the corruptions by interest and passion make necessary."[12] For Niebuhr, state capitalism was the means of securing such a system, particularly since it occupied the middle ground between the utopian extreme of Stalinism and the ruthlessness of laissez faire capitalism. Hence, in helping to develop the post-World War Two liberal consensus Niebuhr did not rely on the state to protect bourgeois individualism, but instead looked to the state to ensure the balance and harmony between various interests, which he saw to be the particular genius of democracy.

But this did not lead to a transformed society, nor did it significantly alter the privatistic notions of politics long fostered in bourgeois society. Whatever may be said for the state as an active agent in alleviating material suffering and economic insecurity, the conception of politics that identifies state activity with political activity is restricted, because political fulfillment and public activity become equated with the affairs of the state. As a result, political participation is restricted to the process stipulated by the state, namely the vote. This narrows self-determination and mass participation to limited forms of pre-set political activity conducted sporadically. Politics becomes tantamount to state activity, and precludes, rather than enhances, the kind of full, public participation that is needed to destroy bourgeois privatism. Societal self-determination, that is, public action in its fullest sense, is sacrificed to electoral activity at the level of the state. Thus, when Niebuhrian liberals allied themselves with the state they reformed capitalism along economic lines, but did not effect a true democracy. The basic assumptions and goals of bourgeois civil society have remained in force.

*This position was reflected politically in the Progressive Movement, which demanded greater state activity in order to restore economic competition and guarantee American individualism.

3

The political theologies associated with the effects of early capitalism and with reformed, state capitalism have remained the major expressions of Christian political thought in America. Neither, in my view, points to a historical transcendence. The theology of resistance that has emerged, however, deserves consideration as a unique theology quite different from previous political theologies.

The theology of resistance, particularly as it has been elaborated by its two most articulate apologists, William Stringfellow and Daniel Berrigan,[13] offers "the state of resistance as the state of life itself."[14] That is to say, resistance to inhuman authority, particularly the state, at once exposes the inherent idolatry of the state, participates in the ultimate act of Jesus' sacrifice, and establishes at the deepest human level freedom and integrity.

Resistance theology leads to no ordinary politics. In fact, it is suspicious of political processes and political ideologies. The latter, it is held, all too often ignore the specifically human problems which alone must be resolved if political or social reality is to be stabilized as an order of freedom. Thus the theology of resistance draws on Thomas Merton:

> The basic problem is not political, it is human. . . . Political lines and barriers . . . are largely fabrications. . . . There is another dimension, a genuine reality, totally opposed to the fiction of politics: the human dimension, a dimension which politics pretends to arrogate entirely to itself.[15]

This political theology, therefore, is primarily concerned not with one or another political or economic form—which are but covers for the heretofore irresolvable dynamics of the human dimension—but with the basic matter of the soul. "Moral process . . . escalated ethical improvement, or social engineering or American dreams, or exportation of techniques. We have had enough of that; we must speak of something other, closer to the dark roots of our existence, to beginnings, to the heart of things."[16] Political resistance which is based on a lively conscience and which rises up in opposition to the power and arrogance of the state is, in itself, a form of salvation. Daniel Berrigan's political flight, for instance, was not the signal for revolution but a spiritual event which was "to become the occasion of rebirth, renunciation of wealth, conversion of heart."[17] Hence, resistance is not so much a political strategy leading to political ends, but a contextual event which lays the spiritual foundation on which a new human politics can eventually be built. The theology of resistance is, in the last analysis, a spiritual theology, because it seeks to create that freedom of the self, that rebirth, which is the goal of all history. "We are trying to get reborn . . . to allow the condition of rebirth a free play. To stand apart from the crushing weight of distraction, affluence and corrupt reward which is the reward and revenge of the world on those who fight the world."[18]

In the political imagination of the theology of resistance, Jesus' opposition to corrupt and blind authority and the defiance of Rome by the early Christian martyrs take on great significance.[19] Their struggles against the satanic power of political authority are definitive struggles for all people of conscience. In addition, their commitment to non-violence substantiates the contention that they are a humane alternative to the greed, corruption, and violence of power-hungry political authority. Jesus, the early Christian martyrs, and all others who witness for conscience exist as prototypical examples of peace and love, standing over against a strife-ridden world. For this reason Stringfellow suggests that the struggle for personal and political integrity against the demonic power of the state is not just an ethical matter concerning the extension of good in an evil world, but is in substance the eternal struggle of life against death, of resurrection against the power of death. The theology of resistance points to Jesus as the model for the transformative power of life in a world given over to death.

But does the theology of resistance lead to any such transformation? Does it embody a truly historical transcendence? For two reasons I think not.

In the first place, the particular transcendence offered by the theology of resistance is not political in any ordinary sense of the word, that is, it is not primarily concerned with the shape of the public life. True, the apologists for resistance counsel political action—usually resistance to state authority—but not for reasons associated primarily with specific political or economic form. Instead they subsume politics under spiritual *askesis* and relate political action, not to political effect, but to the demonstration of true humanity which purportedly underlies all politics. Politics, and for that matter history, is collapsed into the more promising search for salvation in the soul. The theology of resistance is a moral or spiritual theology set within a political context; it seeks to transform the political realm by means of a primary human conversion.* As Thomas Merton has suggested, this assumes that the political dimension is a fiction. Thus, little attention is given in resistance theology to the autonomy of the political realm, its development and history, and the objective state of its laws. This means that, apart from slogans, the question of the form of earthly justice receives scant consideration. But one can ignore the full dimension of political reality only at the greatest peril. Politics has its own life and cannot be reduced to any so-called human dimension; rather it must be confronted on its own terms. By ignoring the complexity of political life, the theology of resistance perpetuates the divorce between theology and politics.

*Ironically, in a manner not dissimilar to that of evangelical Christianity.

Secondly, the theology of resistance contributes to a serious misreading of the political situation of Jesus and the early church. Both Jesus and the early martyrs are seen as resisters to the demonic power of the state. This is not completely accurate, however, for on the one hand the all-encompassing reality we now ascribe to the modern state was not present in first-century Palestine, and on the other hand Jesus' primary dispute was not with Roman officials—that is, with the state—but with the customs and authority of Jewish civil society. Jesus was not a revolutionary or a martyr for non-violence; rather he was a prophet in the apocalyptic tradition who clashed with the Jewish religious tradition. It is wrong to limit Jesus' role to that of a political rebel (for which there is hardly any scriptural evidence), or a nationalistic patriot, or a non-violent anarchist testifying to the supremacy of conscience. Similarly, the early Christian martyrs were not challenging the state, fostering national uprisings, or espousing the end to Roman society. They asked only to be left alone, hardly a radical position.

This is not to say that Jesus' life and teaching are without revolutionary implications. Clearly, they have radical consequences, but not in the way the theology of resistance sees it. Jesus' political significance is not to be found in his relationship to the state or in his witness to conscience; rather it is to be found in his relationship with the Jewish social structure and its political aspirations concerning the coming kingdom of God. Within the context of the prevailing tradition, Jesus' apocalyptic hope that the kingdom involved an earthly transformation in which the poor and despised were centrally favored was clearly unacceptable. By linking the promises of God with the fate of society's outcasts, Jesus at once undermined sacred customs and threatened the social order. The ruling strata of Jewish society could not ignore such a challenge. It was with civil society and not the state that Jesus was at odds. And it is in this context that we shall find Jesus' political importance. When the theology of resistance narrows politics to the issue of resistance to the state, that is, equates public affairs with the affairs of the state,* it distorts the true political nature of the Gospel and confuses the responsibility of present-day Christians in the political arena. The primary difficulty with resistance theology, therefore, is that it confuses the state with society, resistance with politics, and the non-violent aspect of Jesus' life with the full range of his ministry. As a result, the theology of resistance fails to point to a true historical transcendence.

---

*This confusion can be traced back to Karl Barth's 1938 essay "Church and State,"[20] in which the great German theologian tends to equate politics with state activity. Jacques Ellul rightly argues that "there is a world of difference between the state and political activity," and that Barth has been a primary source of this confusion.[21]

4

Political theology must still overcome other major obstacles if it is to embody a genuine historical transcendence. These difficulties are related to whether the Christian tradition can remain truly historical in its basic orientation or must succumb to some mystical interpretation of existence.

One of the great temptations of modern theology is to promote a religious understanding of life, one that views the basic dilemmas of the human situation as personal or human problems existing apart from political life. The anxiety or alienation of the self is, in this light, understood to be endemic to the human condition and in need of a specifically religious answer; transcendence is a purely religious category and refers to the power of theological symbols to resolve problems related to the quixotic nature of existence. History is no longer held to be a meaningful category of existence because it has ceased to be seen as the locus of ultimate meaning. That function has now been taken over by the so-called religious dimension found in the troubled soul or alienated self in its dialectic relationship to a God who exists apart from or above history.

This approach is particularly appealing to Americans who have long operated on the model of the isolated individual as the most basic substantive reality. As a result Americans continue to find it difficult to understand social reality in any meaningful sense. Likewise alienation for most Americans is a matter of the problematic nature of the self or a result of tensions at the interpersonal or familial level. Alienation is only rarely related to man as a laborer or as a member of an exploited class.* Any public form of alienation is only imperfectly understood, while essentially private forms are readily comprehended, which causes Americans to search for religious or mystical answers, i.e., answers dealing with the self or the soul or the family.

It should be acknowledged, however, that the attempt to locate meaning in the self or in the specific "human" dimension is an understandable response to a particular set of dilemmas which plague all people who live in time. Transiency, finitude and death are real problems haunting the human enterprise. As such they are indeed theological problems that cannot be

---

*One of the perplexing riddles of American life is how the frontier myths of individuality and subjectivity exercise such a powerful influence on a people whose industrial work existence is now thoroughly social or collective. Part of the answer lies in that cultural ideas even though drawn from an entirely different era remain powerful due to the influence of the media in American life. All the organs of popular expression in America are thoroughly bourgeois in their ideology and permit no extensive opportunity for different cultural ideas or myths to be presented. But further these myths remain powerful because they purposely are applied not to the work situation of the audience (television, for example, hardly ever portrays people at work) but to their non-work time, to the private sphere where they may still operate.

ultimately explained in socio-economic categories.* The persistent appearance of these factors in spite of all political solutions testifies to their endemic nature. However, the answer to these problems cannot be found by separating them from the historical context in which they manifest themselves. Nor is it possible to overlook that even their interpretation is colored by specific historical factors. To set up, therefore, some exclusive religious means by which a particular religious transcendence meets these basic problems without reference to the historical nexus in which they are imbedded, through which they are manifested and by which they are understood, is to participate in illusion. Further, to locate meaning and hope within the specifically religious dialectic of self-God or alienated existence-transcendent meaning is to deny the full reality of man and history. Death and transiency are firmly planted in the flow of history and are very much related to such matters as work and class. Only a complete transformation of historical reality, which in turn means a specifically historical understanding of existence, can establish a true human community and solve the problem of human alienation.

Much of what has been said corresponds to the long-standing theological tendency to interpret sin in exclusively ontological terms—as opposed to articulating it in its full historico-sociological dimension. By relating sin to the human condition per se in the sense that all earthly activity then becomes inherently problematic and all earthly hopes for justice impossible, theology has shortchanged the great questions associated with human freedom.

> In its official interpretation Christianity justified the discrepancy between the principles of Christ's teaching and reality on the grounds of the corruption of human nature, which made it impossible for the Kingdom of God to be realized here on earth.[23]

As a result of ignoring the sociological aspects of sin and favoring an ontological interpretation, the hope associated with the Biblical image of the kingdom of God was quite literally banished to the other world, with the matter of human justice becoming, theologically, incidental as well as being divorced from the question of the destiny of world history.

Into this vacuum in which human justice was not bound up with the question of history, moralistic visions have come to dominate the discussion concerning the form of earthly life. Moralistic conceptions assume that historical change is a relatively straightforward matter in which the witness of conscience or the power of moral suasion is sufficient for historical transfor-

---

*"On certain points," writes the Marxist philosopher Milan Machovec, "I can admit . . . that I do not know. I do not know, for example, how to deal with death in a Marxist way. I know that . . . on this all too human point the Christian tradition has achieved more than . . . Marxist atheism."[22]

mation. Unfortunately history has rarely been moved by such strategies. In the first place moral visions too often are drawn arbitrarily from the utopian fantasies of the mind, or else they arise without any regard to the historical process—its tendencies and possibilities. Secondly, history cannot be transformed by posing simple moral solutions over against a so-called evil world. Rather a full understanding of history as a process with its own potential for renewal, and a full confidence in the God who guarantees such a process, are necessary for a radical historical transcendence.

It should be noted, however, that I understand the popularity of both religious and moralistic conceptions of history not as incidental or arbitrary but rather as a product of the more general disintegration in the West of history as a comprehensive category of meaning. This crisis has been implicit in Western life and thought at least since the Enlightenment and haunts us today.[24] I am suggesting that the a-historical tendencies in understanding existence are impacted in the bourgeois world-view itself.

It was bourgeois liberalism that confidently assumed that the world was ordered and changed by the organization and effort of human good will and that the simple exercise of autonomy (divorced from crude or religious superstition) was in accord with the laws and goal of history. In other words bourgeois liberalism supposed that in winning autonomy man was at the same time gaining history. But nothing of the sort occurred. Save for the belief in progress, which lasted but a short time and which at any rate was not adhered to by the overwhelming masses of people, the belief in the efficacy of human autonomy went unaccompanied by any corresponding trust in history. Confidence in history had been rooted in belief in God, but when the Christian world-view collapsed, the seeds were planted for the eventual eclipse of historical confidence. A belief in human autonomy is nothing but a belief in the power of man and does not link up with a belief in history; on the contrary it belies a loss of confidence in history. This fact was only obscured by the doctrine of progress, a secularized belief in history, so that the eventual divorce of man from history was simply forestalled. By the twentieth century, however, this divorce could no longer be concealed; and with the collapse of confidence in history, brought about by numerous factors, the belief in human power came to be what it had always essentially been, a desperate faith in the autonomous strength of the individual will. Thus secularism became not what its original progenitors had hoped: confidence in man's power to order a new history; but instead it devolved into a hysterical flight from history, a flight which as it lost the world and history turned with ever greater desperation to the powers of the self.

The isolated self then became charged with the responsibility of marshalling good will for the creation of a new world, for the self was now the basic vantage point of all judgments. But since there was no linkage with the historical process and no confidence in history, the self was left in relation to nothing and, therefore, found itself without a vision, without a past and without a future, i.e., without that which is necessary for the creation of anything new. As a consequence of being riven from history the self was led to the repetition of the ordinary and of the known.

As a result the contemporary technocratic form of bourgeois liberalism has come to be the final resting place of all the great hopes of the bourgeois epoch. Under the prompting of technology modern liberalism has translated human autonomy into the extension of present processes. This belies its essential enclosure in the tyranny and form of the present. What else has it? Neither dreams, history, nor a vision of the future. It has only the individual thrust upon the manic exercise of will. But without confidence in history, will works itself out either in reform, which is the bland extension of present processes into the future, or despair, which is the inevitable plight of the isolated self. Neither the courage-to-be of contemporary existentialism nor the steel-willed activity of the modern technocrat can overcome the immeasurable loss man suffered when history as a category of meaning and hope was destroyed in the bourgeois age.

5

In the essays that follow, the concern for a true social democracy will be explored within the context of the American national experience. It remains to set the stage for these essays by noting the pattern of thought that ties them together.

First, a good deal of attention will be paid to Christian theology for the simple reason that any meditation on history presupposes some prior commitment and understanding. To claim that history is an arena of meaning is itself a commitment which is based less on the raw material of existence than it is derived from an a priori apprehension. Christian faith is, for this writer, that informing belief system which illuminates the course of history and establishes its ultimate importance. In this regard the central New Testament symbols of resurrection and crucifixion are crucial for historical understanding. It is the resurrection of Jesus that establishes the idea that the destiny of all people lies in historical transformation. However, since at all times history is plagued by misery and despair, the Christian understanding of resurrection is intertwined with reflection on the crucifixion. The resurrection points to the fact that life is ultimately not tragic, while the crucifixion points to the ambiguous quality of all human life. This is as true at the political level as at the personal level. Thus, theology continues to meditate on personal and political existence as it moves between the poles of tragedy and hope, despair and faith.

Secondly, since it is my desire to develop a political theology I will spend a good deal of time reflecting on the American political economy and developments within American political and social ideology. I continue to be perplexed by the absence of attention to strictly political matters among those Christians who purport to be doing political theology. By this inattention they betray a lack of true historical consciousness and rob the Gospel message of its historic hope. It is not the task of theology to transform itself, but to consider the dynamics of the transformation of human existence.

Furthermore, if there is to be such a transformation, I do not think it will be on the basis of a theology that seeks simply to justify resistance to evil. It will entail the search for Biblical insights into the nature and form of earthly justice, insights which, I am convinced, go beyond vague appeals to justice and truth. In this regard I hold equality to be a central Biblical injunction.* It is equality, or the lack thereof, which stands at the heart of present political conflict, and the vision of human equality will inform our search for a new human society.

Thirdly, in the later essays I will discuss a Christian approach to history. In my own understanding I place great importance on signs. I do not see history simply as a linear process based on the model of some scientific or moralistic evolutionary scheme. I take the course of human events to be jagged and unpredictable—but by no means pointless. Rather, I believe that signs which appear or, better, irrupt in history are meaningful. Signs occur in history which point to history's ultimate end. Hence, it is not the Christian's task so much to convert people to Christianity, as to discern and testify to those movements or events which reveal God's ultimate purpose for all people. In Christian remembrance the life, death, and resurrection of Jesus remain the ultimate signs of God's purposes for man, and those signs against which all other earthly signs are to be measured.

In this regard I lay great stress on the importance of liberation struggles throughout the world as signs of hope. I take it to be the most narrow kind of parochialism to think that the course of world history is the same thing as the history of the Western world. The progressive upheavals of our time have

*To anticipate the argument that appears in later chapters, I wish to point out a crucial distinction concerning the concept of equality. " . . . Equality of opportunity can mean very different things. It can mean an equal right to a fully human life for all who will exert themselves: on this interpretation it comes to about the same thing as the classic democratic vision of an equal society. Or [it] can mean an equal legal right to get into the competitive race for more for oneself: on this interpretation it comes to about the same thing as the classic liberal vision of the market society. . . . Everyone can be in the race, indeed everyone has to be in the race. But . . . everybody cannot be in it on equal terms. For in the nature of the capitalist market society there must be some who own the capital on which others must work."[25]

generally occurred outside the Western orbit and may very well continue to do so. One need not romanticize the so-called third world, nor see it as the source of salvation for the West, in order to understand the tremendous significance for human liberation that these struggles have.

Lastly, I wish to make it clear that I closely identify socialism with Christian hope. Implied in these essays is a great sympathy for Marxism. In this sense I do not hesitate to take an ideological stance in political matters. I am not at all impressed with the almost overwhelming opinion of Christian writers that Christianity is inherently non-ideological. This strikes me as merely another reflection of the bourgeois view that reality and progress are simple matters of pragmatic adjustments which are unrelated to ideology. In fact, even this position is an ideological one, since pragmatic solutions always end up serving certain interests at the expense of others, and reflect a particular view of how and for whom society is to be organized. As a socialist I accept, with some reservations,* a class analysis of society, and hold to the crucial importance of socio-economic matters for understanding the course of political history and political ideology.

I am further impressed with socialism because it echoes politically the Biblical dialectic involved in the relationship of the kingdom of God to man's freedom. Biblically, because God wills to bring about his kingdom, man is inspired to work for its completion. Hence, faith in God's providence, far from leading to earthly resignation, excites earthly confidence and increases human effort directed toward justice and equality.† It is not confidence in God, but the absence of such confidence, that breeds earthly resignation. The socialist view that the proletariat will emerge victorious from the struggle of history likewise combines confidence in history with human effort. It is bourgeois liberalism that has dissolved this dialectic, by substituting the achievement of the individual for the transformation of the totality of human affairs as the goal of human history. Therefore, human will has been exalted without any corresponding exaltation of history. As a result loneliness and ennui have appeared in our time—the reverse side of the coin of bourgeois activism. For this reason one can only note with sadness the persistent effort of many Christian activists, long unaware of such factors, to make moral conscience and the almost hysterical effort of the will the substance of politics. They have simply built on the weakest of liberal foundations.

---

*The reservations being, first, that I understand the working class to include more than blue-collar workers and, second, that the phenomenon of class should not be understood in narrow economic terms but includes a cultural dimension also.

†"Among people in the history of Christendom who have believed in a very strict predestination, like Cromwell for example, and the Puritans, it certainly did not produce laziness. . . ."[26]

But to the degree that contemporary socialism has deteriorated into tyranny, thus further rendering questionable both hope and confidence in the course of history, could it be that historical confidence should be restored, not by reference to liberalism or to present-day socialist experience, but from that source within Western history whence even socialism derived its basic dialectic—namely, Christianity?[27] If so, then the ironies of history which the great Reinhold Niebuhr delighted in would once more have visited our beleagured age.

PART ONE

CHRISTIAN ETHICS

Chapter One

The TRANSFIGURATION of TIME and the ETHICS of EQUALITY

For nothing can happen to birds that has not
happened before: we though are beasts with a sense of
real occasion, of beginnings and endings,
   which is the reason
we like to keep our clocks punctual, as nature's
never is. Seasons she has, but no calendar:
thus every year the strawberries ripen
   and the autumn-crocus
flares into blossom on unpredictable
dates. Such *Schlamperei* cannot be allowed an
historian: with us it's a point of honor
   to keep our birthdays
and wedding-days, to rejoice or to mourn on
the right one. . . .   —W. H. Auden

The more successfully the good and right assume concrete form, the more
they become evil and wrong.   —Karl Barth

1

Man lives in time.[1] Not time as the word has come to be used, a duration
locked between beginning and end, but the constant series of instances which
greet women and men on their pilgrimage toward death. Existence is characterized by the decay and disintegration inherent in the perpetual flux pressing
in on man at every moment. The very cadence of life—birth, growth, decay
and death—testifies to the ceaseless flux of instants which men and women
experience as the present. Time, therefore, is not the duration we measure as
an objective, self-contained unity, but the category and form of our existence
as that existence is continually threatened with disquiet, anxiety, insecurity,

meaninglessness, and decay. This is why the ancients were unable to characterize time as meaningful. Only the gods in the realm beyond time possessed ultimate meaning. Sophocles has Oedipus say:

> Only to gods in heaven
> Comes no old age, nor death of anything;
> All else is turmoiled by our master Time.
> The earth's strength fades, and manhood's glory fades. . . .[2]

Transitory time was made up of cyclical happenings which recurred in a kind of endless, eternal rhythm. Ancient peoples knew this existence as *fatum*. It was impossible to conceive of time as a thing of meaningful duration. The Biblical story testifies to this when God says to Adam: " ' . . . you are dust, and to dust you shall return' " (Gen. 3:19). Here the Bible points to the problematic quality of existence and, above all, to its relation to death, man's final destiny, which casts the ultimate shadow of meaninglessness over all existence.

In the scriptures the insecurity of Adam leads to the fratricide of Cain and the building of a city (Gen. 4:1-17). Man's social existence begins. But man's social existence is the objective counterpart of man's finite state and bears the marks of man's fear and insecurity. It is part of man's being to fashion a world, but that world is not immune to the finitude that characterizes man's life in time. Cain built a city which was characterized not only by human prowess (a sign of God's preservative grace) but also by Cain's status as a fugitive, a man in rebellion and insecurity. All of man's social life is marked by the objective presence of the misery and decay of time.[3] Therefore, time is the category of man's social *and* personal existence as it is perennially threatened with disintegration, oppression, and futility. The totality of man's existence, the complex interrelationship between personal, cultural, and political expressions, manifests and reinforces at every level the peculiar arbitrary and transitory quality of each instant of human life. In such fashion men and women are prisoners of time, prisoners of the endless decay that envelops them personally and societally; prisoners to the signs of death.

If time is but transitoriness and flux, that which follows upon the present is more mysterious and frightening than the present. Like the present it is filled with misery and futility, but, in addition, it is closer to death. Thus, a threatening future is part of living in time. But further, it leads to the paradoxical situation in which men and women, in order to preserve themselves from a dark and mysterious future, project the present, with all its problematic quality, into the future. A present that is known is better than an unknown future. As Rubem Alves notes:

Set in the provisional and finite context of human life, man fears the future. . . .

The future is the possibility of death. . . . since [man] cannot trust, the reality of insecurity and death become the *factors,* the powers that create the fact of his behavior. . . . man . . . finds himself with the titanic task of avoiding the future over which he has no control, by absolutizing his past and his present. . . . He wants to be like God . . . the creator of his own history. . . .[4]

Ancient man possessed little notion of extended time and therefore lived in an eternal present. The ancients constructed a ritual system modelled on the rhythm of nature in order to aid women and men on their pilgrimage to death. This system recognized the despair of time, even as it attempted to ease this despair through ritual cooperation with the transitory rhythm of life in time.

It remained for Israel to shatter the meaninglessness of existence by making time a category of meaning.

Israel conceived of her life with God, not in terms of the decay inherent in the rhythm of nature, but in terms of certain promises her God had made and fulfilled in the events of her tribal and national experience. Israel's attention shifted from the rhythms of nature to the cataclysm of events, thereby introducing a new mode of human understanding. To conceive of events as themselves constituting the meaning of existence broke with the past. Clearly, events partake of the futility of time. But if God had signified ultimate meaning by making and keeping promises regarding earthly events, then time was something more than despair, repetitious flux, and decay. The specific ability to make and keep promises shatters all naturalistic and tragic conceptions of life because it introduces the possibility of new starts and destroys the tyranny of oppressive and self-evident regularity. It provides for the possibility of meaning within human events.

Because of Israel's faith, to which we in the West are heirs, time was transformed. Nothing in time could reveal the destiny of man; nothing in the natural processes of life could lead to health. But the meaningfulness of time was disclosed from beyond itself by a God who attached ultimate significance to events he had promised to bring about. This disclosure took place within the flux of time, but it occurred as a transfiguring power, a liberating force. Time with meaning became history.

For Israel, therefore, time became a duration, a period with a beginning and a future. If events and the promises that precede them are of ultimate significance for men and women, then the procession of particular linear moments takes on importance. The events of time reveal the ultimate destiny of man. What we call history is time that has duration and has acquired meaning. For Israel, time retained its potency as endless flux, but since it was also composed of meaningful events, it had been transfigured by the promissory power of God. Time itself could not deliver meaning to life, it could only exemplify despair; but when Israel announced a God who made and kept promises, time was given a beginning and a future; a meaning was affixed to it. Time remained itself, and yet it was transfigured by a God whose word and activity in human events changed it *from flux into history.*

2

At first Israel conceived of time much like her neighbors did. In Genesis, for example, we read: " 'While the earth remains, seedtime and harvest, cold and heat, summer and winter, day and night, shall not cease' " (Gen. 8: 22). Time was a recurring series of happenings with no beginning or end, and signified only the repetition and circularity of nature. Israel's escape from Egypt and her journey to the land of Canaan, however, engaged her in a specific remembrance quite different from that of her neighbors. These events helped to define the nature of Israel's God and in turn created her national life. For this reason, after Israel settled in Canaan, she transformed the old Canaanite agricultural festivals into historical celebrations of her sacred past (Exod. 23:15; 12:1-15). Gradually Israel wove together all the great events of her past into a comprehensive whole (Deut. 4:37-40). These events determined the shape of her life, however, not simply because they happened, but because they occurred within the context of word and promise. Arbitrary happenings, however marvelous, do not make history. For Israel, God spoke a word of promise and then fulfilled that promise in time (Exod. 7:17; 8:20-22). This is what gave the events of time such significance. It caused Israel to look upon time as more than transitory flux; it was duration pointing to meaning.

But sequential happenings, however important, don't necessarily lead to compelling meaning. Attention to past events may take on the character of circularity and become merely the substance of liturgical repetition. It is but the prelude to understanding time as history.

Historic time, that is, time as linear duration—beginning and future—*with comprehensive meaning* was primarily the product of the prophetic movement and literature which arose from events surrounding the destruction and exile of Israel. The prophetic movement declined to assign ultimate meaning to the events of Israel's past. It accepted the end of Israel's national life as a part of what it meant for God to be God and for Israel to be the people of God. This meant that it was no longer possible to understand God in terms of past events nor in terms of the inevitable development and growth of Israel as a nation. The destruction of Israel buried older understandings. (Further, it prompted the understanding that had Israel's national prosperity been directly controlled by the extent of her faith, then it would have made God dependent both upon Israel's success and upon a particular stage of his own activity, namely, his time with Israel in the past.) In the midst of collapse the prophets had nothing to hope for save that God would act out of the future. For them the sacred past did not create meaning, save as it was a sign of the nature of Yahweh as a God of events, and as it was a paradigm of God's essential faithfulness. The later prophets determined God's faithfulness in terms of what he would do in the future. They rejected the principle of temporal continuity as ultimately significant and fell back on a daring hope that a new and mysterious liberation would come out of the future. In this they transformed the understanding of promise. They moved beyond the idea of simple regularity and associated promise with a dramatic, discontinuous future. They associated it with the freedom of God. Time was lifted into history when the later prophets directed Israel's attention toward that which was to come. Meaning was not located in a sacred past which could be swallowed up in a cyclical pattern of liturgical remembrance. Instead historic time was open and directed toward the future.

A belief in historic time leads to the question of the ultimate meaning of time. Prophetic hope, though directed toward the future, held that human fulfillment would come in history (Isaiah 2, 11). However, this view was overtaken and altered by Jewish apocalypticism. Apocalypticism (which owed a great deal to the thought world of Persia) appeared in Judaism in the book of Daniel, which dates from around 160 B.C. Apocalypticism was deeply pessimistic about the human condition. It moaned despair in the face of a world seemingly unable to establish justice. Apocalyptic writers found ultimate meaning in an end to history itself. Apocalypticism deepened the prophetic understanding of linear history by developing a view of universal history—time from beginning to end—with history leading to a cataclysmic end in which God himself would once and for all render a judgment on human affairs. The future age of final judgment and salvation was quite discontinuous with the present age; the present was too much given to evil and misery, the new age would vindicate God as he established universal justice on a new earth. For apocalyptic thought, standing on the verge of the final dispensation, the present was not the anticipation of the future, nor was it related to a golden past; rather it was dialectically related to the new age. The dialectic found in the prophetic writings, in which judgment was pronounced in the midst of prosperity, and hope in the midst of despair, was intensified so that the present age of misery was seen to contain the signs of the final end to all misery.*

---

*"The simplest solution is that in the world there is always an exodus that leads out of a particular stasis and a hope that is linked with dismay" (Ernst Bloch).

Apocalyptic thought provides the original context for understanding the life and teachings of Jesus of Nazareth. Even though Jesus was not an apocalyptic preacher in the dire and dark fashion of John the Baptizer, the teachings of Jesus and the context of expectations in which they are set are plainly apocalyptic.[5] Jesus preached the coming of the kingdom of God, namely the imminent earthly reign of God in which the present age would give way to a new transformed age (Mark 1:15; 13:14-37). In the crisis provoked by the impending reign of God, judgment awaited some (Matt. 24:37-41) while salvation was the fate of others (Matt. 5:1-17). Jesus preached as if men and women lived in the last days; thus the time of decision was at hand for all people (Luke 12:8-59). As if possessed of divine authority, Jesus preached that God's coming kingdom seriously contradicted present social and religious practices (Matt. 5:27-48). On this basis he contravened the sacred Jewish law by associating with outcasts and sinners. Further, he preached an uncompromising ethic of love which extended even to those considered hateful enemies (Matt. 5:44). Above all, however, his work was carried on amid signs, miracles, and wonders pointing to the end of all history and the beginning of God's final righteous rule.

When Jesus rose from the dead, the event was interpreted by his earliest followers as the beginning of the end of the world. According to Paul, Jesus was the first to rise from the dead, thus fulfilling apocalyptic expectations. The general resurrection to judgment and salvation would soon follow. After that, God would be "all in all" (I Cor. 15:20-28). But further, in light of these expectations, Jesus was pictured as the final meaning to time. The resurrection authenticated his preaching about the kingdom, his relation to the law, and his radical ethic of love. Jesus, himself, was the determinative sign of the new age come to earth. With the resurrection of Jesus the despair of the world had been overcome, the destiny of the world revealed, and the final fulfillment of all things definitively presented. In Jesus, the goal of history as well as the end of the power of time (death) had been revealed. Time itself was redeemed, now made fully into history.

However, Jesus altered apocalyptic expectations in a very significant way. The full complement of apocalyptic hopes remained save that the world did not come to an end. The historical process was not destroyed. Jesus had risen from the dead to life. Death, the final power of time, was overcome, not by cosmic catastrophe, but by life, namely the transfigured life of Jesus. The interim period between Jesus' resurrection and the final end of the world, therefore, was not simply an incidental prelude to the final conflagration. It was a time of immense importance; a time of work and preparation. As such Paul assigned it great significance, pointing to the necessary salvation of Jews and Gentiles before the end (Rom. 9–11), suggesting that earthly affairs and not the cultic world of religious spiritualism and fantasy was the appropriate arena within which to exercise true worship (Rom. 12), and arguing with the Christians in Corinth that a full human existence was characterized not by worldly escape but by hope in historical transformation (I Cor. 15:20-28).

Of course, for Paul the present age was "perishing," under the sway of "principalities and powers" (Rom. 8:38). Life in time remained problematic. However, the death and resurrection of Jesus had revealed the final goal of earthly existence, the destiny of human life. And since Jesus had lived in time and suffered his fate among women and men, it followed that the tyranny of time was definitively broken in time. The delay in the appearance of the final end to time served only to spotlight the importance of earthly life and the promise of human destiny in that life. Paul, therefore, laid the groundwork for a continual tension between time and the end of time, between the form of the new age already prefigured in Jesus and the present age. In this tension the central point was not the hope that the present would be quickly and forever swallowed up by the future, but was rather the relation between the now and the not-yet. The delay before the end of time, therefore, served to spotlight the life and activity of Jesus, increased the importance of historical activity (now that time was seen fully as history), secured the significance of Jesus' life as a norm for historical judgment, and established a continual dialectic between the present and the future, time and history.

The transfiguring of time in the light of the end of time renders this present age under judgment. So it has been with every age. Jesus, as the end of history, is fulfillment, and in light of this fulfillment the pretensions of every age are exposed. Each age proclaims its virtues while masking all its crimes. For all human epochs were built by the children of Cain; they were erected out of rebellion, insecurity, and meaninglessness. The proleptic occurrence of the goal of history in the resurrection of Jesus means that death has been overcome and a new destiny provided for women and men. The tyranny of time, while not banished, has been overcome, opening the way for men and women to become new creatures. Likewise the projections of man's futility—institutions and social arrangements—are now robbed of their ultimate wretchedness. Man now possesses a new chance to break the cycle initiated in this projection. It is man who makes history, Karl Marx said; thus the promises of God, fulfilled in Jesus, stand now as man's destiny. To live in Jesus, that is, to live from the end of history, is to judge the misery and exploitation of this age. It is to live in the midst of true history.

And yet time remains. Always, " . . . the power of man finds its limit in the disintegrating temporality of his creaturely existence. . . " (Lampert). Whatever new hope or new beginning is found among women and men, it is bound to be tainted by the misery of time. The transfiguring of time provides the judgment and hope of this age; but so long as time exists as the locus of creaturely existence, justice will always be proximate justice and freedom will only be partial freedom. So long as time exists, men and women can live in the hope of liberty but they will never possess it; they can expect peace but will fall short of achieving it. God alone is the unity of all history, he is the final promise of all things, and toward the future of his majesty all things strain in conscious or unconscious hope and trust.

Wolfhart Pannenberg has summed it up eloquently:

"Salvation" means nothing else than the fulfillment of the ultimate destiny toward which man is aimed. . . . Salvation is the wholeness of his life for which he longs but never finally achieves in the course of his earthly existence. No one on his own initiative can make life complete, "whole," since the slightest discrepancy must destroy the whole. . . . Only through the granting of salvation . . . is the essence of man realized; for the essence of man is not to be sought in what is already realized in man, but it still comes to him from his future. The essence of man is the destiny that still lies beyond the empirical content of man's present and that always lures man beyond everything at hand for man. Salvation is obtained when the destiny of man becomes identical with his present existence, when man is united in his present with his past and his future. [This] is not possible without concurrence with the world and without community with other men. . . . in the life of the individual man, it finds no ultimate realization this side of death. The question about the fulfillment of man's destiny remains open beyond the death of the individual. The wholeness of his life in unity with himself, the world, his fellowmen, and God can come only in the resurrection from the dead, which is hoped for.[6]

3

Most people conceive of personal or political ethics as a simple matter of doing right or avoiding wrong; of obeying to a greater or lesser degree some legal or ideal norm based on reason. In this way the word *saeculum* implies secular ethics, the ethics of the age, the norms of an age committed to its own ultimate goodness and prosperity. Women and men are urged to act according to the given norms of the age and the particular needs that the age may have. It is assumed that the final meaning of existence is contained within the parameters of the age and the imagination that supports and extends it. The age, it is argued, contains no inherent tragedy, no incessant wound, no unconquerable evil and, therefore, men and women may legitimately, if not necessarily, draw from it the inspiration to live and act. Of course, secular ethics acknowledges the existence of evil and the need for reform, but ethical problems are seen only as maladjustments which challenge the good will and ingenuity of men and women.

Evaluations of the overall shape of the age are characteristically made by balancing the so-called good against the so-called bad. It is believed that this sensible procedure offers an accurate picture of the health of the age. In fact it does nothing of the kind. Since the norms, categories, and information are inevitably provided by the dominant groups of the age, evaluations reflect, not the truth about an age, but the legitimization of dominant groups. The rulers of each age construct ethics for their own benefit. Even reformers who wish to alter the shape of an age generally diverge little, methodologically, from the groups they wish to replace. Reformers may offer new norms, but they too realize that, once new norms have been put forth, the best way to guarantee control and leadership is to conduct ethics by summing up good and evil, and by balancing the two in some neat fashion ultimately designed to promote the stability of the age.

Christian ethics is eschatological in that it draws its power, norms, and judgments from the end of time. In this manner it is preserved from the self-sufficiency, deceit, and smugness of secular ethics. According to eschatological ethics, all human action is judged in relationship to the end of time. Every age is judged by norms and standards which the age, because of its ultimate desire to preserve and justify itself, cannot and will not recognize.

History, Karl Marx noted, is the history of tyranny. Both bourgeois moralists and Christian liberals have seen this as a harsh judgment on the slow but sure progress of humankind through the centuries—the decline of superstition, the gradual alleviation of suffering, and the extension of rationality and civilization. They insist that, on the whole, good has been more evident than evil. Indeed, it is argued, severe human problems remain but the tendency is for man's goodness to extend itself and for human evil and suffering to recede. The judgment of God from the end of time upsets such schemes. Justice cannot be determined on the basis of a relative comparison. In the first place, such comparisons are inevitably self-serving and are designed to ensure the dominance of ruling groups. But more important for Christian ethics, the mere existence of misery, fear, poverty, cruelty, and oppression condemns the age itself and exposes its optimistic claims as false. Each nation and community is a whole, and the presence of degradation invalidates the claims and posture of the whole. In any situation of imbalance (and every epoch has been characterized by imbalance and inequity) the poor and despised stand in place of the well-to-do. Without the poor as a cushion, the inequality of the age would dictate that the wealthy take their place and sink into chaos and despair.* The vicious structural inequality of the whole which characterizes every age cannot be erased by any kind of average between good and bad deeds, by a balancing of good and evil or by any

*This accounts for Martin Luther King's insight that mankind will not be free until the poor and oppressed are free.

appeal to progress. Instead, the oppression and misery of the stricken testify to the despair of the whole, to the tyranny of history, namely to the decay of the present order in the face of the judgment of God.

Christian ethics is related to the struggle for the victory of life over death. Death in all its forms renders people and their institutions vulnerable; death is the pervasive power operative over all life; death is present as the demonic force at every point in existence. Christian ethics looks to action based on the conquest of death, on the breaking of death's power in the world. To reduce ethics to matters of reform or to such slogans as "obeying the law of love" only assumes that this age is generally healthy and simply in need of benign good will. So long as men and women live in time such notions will leave them enslaved, without hope, deceived and despairing. For the Christian, ethical decisions are made in light of the radicality of the end of time, "whether they represent a manifest destiny, which may be a judgment as well as a promise; . . . [whether] they represent, as it were, the end of history in fulfillment of its actual end."[7]

The ethics associated with such an apocalyptic hope is dualistic. It places the justice of the future of God over against the cruelty and oppression of the present age. However, this is a special sort of dualism in that the apocalyptic hope is grounded in the proleptic appearance of the end in time—that is, the appearance of Jesus in the world of man as a sign of judgment and hope. Hence, apocalyptic dualism does not suggest an ethic based on the confrontation of two separate ages in which the present age will be brought to dissolution by the power of the new age. It is an ethic for the time between the resurrection and consummation; it struggles to reveal the form of the future in the present, the reality of the resurrection within the flux of time, the reversal of the power of death.

In this regard the dualism derived from apocalyptic thought is intimately related to the issues of history and justice, while traditional Christian ethics based on incarnational thinking has been obsessed with the problems of essence and law. Traditional incarnational thought* was a product of the sphere theology adopted by the early Christians from the thought world of Hellenism. Two spheres or realms were seen in juxtaposition with each other. The realm above—the gods or God or spirit—was separate from the realm below—darkness or matter. The perennial problem for theology was how the two realms were related. In traditional thought the incarnate deity entered the world of matter, transformed it with spirit, and provided the basis for the

---

*Incarnation is a metaphor of grace. It adequately points to the extravagance of God's love in embracing the human condition. No other metaphor has so powerfully captured this incredible intention of God. But this metaphor still is an incomplete one because it is related to the question of the relationship of matter and spirit, a question which is not central to the issue of ethics. Thus, incarnational language and thought cannot be retained without at the same time suffering a lack of rigor in ethical matters.

claim that the world was essentially good. This in turn made it possible to establish an ethic of law which manifested the basic goodness of the world. However, this extreme form of incarnationalism on the one hand admitted, but on the other hand didn't really deal with, the basic assumption of sphere theology, which was that matter was essentially evil (otherwise why would it need to be transformed in the first place?). It was possible, of course, to suggest that the incarnation was only a temporary phenomenon. In this way God could remain essentially divorced from an evil world and ethics could become a matter of divine law hurled, as it were, at an evil world. As a result of this dilemma, incarnational ethics has swung between two alternatives. One alternative suggests that the essential incorruptibility of God prevents complete identification with the world of matter, thereby leading to an ethic of escape from the materiality of existence to the realm of the spirit. The other suggests that the incarnate God enters fully the world of matter in the flesh of Jesus and transforms matter into spirit. This leads to a total identification with earthly life and provides the basis for a naturalistic ethics. In both cases the form of the world is left essentially intact. It is no surprise, therefore, that the history of traditional Christian ethics has been characterized by an adherence to the status quo and has generally left uncontested the injustice, cruelty, and inhumanity of every age.

The protest of the Enlightenment against the Christian Church was launched from within the framework of incarnational thinking. The *philosophes* correctly sensed that most of Christian ethics assumed that matter (and natural man) was evil. As a result they asserted the natural goodness of man as the basis of future perfection. However, insofar as the apologists for the Enlightenment rested their case on the essential goodness of man and the world, they were simply taking up a variant of traditional naturalistic theology and were soon to fall prey to the same problems that beset any such theology, namely, the identification of goodness with what is. In their case this was the new, scientific bourgeois epoch.

Spherical thinking makes a metaphysical evaluation of man and the world, but it is static, inherently lacking in prophetic or critical capabilities. Its major concern is whether the world is intrinsically evil or not. In contrast Christian thought, informed by apocalyptic hope, is not concerned with the question of essential evil or essential good, but with the justice of God. It focuses on the action of men and women in relation to the approaching end. The future of God is related to the ethical shape of the world and not to its inner essence. Thus every age stands under judgment. This judgment is related, not to law or morality, but to the revelation of God's sovereignty, which exposes the corruption of the age to the light of the kingdom of the new age. Christian ethics rests on the distinction between this age and the age to come, not on the distinction between matter and spirit. And it draws its power, hope, and vision from the future of God already present in the resurrection of Jesus. This act is the judgment of the age even as it is the anticipatory transformation of the earth. E. Lampert writes:

> . . . "static" dualism spells resignation in regard to temporal and historical reality. Christianity . . . conceives of this relation as one at once of co-inherence . . . and of tension which presses towards a solution. Such "dynamic" dualism is really a struggle for *visibility*. Our present order is a reign of the temporal which conceals the visibility of God. . . . But the emergence of the new order is to be a visible disclosure of God's Kingdom, which until then is kenotically hidden within the ambiguities of Time. The final consummation, then, is a visible disclosure of the Kingdom, a rending of the veil in order to make manifest a hitherto invisible presence.[8]

Setting ethics within the context of expecting to see God coming, at once relates earthly action to God's eschatological work, hence to God himself, and also provides the basis for a radical critique of the injustice of every age. The substance of Christian ethics, therefore, is action which overcomes the power of death. This is a sign of the end of the world, a dramatic reversal of injustice and oppression.

> Every truly creative act of man must . . . be regarded as an eschatological act which "ends" this world and inaugurates a new one. "If you feed the hungry," writes [Nicolas] Berdyaev, "or free the oppressed, you are committing an eschatological deed, and you are 'ending' this world so full of hunger and oppression." Each truly creative act is a historical fulfillment, a coming of the End, a transcending and transforming of this spellbound, stricken world of ours.[9]

Of course there is a tendency in an ethic so strongly apocalyptic to disparage any form that an historical epoch takes. A strong belief in judgment from the end of time casts serious doubt on all human actions and all forms of human life. In light of the end, it is perfectly clear that man's earthly affairs remain stricken and imprisoned in misery. Certainly, no human age or human action can provide the ultimate meaning of existence nor erase man's bondage to time. With Paul we might very well desire our release from this world (Phil. 1:23). But the paradox of grace is that Jesus was raised in time. Thus, by virtue of this sign, we have been granted life until the final consummation, and the interim period becomes more than just an accidental moment, our hopes for justice more than fleeting hopes, and our human actions more than time-filling exercises. Christian ethics is directed toward the transfiguration of the earth because we have been granted life and because Jesus was raised in time.

Because of Jesus' resurrection the end of time is not just the judgment of time. The ethical consequences of the resurrection fulfill time. There is no complete fulfillment in time, however, since the new norms introduced by the resurrection must work in time. They are subject to time and the despair it brings. The ethical consequences of the resurrection lead to a radical conception of human justice; but even as Christians strive to act out that radical stance, the ambiguity of time seen in the light of the end reminds them that all temporal ethics, however closely related to justice, fall far short of redemption. On occasion, human actions may partake of the glory of the end, but they do so momentarily, as parables. No time will ever find the true peace and justice that is redemption. But God's sovereign acts do transform our time with interruptions, new starts, moments of consummation and sporadic parables of fulfillment. As Ernst Bloch has noted, "every moment contains . . . potentially the datum of the consummation of the world."

The Biblical story makes clear that the resurrection of Jesus is the definitive sign of the end of the world, the final power over death. Too often, however, the meaning of this event has been mistakenly limited to matters of individual salvation or morality. In America, for example, the religious preoccupation with personal salvation or with individual moral rectitude has blinded women and men to the full power and depth of the resurrection. The resurrection lifts time into history, by judging the earth and revealing the eternal destiny of mankind. Further, the resurrection is the definitive earthly sign of God's victorious struggle to become visible in the overthrow of death. It signals the shift from the old age to the new age. Since justice is the main concern of ethics, it should be plain that the shape of each epoch—the network of institutions, relationships, and ideologies that characterize life in time and give form to the age—is of paramount importance. The reduction of ethics to matters of personal forgiveness or individual righteousness occurs when the resurrection is divorced from its apocalyptic setting and is regarded simply as the highest example of love or sacrifice. Ethics deals with the form of the age and is not just a matter of simple understanding or good sense. All of Jesus' teachings and parables are set within the context of the coming transformation of the world, they are not universally applicable moral injunctions. Neither simple morality, human love, nor better understanding is the substance of Christian ethics. Its substance is the expectation of the end of the world.

The church is the form of the new age, the shape of the end as it appears in time. Therefore, in the New Testament, the implications of the resurrection are worked out *as* the church as well as *in* the church. It is most important to recognize the church as the primary focus for working out the implications of the resurrection.

The New Testament church conceives of itself as the new world in the midst of a decaying, perishing old world. "The faithful *are* the world as it has been recalled to the sovereignty of God, the company of those who live under the eschatological justice of God, in which company, according to II Cor. 5.21, God's righteousness becomes manifest on earth."[10] Unlike modern Christians, the New Testament writers do not think of the world as an abiding, self-contained reality which the church addresses concerning justice or peace. Instead, the world is pictured as disintegrating, given over to death and yet penetrated by the power of the resurrection—of which the church is the sign, the mark of the new age. The church demonstrates the visibility of God's sovereignty in time. The New Testament church is, therefore, a body of witnesses, testifying to the presence of the end of the world; it is not a body of moralists offering political advice to a self-sufficient world. The inner life of the New Testament church reveals the form of the new age. Of course the scriptural writers still perceive this reality to be eschatological; the norms they derive from the resurrection are never fully practiced or obeyed, but instead are visions drawn from the end of time. Further, these norms are never simple matters of principle. They are signs of the power of God. The church commends conformity to these norms as a matter of obedience to the victorious appearance of God, not because they are laudable principles. Thus for the New Testament church the resurrection is the means of discerning the majestic power of God at all times and in all places. The ethical task of Christians is to identify the signs of the end in their elusive and paradoxical appearance.

The resurrection was bound to have some effect on the form of the common life of the Christian community. Of course it can be argued that the early church simply copied Old Testament forms or borrowed from the surrounding Hellenistic culture to forge the shape of its common life. But this overlooks the fact that the church was conscious of being the "new" Israel and was very hostile to the "worldly" forms of contemporary life. Undoubtedly the church borrowed from the scriptures and from Hellenism, but these forms were continually altered by the church's consciousness of being the people of the "last days."

Nor was the church's common life a secondary matter, developed pragmatically or helter-skelter after the primary business of conversion had been attended to. There was no distinction between the form of the church's life and its belief. Their common existence took a form that flowed directly from the proclamation that God had raised Jesus from the dead and made him Lord.

For this reason, Rudolph Bultmann is wrong to suggest that the radical egalitarianism, which was the most prominent mark of the primitive community, was only incidental and unimportant.[11] Faith and life, ethics and belief, confession and form were inseparably intertwined in the life of the early church. To have faith in the power of God was to demonstrate that power in the forms of human life.

For the early Christians, to confess that God had revealed his sovereignty over the world through Jesus' resurrection was, at the same time, to confess that by adoption and grace one had become a son of God and a brother to other Christians. Jesus had procured standing for man before God, and thus women and men entered a new relationship with one another. Jesus had made them his friends (John 20:17) and his brothers (Matt. 12:50; Mark 3:35; Rom. 8:29); and this made them friends and brothers to each other. To be sure, this was no natural brotherhood but one that existed by the grace and favor of God, and received its ultimate power from the life of God which Jesus shared fully after his resurrection. It augured an egalitarian existence quite foreign to the hierarchical political and social life of the surrounding world. To believe was to be a brother or a sister. This was a sign of the very goal of human life; only now it was operative in the life of the community. Thus, Paul's usual form of address to the church is "brother," an appellative that continued in church use to the annoyance of those outside the church. In the second century, for example, the Roman official Minucius Felix commented about Christians with obvious disdain: "They call themselves brothers and sisters and love each other without knowing each other." [12] Writing in the same century the satirist Lucian was even more contemptuous:

... their lawgiver ... persuaded them that they are all brothers and that once converted ... they should worship that executed sophist and live in accordance with his laws. They therefore despise everything equally and hold everything in common, having accepted such ideas without a soundly based faith. [13]

But it *was* a soundly based faith which clearly demonstrated, to the consternation of worldly authorities, that the faith that beseeches the end of the world inevitably leads to the transfiguration of the values and behavior of the world.

The church remembered that Jesus had forbidden his disciples to claim for themselves the title of "rabbi" or "father" or "master." "You are all brothers," the writer of the second Gospel has Jesus say. The Christ, alone, is master, teacher, and rabbi (Matt. 23:8-10). For the Christian to claim supremacy in anything was to reflect the spirit of the world and betray the community and its Lord. Thus Paul, aware that Jesus was the unity and wisdom of the community (I Cor. 4:7), exhorted the church to reflect on the crucified Christ and on their equality in the body (I Cor. 3:7-9) and not to claim superiority in any thing (I Cor. 8:2). Service was to characterize those anxious to assume leadership: "Whoever will be greater will be your servant," Jesus counsels in Mark's Gospel (10:43). The church is a community of equals in which there is no authority save that of the Spirit. No one is to put himself forward as a teacher (James 3:1), but rather each should remain a part of the body under obedience to the same Spirit.

Of course there are differences within the community and obviously there are varying degrees of skill and talent present in the body of believers. But where the world takes these distinctions and builds hierarchical structures and forms upon them, inevitably exalting some over others, often according to class or money, the church is to organize the talents of women and men in different fashion (James 2:1-4, 9).* The gifts of the Spirit are manifold, and those receiving and exercising gifts are to use them to build up the entire body (Eph. 4:12, 16; I Cor. 12:25-26) rather than to establish rank and privilege. Paul sees distinctions of talent and skill as different functions and callings, not in terms of rank and hierarchy (Eph. 4:7-11; I Cor. 12:8-11). The value of work is determined by how well it serves the brotherhood, not by how it serves individual standing. There are to be no distinctions of rank, privilege, or status within the body, only different styles of service. The modern notion that communal well-being is the sum total of individual interests could hardly be further from the New Testament idea of community.

The resurrection has made Jesus one with the power of God, and the mystery of this unity is expressed in the church through the unity of the church. The communal polity of the church is therefore not incidental, but the very core of the new age's power visited among men. Christ himself works through the community, taking form in their collective life in a stricken world (Eph. 4:4-6; I Cor. 12:5, 6, 11). That is why the body of people called to be the church is described as the body of Christ himself (I Cor. 12:12).

Equality in the body has a further basis in that in the resurrection God had overthrown the "principalities and powers," the demonic forces resident in the institutions, structures, and forms of the culture, which held men and women captive and alienated them from themselves and from God (Col. 2:15; Eph. 1:21; 3:10; I Pet. 3:22). Jesus' resurrection meant, therefore, the overthrow of a world organized according to distinctions of power, wealth, status, or knowledge. In contrast the church would be characterized by powerlessness, service, and humility (I Cor. 1:19, 25-27; II Cor. 11:30; 12:9-10), for these are the values implicit in structures built to embody communality and equality. The end to authoritarian rule and worldly values leading to privilege and exploitation gives way to the new age of brotherhood made possible by the destruction of the demonic powers. Thus Paul can exuberantly confess:

---

*The Barmen Declaration of 1934 echoed this Biblical insight: "The different offices of the Church give no justification for the privilege of some over others, but for the service entrusted to the whole fellowship and required of it" (Section 4).

There is neither Jew nor Greek, there is neither slave nor free, there is neither male nor female; for you are all one in Christ Jesus (Gal. 3:28; cf. I Cor. 12:13; Col. 3:11).*

The radical egalitarianism of the Christian life and its inherent relationship to the central confession of faith is strikingly manifest in the matter of property relations. Whereas Jesus apparently neither encouraged nor condemned ownership of property, we find that in the early church, property is held in common (Acts 2:44-45; 4:32-37). When Ananias and Sapphira hold back part of the proceeds from a property sale which they were to bring for common use, they are struck dead by the prophetic utterance of the apostles (Acts 5:1-11). This story draws added attention because it is here that scripture first mentions sin in the nascent community.

The sharing of property and wealth is not a goal in itself. Rather it manifests a lack of concern about possessions and points to a dependence on the grace of God. " . . . Recall the former days," writes the author of the letter to the Hebrews, "when . . . . you joyfully accepted the plundering of your property, since you knew that you yourselves had a better possession and an abiding one" (10:32, 34). Paul related equality and poverty and links them with the crucifixion:

> For you know the grace of our Lord Jesus Christ, that though he was rich, yet for your sake he became poor, so that by his poverty you might become rich. . . . I do not mean that others should be eased and you burdened, but that as a matter of equality your abundance at the present time should supply their want, so that their abundance may supply your want, that there may be equality. As it is written, "He who gathered much had nothing over, and he who gathered little had no lack" (II Cor. 8:9, 13-15).†

The commitment to equality not only implied forsaking rank, status, and wealth, and a mandate to share goods and property, but it also implied the establishment of human relationships on an intrinsic basis (Heb. 8:10-11). The source of the unity of the Christian community was the Spirit. It was the Spirit who signified the bond of the new age, the sign of the presence of the

---

*It has been suggested that this saying is a gnostic formula which Paul tried to combat. This is true only to the extent that the saying was taken without any eschatological reference. Paul did not quarrel with the saying per se, he only wished to make clear that this mystical reality does not actually exist under the conditions of existence, but is an eschatological reality breaking, parabolically, into the present.

† The collection for Jerusalem which is the setting for II Cor. 8 and 9 was not simply a matter of charity shown to the poor in Jerusalem. It perhaps entailed that; but equally important was that the offering both recognized the importance of the mother church in Jerusalem and was meant to symbolize the equality of gentile Christianity and Jewish Christianity.[14]

end. The Spirit was from God even as the salvation of man and the unity of the church was seen as a miracle. Since the Spirit was from God and not from man, it was impossible for the community to claim any human works, actions, or achievements as the basis for its life. Salvation had been conferred from outside as a gift. It was only natural to conceive of human relationships in intrinsic terms. This was not because of any belief in universal dignity or the presence of a divine spark in man. Instead it was fashioned from the solidarity of sinners unexpectedly redeemed by the majesty of God. Jesus had been made to share the sin of men and women, and on their behalf God had raised him (II Cor. 5:21; Heb. 4:15; Gal. 3:13). Therefore what outward measure could establish human relationships, save the cross and resurrection of Jesus? How could sinners establish external works and accomplishments as a guarantor of salvation? Only intrinsic relationships could be fostered among Christians as a response to the grace of God (II Cor. 10:12-15), relationships that embodied the virtues of humility and service, peace and love, joy and simplicity; relationships built on the recognition of a common salvation with one's brother or sister. In this fashion intrinsic worth was established among the early Christians as an eschatological sign.

The evaluation of man on the basis of extrinsic marks, characteristics, or accomplishments finds its most severe and ugly expression in the institution of slavery. The early church clearly tolerated slavery in the world (I Pet. 2:18-25; Col. 3:22-25). But again it should be noted that the church did not see itself addressing the world with moral or political advice. The world was perishing; the new age was dawning in and as the church. Certainly Christians had to wend their way through the corridors of the decaying world and thus had to conform to this reality. But the church was the form of the new world and it was here that God's will was known. Thus, in the only instance we have in the New Testament where slavery is raised as an important issue, we find Paul writing to Philemon concerning the slave Onesimus, whom Paul is returning: "[Receive him] . . . no longer as a slave but more than a slave, as a beloved brother . . . " (Philemon 15-16). Within the church slavery is cancelled. In its place we find the characteristic appellative, brother.

Finally, the consequences of the resurrection led the church to manifest a solidarity with the poor and outcast. Indeed, the early church was made up mostly of people drawn from the lowest ranks of society. The New Testament's bias was clearly toward the poor. One can hardly find a good word in it for the rich. This bias arose in part because of Jesus' friendship with the outcasts of society, and echoes the strong sense of social justice found in the Prophets and elsewhere in the Old Testament (Amos 2:6-7; Jer. 22:16; Job 5:11-16). But more than this, solidarity with the downtrodden was derived from the fact of the resurrection. When the early Christians confessed that Jesus was raised from the dead, they were proclaiming publicly the resurrection of a criminal and an outcast (II Cor. 5:21; I Pet. 2:24). When Thomas exclaimed, "My Lord and my God," the confession expresses not only wonder at the conquest of death but also surprise that God would vindicate this particular man, Jesus, the criminal (John 20:26-29). After all, Jesus had preached the arrival of the kingdom to the forsaken, to those whom the Jewish law had excluded from the promises of God. Thus Jesus was arrested as a blasphemer. His trial by the Romans was probably for sedition. It is of little wonder that Jesus was pictured as accursed, forsaken, and given over to shame (Gal. 3:13; Heb. 12:2). Jesus' resurrection did not cancel out this reality. On the contrary it vindicated and confirmed it. The two central realities of Jesus' life—his forsakenness and his glorification—were seen as inseparable. Thus his followers testified to the new age when they experienced glorification through humiliation and abuse. This was the way of Jesus. Inevitably, Christians were drawn to the sick, the poor, to those hungering for liberation (Luke 4:18-19), and to those in prison (Heb. 10:34; 13:3). The Christians themselves were poor, sinful, despised, and often imprisoned. They could hardly forget that the kingdom had dawned in the person of a criminal, an accursed, stricken outcast. The new age would necessarily appear in and from the outcasts. Thus the church could not proclaim a faith apart from this reality. To do so would be tantamount to separating belief from earthly consequences, faith from God's power to manifest justice on earth. The Christian remained a sinner who worshipped a God whose inner reality had been revealed in the life of a forsaken criminal. Thus Paul could say:

> For consider your call, brethren; not many of you were wise according to worldly standards, not many were powerful, not many were of noble birth; but God chose what is foolish in the world to shame the wise, God chose what is weak in the world to shame the strong, God chose what is low and despised in the world, even things that are not, to bring to nothing things that are . . . (I Cor. 1:26-28).

If the lowly are chosen to shame the exalted, then the hope of the new age is directed toward the poor and oppressed since their liberation is a sign that the powers of death which enslave sinners and outcasts have been publicly overthrown. The resurrection hope is that "The last will be first" (Matt. 20:16), that the poor and downtrodden will be the inheritors of the messianic age (Mark 12:1-12; Matt. 22:1-10; Luke 15:1-2, 24-32), that criminals will enter paradise (Luke 23:39-43). The church's inner life manifests this reality by honoring the weak (James 1:9; I Cor. 12:22-24). It is among such as these that the signs of the promise of the new age are to be found; for it was so with Jesus, the pariah.

> Listen, my beloved brethren. Has not God chosen those who are poor in the world to be rich in faith and heirs of the kingdom which he has promised to those who love him? (James 2:5).

4

The recession of apocalyptic expectations, and the general decline of Jewish thought in the face of Hellenistic influences, significantly altered the role of the church in theology and ethics. Even today we live as the heirs of this change. In time—and this is clearly reflected in the scriptures themselves—the church came to see itself less as a sign of the end than as the end itself. Instead of waiting for and effecting the transformation of the world—of which it was the sign and pledge—the church began to proclaim *itself* as the transformation. The mission of the church soon shifted from the proclamation of Jesus in the context of the expected end, and became, as the end itself, the gathering place for all mankind. Sacraments, cultus, and leadership came to be perceived less as parabolic events in anticipation of the end, and more as marks of religious observance for those saved from the world. The church began drawing people from the world rather than preparing them for the transformation of the world. Whereas Paul had taught that true faith and the effect of worship were found in the midst of jeopardy, that is, in the midst of a world caught in a cosmic struggle, the church soon relegated worship to the sphere of the sacred and commended the church as the place of safety. Inevitably, the church took form as an institution and lost its pilgrim character, its sense of temporality and its reliance on the Spirit as the bond of the new age. As an organization with a defined leadership and sacred tradition it came to face the world as one self-contained reality standing over against another. The world was soon accepted as an abiding reality which was to be dealt with by the church as another separate reality. Christian ethics has functioned ever since within the context of the church-world dichotomy.

Incarnational thought gave point to this development by applying its essentialist designations to the church (good) and to the world (evil). As a result the ecclesiastical expressions of prayer, sacraments, and priesthood were elevated above the worldly activities of politics and economics. Incarnationalism served as the theological and ethical expression of the doctrine of "two realities."

This doctrine continues as a basic assumption in the modern church, which has separated itself even further from apocalyptic thought. For liberals in the church, Christian ethics has increasingly become a matter of what advice the church should give the world about social, political, or moral problems. Ethics has become the application of "Christian principles" to social and political affairs, that is, it has become the instruction of the world by the church, now euphemistically called "the church speaking to the world." In reaction, evangelical churches place primary attention on the matter of saving faith apart from "worldly" adventures. This faith, however, is considered a religious or churchly matter and, therefore, demonstrates the Evangelical's acceptance of the church-world dichotomy. For them salvation remains, fundamentally, withdrawal from the world.

According to eschatological thought the church remains a distinct body within the world but is at the same time a part of the whole perishing earth. It is in no sense an entity apart from the world. The church's distinctiveness lies in its relationship to the world's end. Its task is to identify and proclaim the signs of the end. It is not meant to be an advisor to the world, as if the general good health of the world needed only some sound advice in order for it to maintain itself. Further, the internal life of the church fails to exhibit any difference from that of the world at large. Greed, corruption, illusion, and death are as much a part of the church's inner life as they are rampant elsewhere, thus depriving the church of any claim to distinctiveness. Indeed, there is little evidence that the New Testament church could claim uniqueness by virtue of its behavioral purity. It, too, was wracked by corruption, as Paul's letters make abundantly clear. What was distinctive about the church was the presence of the Word of God which testified to the end of the world. The dilemma of the modern church therefore is found, not in its moral corruption—however reprehensible that is—but in its inattention to its primary task of testimony. Thus the church has divorced itself from the end and has given up its task of being a promise of the world's destiny. Instead it has become an agency of advice.

Many modern liberals have taken a further step by commending action in the world on the grounds that the essential goodness of the world has undermined the basis for the old church-world dichotomy. But by prompting action on the basis of optimistic assessments of the world's life, liberals inevitably are drawn to reformist politics which do not significantly alter the status quo. The reason for this is that optimistic evaluations of the world almost always blind men and women to the depths of the human dilemma. The world is neither good nor evil; it is held in check by demonic powers (I John 5:19). At all levels the powers of death threaten to be victorious. The world is perishing because of the presence of death in all its guises. It is not an imminent end, nor any essential evil that keeps the world in decay and misery; it is the powers of death that hold sway. Against them God is locked in combat for the life of man.

We no longer expect an imminent end to the world, nor should we. But judgment is still present in our time, as is God's struggle to become visible in triumph. In this struggle the church becomes the sign of God's victory only in its confession of the end and in its willingness to gather around the signs of the end wherever and whenever they appear. This is the heart of ethics.

But where are these signs to be found? In our time they are to be found, mainly, in the life of politics and social affairs. Not only has the delay of the *parousia* given time value, as we suggested earlier, but it has also focused our attention on the life of the total world. The original apocalyptic tradition operated from within the framework of eschatological expectation. But it did so, not because religion was a separate area of life—as was gradually to be the case when apocalyptic thought gave way to Hellenism—but precisely because it was the determinative area of man's life and possessed the same formative power that politics and economic and social organization do in our contemporary world. Therefore, unlike Hellenism (of which we are still the modern heirs), apocalypticism invites us to see that the struggle for the world's life is taking place in the social and political arena, namely, in the arena where power exercises its most devastating hold over human life. The collapse of imminent expectations allows us to focus on political and social reality and on the dialectic struggle of sin and grace, death and life being carried on there. It is there that the signs of the transformation of the world will arise; there that the decaying nature of the world gives rise to the ironic and wondrous appearance of God.

It remains the Christian's task to witness to the signs of this transformation. The Christian is not primarily concerned with church renewal or political reform or service to the community or a variety of other similar activities, though, of course, these things are necessary in the world (Luke 17:7-10). The Christian's first task is to discern the transfiguring power of the Lord in the political and social formations of the age and to gather in action around them. Yet even as this is done, it remains that these signs are true signs only insofar as they are related to the pre-eminent sign of the world's future—the resurrection of Jesus. The present-day signs of God's sovereignty must be identified in terms of their relationship to the resurrection and to the norms of the resurrection. Insofar as the raising of Jesus and its consequences are the central witness we have to God's power, we are beholden to measure every contemporary event with the Biblical witness of God's decisive act in Jesus. Further, we are constrained to confess in the midst of political and social affairs. The signs of the end may occur in our common life apart from the church and without any prior presence or comment of Christians. God is hardly restrained in such a fashion. Yet if these great occurrences are to receive their fullness they should not be received apart from the confession of Jesus. On the one hand, signs need to be identified as manifestations of the majesty of God in order to inspire men and women to action. On the other hand, signs must be restrained from claiming ultimacy which, by their very nature as pointers and not full reality, they do not possess. Only faith in Jesus and in his future with God can end this world so full of misery and decay. This is the distinctive message of Christianity.

PART TWO

THE DILEMMA
OF THE AMERICAN
POLITICAL
ECONOMY

Chapter Two

The SOVEREIGNTY
of INEQUALITY
in the AMERICAN SYSTEM

An unstratified society with real equality of its members is a myth which has never been realized in the history of mankind. ... The forms and proportions of stratification may vary, but its essence is permanent.

Pitirim A. Sorokin

Politics is a matter of who rules whom.   **V. I. Lenin**

We cannot join economic inequality and political equality.

Walter Rauschenbusch

Social justice is not a panacea for the world's ills.   **White House aide, 1971**

1

The theory of political democracy has always held that the political form of the state should involve equality among its members. Yet the theory and practice of capitalist economics espouses inequality as a necessary characteristic. Thus it is that capitalism and democracy are fundamentally contradictory systems. Under capitalism the capital-owning class endeavors to protect its economic advantage by institutionalizing inequities in wealth, power, and social roles. All the while, democracy hopes for an equality beyond the formal equality enjoyed in the ballot box. Insofar, however, as capitalism and democracy are coupled, the dream of an egalitarian republic is merely a dream. You cannot have equality and capitalism.

In fact, inequality is endemic to capitalism. This is the real exegesis of the concept of the "free market." As Robert Heilbroner has pointed out, "in a market run society ... it is the distribution of purchasing power that sets the effective demands to which social effort will cater."[1] A "hierarchy of remunerations," namely differentials in income designed to promote incentives toward economic effort and consumption, is the motivating power in capitalism. But this "hierarchy" lacks any means to guarantee equality. "The price mechanism," notes W. A. Lewis, "rewards people according to the scarcity of resources that they possess, but it does not itself contain any mechanism for equalizing the distribution of scarcity."[2] The result of this is unequal access to capital and its attendant privileges and the inevitable maintenance of a class system. According to its own laws, capitalism rewards some while penalizing others.

In the early years of the American republic the contradiction between the inequality of capitalism and the equalitarian dream associated with democracy was not fully perceived. In large part this was because the doctrine of equality held by the early settlers was a means of overcoming the remnants of feudal-aristocratic practice in America. The doctrine was employed, not against capitalism, but against notions of rank, privilege, and social status which the old aristocratic order had articulated and which, consequently, served as artificial barriers to the ambitions and energies of restless pioneers. Hence the belief in social, political, and religious equality was admirably fitted to the aspirations of women and men eager to build a new continent. This prompted the aristocrat Alexis de Tocqueville to remark that "equality . . . was the fundamental fact [of American life] from which all others seem to be derived."[3]

Characteristically, when the question of full, white, adult male suffrage was debated in the American states in the 1820's and 1830's, the vote was presented as the extension of the inherent equality of man. This doctrine was embodied in the notion of natural rights, that is, in the view that men possess an essential equality apart from the outward signs of rank, privilege, or noble birth. Quite pointedly the proponents of an extended franchise refrained from suggesting that the widespread vote would be used to challenge the unequal division of property, though, understandably, opponents of the issue feared that this was the prime motivation in attempting to extend the vote. Characteristically, in the debate, equality referred mainly to the absence of class distinctions and privileges long associated with aristocratic standing.

But even as the doctrine of equality was successful against the old aristocratic assumptions, it remained a limited doctrine when it came to confronting the economic inequality of American capitalism. The concept of equality, in fact, did not apply to economic life. "I know no other country," declared Tocqueville, " . . . where a stronger scorn is expressed for the theory of permanent equality of property."[4] If egalitarianism were extended to the economic sphere it would, or so it appeared to aggressive and ambitious settlers, provide an arbitrary restraint on rapid economic advancement. And above all America was about economic success. Hence the doctrine of equality proved a useful weapon against aristocratic pretensions by locating human value in the inner equality of all people before God or with each other, but it was summarily discarded when it came to economic affairs.

This, in turn, made it easier for monied classes to rise to prominence. As they advanced they proclaimed, in traditional anti-aristocratic fashion, the inner equality of all people. So long as there was a certain absence of pretension and overt snobbery in their move to the "top," they were in conformity with the canons of social equality long associated with American egalitarian hopes. Since the doctrine of equality was primarily social and not economic, any significant challenge to the new privileged elite was invariably muted. Instead of focusing on the traumatic effects of economic inequality, therefore, the debate drifted around issues of style and social behavior. As James Bryce noted almost a century ago:

The equality of estimation—the idea which men form of other men as compared with themselves, it is in this that the real sense of equality comes out. In America men hold others to be at bottom exactly the same as themselves. . . . the admiration felt [for a great man] may be reason for going to see him and longing to shake hands with him. . . . But it is not a reason for bowing down to him, or addressing him in deferential terms. . . ."[5]

More recently, David Potter summed it up admirably:

Some people, according to the American creed, might be more fortunate than others, but they must never regard themselves as better than others. . . . the American people have . . . reserved their heartiest dislike . . . for people with upstage or condescending manners, and for anyone who tries to convert power or wealth (which are not resented) into overt rank or privilege (which are).[6]

Capitalism, therefore, maintained the upper hand economically and ideologically. And if there was an inconsistency between economic inequality and democratic ideals, it was not of great concern so long as the early American economy promised eventual material abundance for all. Whatever anger or resentment there might be at economic inequality could be forestalled in the hope that future affluence would somehow solve social problems.

By the time of the rise of the corporations, however, tendencies toward inequality had become so pronounced that the issue could no longer be avoided. Yet, since the doctrine of equality had never extended to economic affairs, there was hardly any ideological tool available to help refashion America along equalitarian lines. Further, since economic realities tend to shape social and political ideals, it became evident that instead of moving to alter obvious inequities, the primary ideological thrust would be to honor American capitalism by constructing an apology for the necessity of inequality. As a result, economic inequality came to be seen as consistent with

American ideals.* It was pictured as a necessary aspect of economic life which served to spur competition and growth. It was linked with a whole range of ideas—initiative, competition, access, mobility, survival of the fittest—whose major purpose was to suggest that the resentment, jealousy, and greed aroused by economic inequality were central to the successful functioning of a dynamic economy. Indeed, any policy or action which threatened to alter this inequality in any radical way was labelled dangerous to the whole economy because it might brake the initiative and combative spirit necessary for economic advance. This was an ancient notion which went back to the Puritans: "Whoever is for a parity in any Society will in the issue reduce things into a heap of confusion."[7] The Puritans, however, could hardly be accused of wanting a society motivated by greed and ambition. What took place in America was not a careful, rational move from one ideological position to another, but a justifying accommodation to the brute fact of capitalist power. The crude doctrine of inequality served to mask the fact that the upper echelons of the bourgeois class had consolidated their power in American life.

Having come to accept the inevitability of economic inequality, Americans have turned to celebrate the doctrine of political equality as the unique feature of American democracy. The right to vote and the exercise of sovereign power through a republican form of government is put forward as more important than economic equality. And to those who argue that economic life and security is far more important than any ideal associated with the right to vote, the proponents of the superiority of political democracy argue that even economic affairs can be regulated through the ballot. Even James Madison was not taken in by such an argument: "Theoretic politicians . . . have erroneously supposed that by reducing mankind to a perfect equality in their political rights, they would at the same time be perfectly equalized . . . in their possessions. . . ."[8] It is true that the exercise of political democracy has had its effect on the economic order, but it has not been an adequate tool to fashion equality. The class basis of society, in which the highest echelons of the capital-owning class effectively control the political machinery of the state, precludes the use of political democracy to destroy the class structure even if, theoretically, this were possible. Political activity will not compel economic institutions to adhere to the goal of economic equality. As Arthur Hadley noted fifty years ago in language applicable today: "The voter . . . could make what laws he pleased, as long as these laws did not trench upon property right. . . . Democracy was complete

---

*Further the doctrine was transformed into the doctrine of equality of opportunity, quite a different thing. The latter posits creating relatively equal starting positions in the economic race but ignores the fact that the race inevitably produces only a few winners. Thus it means equal opportunity for future inequality.

as far as it went, but constitutionally it was bound to stop short of *social democracy.*"[9] All the political reforms of the last half-century, as helpful as they have been, still leave untouched the class basis of this society and the vast inequity in wealth and power that springs from it.

It was the bourgeois class that elaborated the basis of the modern state by supporting political liberty and equality against the feudal aristocracy. However, the threat of the industrial working class forced the bourgeoisie in America (and elsewhere) to separate political equality from economic equality and to espouse the former while denying the latter, precisely because to grant the latter would be tantamount to surrendering the power they had secured at the expense of their aristocratic foes. That the ruling class in America has shared a great degree of wealth with those classes beneath it bespeaks the great prosperity and wealth which abounds on this continent, but it does not mean that the essential class basis of the society has altered, or that there has been a real sharing of power or, most importantly, that the fifteen percent of the American people who live in poverty have any prospects for economic parity.*

2

All inequality derives from expropriation.[10] In order to sustain inequality in wealth or property, some people must not only take from others but ensure, either by law, custom, or sheer force, that others do not gain enough property or capital to threaten groups in power. Hence the two great formative groups of the twentieth century—the Western capital-owning class and the Eastern Bolsheviks—have relentlessly and ruthlessly expropriated both land and capital from masses of people. While this expropriation flatly contradicts theories of democratic socialism, in no way does it clash with the fundamental notions of capitalism.

There are those, particularly modern conservatives, who look upon the early years of the American republic as a model time in which freedom and equality flourished under capitalism. Perhaps there is some justice in this view, but it can only be held by someone who overlooks the immense degree

---

*It should be noted that significant reform in America has not been due to the benevolence and progressive ideals of the propertied elite. While reform has often been instituted by them, the pressure for reform has always come as a result of the insurgency of workers and farmers. In practically every case the elites managed to institute reforms which at once calmed popular anger and saved propertied privileges. The popular bourgeois notion of historical change coming as a result of the ethical good will of "progressive" business or government (or church) leaders should be laid to rest forever.

of expropriation that was taking place then. Whatever "equality" a white American had with another white American, it was gained at the expense of people of color.* The continent that greeted energetic farmers, mechanics, and shopkeepers was not an uninhabited one; its occupants were a proud people whose customs clashed in practically every way with the dynamic capitalists who stole their land. Since there was little in the capitalist creed that prevented the strong from taking from the weak, the Indians of North America were the first to pay for the success of the American economic experiment. The reduction of the Indian population from over one million in the early eighteenth century to under one hundred thousand in the late nineteenth century, the disruption of an ancient culture and forced removal of whole tribes from their land, characterized capitalist growth in America. While some may speak in terms of racism and others in terms of sheer moral rapacity, the simple, outstanding fact which underlies all sociological, psychological, and moral explanations of white brutality was the need for land, which the Indians had and which white Americans wanted.

In similar fashion, it goes without saying that the black people who were brought to this land as slaves did not enjoy the connection between work and ownership that white people did. The labor of black people built and maintained the American South. And in the North and West black people toiled as the cheapest human labor and laid the groundwork for an industrial empire. Nowhere was the black man or black woman exempt from exploitation, that is, exempt from the process by which employers accumulate capital through the toil and misery of the worker. And nowhere was the black person a part of the American dream of equality. "The classless society," notes the American historian Henry Nash Smith, "of fee-simple empire had no place for the Negro."[12] No place, that is, save as part of a cheap labor pool.

The rise of the corporation as the central economic unit in American life meant further exploitation. Land came into corporate possession and huge amounts of capital were gathered by the new industrial giants, all at the expense of the industrial working class. *In a capitalist economy reward and privilege arise not from the amount, length, or difficulty of labor but from the ownership of property or capital.* Thus it was that the working class built America even though the capitalist class owned it. During America's industrial revolution the worker's wages and working conditions were horrifying. Further, the toll in ill health, anxiety, fear, and personal misery was incalculable. "It is safe to conclude," writes one historian, "that 80 per cent of Americans lived in 1900 on the margin of subsistence while the remaining 20 per cent controlled almost the entire wealth of the country."[13] This was not simply

*In this discussion one should not overlook the fact of poverty in early America. Jackson Main[11] estimates that in the early period thirty percent of the population was "permanently poor."

because of some moral fault of the owners. Rather, it was part of the logic of the growth of corporate capitalism, part of the logic of growth which determined that economic progress would be made at the price of exploitation and misery.

It is true, however, that material exploitation and oppression have lessened considerably over the last seventy years. The decline in absolute misery and impoverishment is a salient feature of contemporary American capitalism. The vast increases in productivity and efficiency over the years have resulted in the creation of enormous wealth which has to an important degree spread throughout the masses of people. As a consequence modern American capitalism has secured the loyalty of the masses through a widespread system of material rewards. And it has rendered obsolete the Marxist projection of the intensification of the class struggle because of the increase in mass misery. In fact, the potential for conflict which was rooted in the class struggle of the early industrial period is no longer clearly visible. Class antagonisms have become latent, and conflict in the industrial system occurs over other issues such as disparity of development (race and poverty) or resentment at manipulative and hierarchical control (the youth counter-culture).

But the decrease in general impoverishment is not the same thing as equality. It is one thing to distribute social wealth more equitably and to raise the general level of well-being; but it is quite another to talk about equality and the end of oppression. However much there might be satisfaction in comparing the present with the past, the most important comparison remains between what is and what will be. Further, it must be remembered that even the shift to relative from absolute inequality does not erase the fact that it is still inequality. As Karl Marx noted long ago:

> The rapid growth of productive capital brings about an equally rapid growth of wealth, luxury, social wants, social employments. Thus, although the enjoyments of the worker have risen, the social satisfactions which they give him fall in comparison with the increased enjoyments of the capitalists which are inaccessible to the worker, and in comparison with the state of development of society in general. Our desires and pleasures spring from society; we measure them, therefore, by society. . . .[14]

There is today a general consensus about the benevolence of capitalism. There is also inequality and the exercise of class privilege. Thus it remains true that, in spite of the lessening potential for traditional class conflict, the capitalist system continues to provoke inequities of a most significant kind.

This is evident in three important ways.

In the first place, the move from laissez faire capitalism to present-day corporate capitalism has been accompanied by increased hierarchical control. The intervention of the state to ensure a minimum degree of economic stability, and the increased rationalization of industry itself, have led to the concentration and exercise of authority at the highest levels. The pressures various reform movements have brought to bear on the American ruling class have often produced fairer wages, and sometimes power is exercised in conformity with, rather than in opposition to, human needs; but these pressures have always been blunted at the point where power would be distributed more equitably and control exercised democratically. Economic reform is one thing, economic democracy is quite another. Thus the inequality of power characterizes modern American society. "Control," former Defense Secretary Robert McNamara has said, "must remain at the top."

Secondly, the protection of the American corporation leads to the extension of class privilege and the institutionalization of inequality. The corporation is the central economic unit in our capitalist society and, as such, receives central consideration in all public policy. If there is to be prosperity, then the health and vigor of this unit must be promoted. Indeed, the essential viability of the corporation provides the outer limit to all activities of the trade unions and of the state. All reform measures must stop at the point where they hamper corporate activity because to proceed further is to endanger the dynamism of the whole capitalist economy.

But the protection of the corporations means also the protection of the class which uses the corporation to maintain its power, namely the upper echelons of the bourgeois class. The corporations do not exist *for* the workers even though jobs are provided and goods or services produced. Clearly the corporations exist for those who own them. And despite generally high wages in many industries it can hardly be demonstrated that there is any equality either in power or in income between workers and managers or owners.* The latter still exercise control and receive a disproportionate percentage of the wealth generated by the corporations. The corporation remains the primary vehicle by which the higher ranks of the capitalist class exercise power and enjoy privilege. And if the economy of the nation is to remain a capitalist economy, it must adjust to this reality. As a result " . . . the prosperity of the capital-owning class," notes Robert Heilbroner, "is a central aim of economic policy."[15] This central aim is registered in terms of legislation, tax structures, and legal arrangements which bias the economy in favor of the corporations and the class they serve.

Consider the following examples:

Oilmen, homebuilders, stock market speculators, investors in tax-free bonds, and others who are at the top of the economic pyramid and

---

*The argument that workers, too, are owners because they hold stock in corporations falls when it is recognized that, according to the Brookings Institution, only two percent of the working class owns stock.

possessors of large capital legally withhold $50 million in taxes annually because of the nature of the tax system.[16]

Backdoor subsidies for industry from tax breaks, incentives, allowances, and exemptions allow big business legally to withhold between $9.5 billion and $15 billion per year from the government.[17]

Government loans to profit-making concerns during the 1971 fiscal year amounted to $250 billion, six times the outstanding credit advanced by all commercial banks.[18]

Railroads ($172 million over five years), airlines ($63 million per year) and shipping ($450 million per year) are all subsidized by the federal government. Publishers get a subsidy in the form of low second-class mail rates. The air space used by radio and television is public property, but the communication stations pay no charge for use of it.[19]

Corporate taxes are reduced $2 billion per year because of the surtax exemption, $350 million by virtue of tax breaks for firms doing business overseas, $325 million by special concessions to firms doing mineral exploration, and $1.3 billion for depletion allowances on natural resources.[20]

In 1971, Harold Geneen, President of ITT, garnered $822,000 in salaries and bonuses. In addition over fifty executives of Ford Motor Company received $5 million in bonuses. In 1969 the richest one-sixth among individual or corporate farmers received two-thirds of all agricultural subsidies, a sum near $2.5 billion.[21]

Business groups and others avoiding property taxes amounts to a subsidy from local taxpayers of over $7 billion.[22]

Five percent of the population of the United States owns the capital—money, securities, land and tools—that produces almost ninety percent of the nation's wealth.[23]

1.6 percent of the population owns eighty percent of the corporate stock held in the individual sector, ninety percent of the corporate bonds and one hundred percent of the municipal bonds.[24]

As a result of the privileges enjoyed by the corporations, the highest reaches of the capitalist class find their power safeguarded. For despite all the reform measures of the last seventy years, as Hans Morgenthau has recently pointed out, " . . . when it comes to the over-all distribution of power in American society, they [the reform movements] all appear in retrospect as essentially futile. . . ."[25] The top twenty percent of the population still gets almost fifty percent of the real national income every year, and that figure excludes the assessed value of capital ownership, which is also highly concentrated in the upper income strata. Indeed, according to Joseph Pechman, there has been no change in income distribution in a generation.[26] It could in fact be argued that between 1952 and 1967 the effective rate of taxation on the rich has actually declined because social security, unemployment insurance, state and local taxes are calculated on a fixed rather than progressive scale.

There is still a third way in which inequality is imbedded in the capitalist system. In a private economy capital will necessarily flow to those enterprises in which there is likely to be a high rate of profit: manufacturing, consumer goods, or consumer services. Areas concerned with public health, public services, welfare, natural resources, and environmental protection do not promise a high rate of return and consequently have been taken over, to a large degree, by public authority. But in an economy which must protect the fortunes of the corporations, capital expenditure in the public sector of the economy cannot be so great that it either removes excess capital from corporations or severely limits their growth.* Thus, for example, in August, 1971, when President Nixon ordered a freeze on all wages and prices, without at the same time declaring a ceiling on corporate profits, he was not being devious or unfair; he was doing what any American President would have to do: safeguard the health of the private economy. In this case, by not ordering a ceiling on profits he was directing money, which could be siphoned into the public sector through taxes, back into the private sector in order to bolster the private economy. Characteristically many Democrats enhanced their popularity by denouncing the President's move, but they offered no alternative, precisely because in a capitalist economy there is none. The imbalance between the public and private sectors of the economy reveals a central dilemma of capitalist society: relative individual prosperity in the midst of decaying cities, collapsing education, spreading pollution, and inadequate public transportation and health care.

Consider the following examples:

During the period between 1938-1968 the federal government, through cheap credit and tax breaks, helped to construct over ten million units of upper and middle class housing while it provided only 650,000 units of low-cost housing for the poor. This prompted a White House Conference

---

*Ernest Mandel has argued that the corporations must always hold back on their support of moves directed toward increasing mass consumption. Too much consumer power tends to lead toward lower rates of profit.[27]

in 1966 to suggest that the entire lower half of the American population is excluded from the market for new housing. And a Presidential Commission noted in 1968, " . . . over the last decades, government action through urban renewal, highway programs, demolitions on public housing sites, code enforcement, and other programs has destroyed more housing for the poor than the government at all levels has built for them." In 1970 the Senate Select Committee on Nutrition and Human Need confirmed this view: "The federal government has proved to be more efficient at destroying low and moderate income housing than at providing it."[28]

In the 1960's the American welfare system reached only one-third of the poor, providing them with only one-half of what they need.[29]

The federal government spends almost $2.5 billion per year on urban freeways but devotes only $175 million for mass transit.[30]

Seventy percent of the federal budget goes toward paying for past and present wars or preparing for future ones. Education receives only $4 billion in federal help.

The main purpose and largest outlay of the Department of Agriculture is directed toward keeping farm prices up by means of large subsidies. The feeding of the poor is only a secondary function. In one year Texas producers, who constitute .02 percent of the population of Texas, received $250 million in subsidies, while the poor people of Texas, 28.8 percent of the population, received $7 million in food assistance. Texas has the largest farm subsidy total in the nation, yet denies food aid to more people than any other state. In 1968, 99 of 253 counties in Texas took no part in the federal food stamp program.[31]

While the average income of an American physician is $35,000 per year, the United States ranks fourteenth among the industrialized countries of the world in the rate of infant mortality. In Watts, California the doctor-patient ratio is 1/2500. And in the United States there are over 5000 communities without a doctor.[32]

The economic imbalance between the public and private sectors (which becomes very serious during recessions because capital is withdrawn almost immediately from public services) is endemic to capitalism. And the great liberal slogan "the re-ordering of national priorities" only serves to substitute a cliché for serious consideration of a structural problem. Even if there were a shift in priorities, the economic thrust would, of necessity, stop short of threatening the private economy. The private sector cannot deal successfully (or on a large scale) with public needs because these needs are not amenable to profit-making. As the Urban Growth Policy Report said, "The development of new communities by solely private means will occur in those rare circumstances where the dynamics for growth in particular areas will afford a timely and reasonable return on private investment."[33] Public authority is blocked from engaging in full-scale work because this would drain capital away from the private economy. In addition, the nation possesses no comprehensive collective ideology which could buttress such a move. After all, capitalism is accompanied by an ideology which focuses on individual concerns and private consumption and success. Any grand scheme to match public needs with public funds will fall short of shifting the emphasis of the economic system from private ownership and planning to social ownership and planning.

> The private form of appropriation makes profit the only aim and driving force of production. It causes the development of the productive forces to be uneven and spasmodic. Production develops by leaps and bounds, not in the sectors where the most urgent real needs are to be found, but rather in those where the highest profits can be achieved. The production of alcoholic drinks, of "comic books" and of drugs takes precedence over the struggle against air-pollution, the preservation of natural resources, and even the building of schools and hospitals.[34]

3

American capitalism has always been subject to cyclical crises which involve large-scale unemployment and slowdowns in material production. This results from a fundamental imbalance in capitalism due both to a lack of planning, and to a commitment to production for profit instead of production for need. Capitalist production is divided into two main sectors: one produces consumer goods, the other produces capital goods, i.e. machinery. Each sector must produce more than it can use. The consumer sector must produce a surplus of goods beyond that used by those employed in this sector so that those employed in the capital goods sector may purchase some. Likewise, the capital goods sector must produce enough industrial machinery both to replace its own stock and to sell to the consumer sector. In order for the economy to run smoothly, there must be a "balance of trade" between the two sectors, with the consumer sector bringing in machinery and sending out consumer goods and the capital goods sector importing consumer items and sending out machines. However, since capitalism has no central planning organ, it possesses no way to keep these two sectors in balance. Consequently when there is a "trade imbalance," there is a crises of overproduction in one sector or the other. And at that point the whole capitalist machinery begins to wind down until some way is found to bring the two sectors into relative balance again. Since 1854 there have been 27 periods of crises averaging 19 months of recession and then 33 months of expansion.

In an important way the development of the corporation was a response to the chaos of laissez faire capitalism. Giant companies are not evil structures arbitrarily imposed on a free, small, natural, edenic political economy. Rather they are a rational response to the instability of a "free market" economy. The corporation possesses the power to restrict competition, control production, prevent falling prices, regulate investment, ensure the depreciation of capital, and determine mass employment; in short, the power to regulate the market, and the power, within limits, to "balance trade."* However, even the move to corporate capitalism did not truly stabilize the economy. Nor did the intervention of the state into the economy. The limits of effectiveness are clearly established: this is a capitalist economy and all efforts toward planning must stop short of threatening the prosperity of the capital-owning class. Thus, unable or unwilling to balance the domestic economy, American businesses have, particularly since 1890, sought to solve their dilemma by creating markets abroad which would absorb the surplus capital and goods produced at home. Since the corporations would not allow for planning toward social needs and equality, they expanded overseas in the hope that ever increasing wealth and prosperity would somehow solve all problems. During the Great Depression, for example, Secretary of State Cordell Hull explicitly focused on expanded trade as a means of relieving the pressure created by excessive domestic production and limited domestic consumption.

This strategy, however, runs the risk of conflict with other capitalist powers intent upon expansion. World War I, for example, was in large measure a clash fought over imperial markets. Similarly, the hostilities between the United States and Japan in 1941 were preceded by a period of intense economic struggle over raw materials.[36]

---

*As J. Kenneth Galbraith so clearly demonstrates in The New Industrial State (New York, 1967), the modern corporation is pre-eminently qualified to bypass the free market. But this has always been true of the corporation. H. H. Rogers, an associate of John D. Rockefeller, noted in 1874, "If by common consent, in good faith, the refiners agree to reduce the quantities to an allotment for each, made in view of the supply and demand, and the capacity for production, the market can be regulated with a reasonable profit for all. The price of oil today is fifteen cents per gallon. The proposed allotment of business would probably advance the price to twenty cents. . . . Oil to yield a fair profit should be sold for twenty-five cents per gallon."[35] Before the Pujo Committee in 1913 J. P. Morgan noted: "I like a little competition, but I like a little combination better . . . without control you cannot do a thing."

4

After World War II the United States emerged as the world's greatest capitalist power. As such she dominated the world economy, and from this position sought to solve her two major economic problems. First, she needed to overcome domestic imbalance by expanding overseas without provoking a world-wide crisis in the form of an indiscriminate scramble among capitalist powers for markets. American economic expansion overseas was facilitated by the injection of capital into the shattered European economy (the Marshall Plan), which ensured markets for American capital and goods, while United States economic predominance precluded any immediate or serious competition for markets.* Likewise, America's overriding power enabled her to secure a second major objective: preventing third world countries from organizing their economies either to block the steady outward flow of raw materials needed for American industrial growth, or to bar American capital investment and industrial sales. Not only could America control the flow of capital into underdeveloped nations (either by means of direct control over private investment and government aid, or through her control of the World Bank and other international sources of capital, all of which are primarily dependent upon the United States for capital), but she did not hesitate to intervene militarily in countries whose policies were considered hostile to American interests. For almost two decades American economic growth and superiority were virtually unchallenged, and her business interests consistently dominated the world market. By the exercise of sheer national power America was able to order the economic world.

But events of the last decade have indicated that American hegemony is weakening. The growth of a vigorous capitalist Europe (in 1970 the total trade of the European Economic Community topped that of the United States), the emergence of an economically aggressive Japan (in 1970 America ran a trade deficit with Japan in high-technology products—heretofore our strongest field—of more than $1 billion), and persistent "disorder" in the countries of the third world clearly demonstrate a challenge to American world domination. As a result the continued success of the United States in the major areas of economic activity has been placed in jeopardy.

---

*In 1946, U.S. direct overseas investment amounted to $7.2 billion. By 1967 that sum had boomed to $60 billion; in 1970 it amounted to $71 billion; in 1971 it was $85 billion. Dean Acheson provided the political rationale for this by declaring before a special Committee on Post-War Economic Policy and Planning in 1944 that unless there were foreign markets to absorb our "creative energy," the nation would sink back into a depression which would necessitate that "we change our Constitution, our relations to property, human liberty, our very conceptions of law. . . ." "Nobody," Acheson warned, "contemplates that." Indeed, no one did then and few do now.

The growth of a competitive capitalist Europe and an industrious Japan is particularly worrisome to the United States. As I noted above, post-World War Two American commercial activity stressed overseas investment in order to provide American businesses with an outlet for their surplus capital and at the same time prepare the market for their goods. This policy was in the tradition of liberal imperialism in that it was designed to throw open markets and encourage free trade as a means of securing advantage for American exporters. But this policy led directly to the economic recovery of Japan and Europe beyond the point where they simply received American capital and goods. These countries soon became successful competitors. As a consequence Japan was able seriously to undercut American prices on the world market while the European Common Market in the 1960's began erecting barriers to block the entrance of American goods.

These nations now constitute a threat to American economic supremacy. This can be seen most vividly in the current crisis over our balance of payments deficit. In the past, American capital outflow (mostly in import purchases, overseas capital investment, and overseas military expenditures) has been offset by returns from foreign investment and large export sales. This is no longer always the case. While yearly returns on foreign investment continue greater than the annual outflow of new investment (in 1970 the surplus amounted to $1.5 billion), the trade surpluses of the past ninety years have in recent periods turned into trade deficits. The trade situation is particularly egregious. Not only are other countries outselling us in durable goods and raw materials, but they are gaining on us in the sale of high-technology items (cars, aircraft, etc.) as evidenced by the 1970 surplus in this area, which was only $9 billion. It is, of course, true that the United States could continue to run a periodic trade deficit if the return on foreign investments could be raised to a significantly high level. In such a case America would serve as the world's creditor. The encouragement given to overseas investment by the Nixon administration (and likely to be continued under Democratic administrations) through the easing of anti-trust enforcement and the work of the Overseas Private Investment Corporation (a government loss-insurance program) clearly indicates the importance given to increased investment abroad as a major component of our attempt to solve our financial problems.

However, since at present we do not have a significant enough income from overseas investment to compensate for other capital expenditures, trade policy has drawn the most attention from policy-makers. At home, greater productivity has been demanded of American workers while the government has urged the formation of Domestic International Sales Corporations (DISC) which provide huge tax breaks for companies increasing their export trade. But even more important have been the concessions wrung from our major trading partners. In an extraordinary show of national power the United States, in the Smithsonian Accords of December 18, 1971, literally compelled its ten leading trading partners to lower trade barriers and revalue their currencies upward so that the United States could once again run an annual trade surplus of $7-10 billion and balance her overall payments. Thus these countries were induced to sponsor the continued acceleration of American foreign investments and overseas military expenditures by overhauling and adjusting their own economies. With his customary frankness, former Treasury Secretary John Connally explained the American position in an interview to *The Wall Street Journal.*

> The most fundamental issue yet to be decided by other nations, Mr. Connally said, is "are they willing to let us have a surplus?" He doesn't think they have yet accepted the idea that the system should be reformed in such a way that would let the United States run a surplus. . . .
>   Other countries should accept deficits of their own, Mr. Connally argued, through such actions as reducing barriers to U. S. goods and diverting resources and employment away from export industries and into domestic social sectors such as curbing pollution. That would help the U. S. economy by permitting more exports than imports, and allow outflows for investment, defense and other purposes abroad. . . .[37]

The Smithsonian Agreements secured a continued (and expensive) defense posture abroad and protected the right of ongoing and increasing American international investments. The expansionist policies which arise out of our domestic imbalances have momentarily triumphed, but only with the crude exercise of national power. And it is clear that the exercise of that power is limited. In addition, the world's capitalist powers continue to grow in strength, raising once more the spectre of intense and perhaps violent competition for world trade and markets. Thus the question remains, How can we guarantee pre-eminence and secure markets ("the size of the foreign market [for domestic and United States firms] is equal to approximately two-fifths of the domestic output of farms, factories or mines")[38] without effective retaliation from our competitors? The use of raw national power is no longer a sufficient device.

It is in this context that one should understand the extraordinary growth and influence of the multinational corporation.* The international corpora-

---

*The American multinational corporation is particularly staggering in size and influence. Sixty-two of the top 100 American firms have production facilities in at least six foreign countries. In addition, about sixty percent of the top 126 businesses averaged one-third of their employment abroad. One-fifth of the total assets of America's largest 500 industrials is invested abroad while the total value of the American business enterprise abroad is $100 billion. The United States has eighteen of the twenty largest world companies; and of the international firms with sales of more than $285 million in 1968, sixty percent were based in America. In 1968, American businesses sold $200

tion is a business organization in which a domestic corporation exercises ownership or control over related enterprises in other lands in order better to facilitate production, secure credit, utilize resources, and control marketing so that profit and development are more easily and efficiently maintained. The giant corporations experienced their most rapid growth precisely at the time the European Common Market was hurting American business by erecting barriers against the influx of American goods. By establishing European branches or production facilities or by controlling European companies, American corporations were able to skirt these trade walls. However, the European action meant that Europeans were questioning the long-standing belief that free trade was a neutral matter. Now they saw it as a cover for continued American economic dominance. Their economic challenge meant that America could no longer rely on the old free trade ideology (nor on a simple anti-communist ideology, since the communists are no longer our principal economic adversary, which helps to explain the eclipse of cold-war hysteria) in order to dominate the world market. Instead, the multinational corporation has become the vehicle of entrance to markets. Moreover, it is a vehicle that attracts various national bourgeoisie and thus creates both an international business structure and an international class fraternity, which threaten to undermine the nation-state. "They are virtually sovereign states operating world-wide and commanding greater resources than many of the governments with which they deal,"[39]   claims Anthony Wedgewood Benns, former Labour Minister of Technology in England.

Not only is the multinational enterprise the natural consequence of a domestic economy whose imbalance necessitates expansion, and not only is the international company a means of securing capital to help our balance of payments, but, more importantly, the multinational corporation is a device that now hopes to order the world market in such a way as to eliminate crude instabilities and competition. It seeks to establish and at the same time dominate a world market free from inordinate imbalances. Thus, what domestic corporations failed to do for the domestic economy—regulate the market and stabilize the economy without sacrificing profit—the multinational corporation purports to do on the international scene.

The international conglomerate claims to point to a post-national world. In this world, national economies give place to the more accurate and beneficial world economy regulated by the giant corporations. " . . . There must be greater unification of the world economy to give full play to the

---

billion of goods overseas of which $165 million was produced outside the United States. So vast is American participation in international economics that the combined output of all firms now exceeds the total revenues of all but two nations. It is estimated that, at the present rate of expansion, by the year 2000 some 300 corporations (200 of them American) will completely dominate the world economy. By 1980, it is projected, these firms will control seventy-five percent of the world's manufacturing assets.

benefits of the Multinational corporation,"[40] argues George Ball. By creating "one world" of business extending beyond national frontiers, the multi-national corporation assumes that matters of resource allocation, capital investment, and technological development, which had heretofore received attention in the competitive and inflammatory world of national ambition, will be more rationally and efficiently controlled for everyone's benefit. Thus the international business firm of the post-national world " . . . will ultimately provide a means of unifying and reconciling the aspirations of mankind—a task which all the politicians have utterly failed to achieve."[41]

What emerges is a vision of a world capitalist utopia. A generation ago Harry S. Truman wished that the whole world would adopt the American system. He may get his wish. With the development of the multinational corporation the old capitalist dream of the free market operating without external interference (in the present case the action of the nation-state), and in accordance with the objective laws of the market, is now projected onto the whole world. The major point is to shift the world economy from that of competing national interests to an international market dominated by the law of supply and demand and presided over by the giant international companies. Of course, it just happens that eighteen of the twenty largest world corporations are American owned or controlled, making it rather a foregone conclusion who will benefit most from the new law of the international free market.

Just when it will happen that the temporary phase of reactionary nationalism (in which it becomes regrettably necessary to protect the world economy by first protecting the American economy) will give way to a true economic internationalism, in which no one benefits at the expense of another, is unclear. Nor is it precisely clear what shape the new world market will take. Presumably it will combine development with equality, though in the past capitalism, while strong on the former, has been notoriously weak on the latter. In fact most of the signs point in another direction. The internationalism and "law of the world market" which the spokesmen and spokeswomen of the international conglomerates speak of as a new utopia are, in fact, the same old instruments of imperialist* power which serve the strong (predominantly the United States) at the expense of the weak. Instead of a new internationalism, the development of the multinational corporation is but a more sophisticated and flexible form of bourgeois class rule.

---

*In the age of the multinational corporation, imperialism refers primarily to the safety of the market for capitalist expansion. *"What matters to the business community, and to the business system as a whole, is that the option of foreign investments and [foreign trade] should remain available.* For this to be meaningful, the business system requires, as a minimum, that the political and economic principles of capitalism should prevail and that the door be fully open for foreign capital at all times."[42]

The raw materials and markets of the under-developed countries are another major concern of American economic policy. It should be noted that at present most third world countries export hardly anything besides minerals and agricultural products. The present exploitative relationship between the American-dominated Western companies and the nations of the third world may give us a clue about the "beneficent" form of the future national economy. Undoubtedly the present is characterized by some of the worst kind of exploitation.

The rapid growth of the American-led Western world and its attendant capital investment policy has brought about a situation in which the countries of the third world are in a perpetual state of economic dependency and deprivation. "By all standard tests—capital, literacy, rise in production capacity—things are getting worse," declared the World Bank in 1967. The materially advanced Western nations do the great majority of business with themselves. A sophisticated industrial base, technical skills, common traditions, ample and relatively stable capital flow, and established consumption patterns determine where investments and interest will go. The United States, for example, does three-fifths of its export business with Europe and Canada. As a result, the countries of the third world pay an enormous price in terms of economic development. The capitalist world economy is designed to ensure Western and particularly American hegemony; the third world does not exist for its own sake, but for the role it plays in the integrated world economy dominated by American corporations. Consequently, the third world has been forced to rely primarily on the production and sale of primary goods (agricultural goods and extraction products, i.e. minerals) as a means of accumulating capital for development. But the prices of these goods are notoriously unstable and particularly subject to sharp drops. Because of the development of synthetics and because service industries and high-technology industries do not require as much raw material, the industrial West does not require the same large amount of raw materials that it once did. Yet, even as the prices of primary goods remain depressed, the cost of transportation (again controlled by the West) rises. And more important, the cost of Western finished products needed by poorer countries continues to go up. As a result, the third world's share of the world export market is shrinking. Between 1956 and 1966, for example, the third world's share of world exports dropped from twenty-five to twenty percent.* Much of this, of course, could be offset if there were a correspondingly high total of foreign aid from industrial countries. However, a large part of American foreign aid is tied to

*The Arab world, for example, imports $800 million worth of goods from the U. S. while exporting only $250 million worth. As a result of this imbalance, due to unfair trade patterns, the Arab world contributes over $500 million to the U. S. Treasury, almost one-fourth of the U. S. trade surplus.

arrangements requiring that recipients purchase highly priced American products. Even beyond this, advanced capitalist nations have been devoting consistently declining percentages of their gross national products to foreign assistance since 1961.[43] As a result of all these factors it is obvious why the United Nations Secretariat should note recently that the annual gap between what developing countries require merely to feed their populations, and what they can expect from selling their products, is now some $20 billion per year.

Of course, some countries would very much like to break out of this dependency relationship and advance rapidly to a higher industrialized stage. At this point, however, with few exceptions (for example, the Arab countries with their capital from oil) the only capital available is from the multinational corporations. Inevitably, if these corporations are to direct the development of the native economy they will do so primarily to suit the needs of the world-wide capitalist economy. The whole process is admirably described by Joan Robinson:

> . . . nowadays the developed nations do not want *their* industries to be undersold; the markets open to would-be developing nations are narrowly limited. Even processing of their own raw material is kept in check by the tariff arrangements which protect processing industries which grew up in the imperialist countries on the basis of colonial raw materials.
>
> The great international corporations which act as buyers of primary products, or set up manufacturing concerns in the territory of the ex-colonial nations, contribute a great deal to their economies. They bring advanced techniques of marketing and production, train labor and subsidiary levels of the technostructure and support the growth of local businesses ancillary to their own. But the spiral of development cannot be set going in this way. The surplus is largely transmitted out of the country in the form of profits. When there is re-investment in expanding the business on the spot it makes a contribution to development, but a high price has to be paid for it. The new capital created on the spot is the legal property of the foreign company and has to pay dividends to foreign shareholders.
>
> The international companies, perfectly correctly from their own point of view, arrange their investments around the world and manipulate the flow of production from one centre or another to suit the requirements of their own profitability, not to promote the viability or growth of particular national economies.[44]

"There are," warns Philip H. Trezise, Assistant Secretary for Economic Affairs of the State Department, " . . . the counterrevolutionaries who consider national loyalties more deep-rooted and enduring than multinational investment."[45] Nationalist feelings, particularly if they are coupled, as they often are, with a socialist ideology, are a threat to the new global economy dominated by American corporations, because such hopes may lead to an economy organized in terms of national goals. Worse, a developing nation may define its self-interest as withdrawal from the capitalist orbit. Apologists for the multinational corporation, using the neutral language of scientific technology, see this possibility as "irrational and inefficient." In effect, however, third world nationalism which prefers to organize its economic affairs apart from the needs of the capitalist world poses a distinct threat to the power of the Western capitalist class. If trade and investment possibilities are seriously curtailed because of nationalist ideology, then Western capitalism and the class it supports are likewise threatened.* Thus the international corporations

> . . . exercise a strong influence, through the policies of the United States and the ex-imperial powers and through the interests of the native capitalists allied to them, to prevent the local government from getting control over the management of its economy through taxation, tariffs or other devices and (above all) nationalization, so as to keep the country open to the operation of free enterprise. This system has been characterized as neo-colonialism, because it deprives the new national governments of the independence which was granted on paper when they were set up.[47]

In order to create stable conditions for the "open door" to capitalist investment and trade, Western capitalists depend upon the services of the various national bourgeoisie. Drawn largely from urban centers where the older, traditional, often peasant values have broken down and the outlines of Western materialistic culture are now forming, the native bourgeoisie have drawn the responsibility of muting nationalistic fervor—or at least making it compatible with international capitalism. This class serves as the major national beneficiary of foreign trade and investment (and hence wealth and power), and thus often finds it in its own interest to serve as a buffer against the anger and militancy that periodically arise from the dispossessed urban and peasant masses. In addition, this class has become the major bearer of Western, materialistic, and consumer values. It is hoped that the social, political, and economic activities of this group will produce habits and institutions embodying the acquisitive values necessary for capitalist development and the emergence of a future consumer economy.

The development in third world countries of a national bourgeois class, able to link up with the higher bourgeoisie in all parts of the world, points to another dimension of modern imperialism. The present phase of imperial exploitation, in which surplus value mainly in agricultural and mineral products is transferred out to Western corporations, is by no means determined to last forever. Only the crudest form of imperialist theory (one that equates

*It is against this background that one understands why sixty percent of the key foreign policy decision-makers in the U. S. government between the years 1944 and 1960 were men drawn from the interlocking world of big banking, corporate law, and large industry, a trend which, according to the Brookings Institution, continues today.[46]

imperialism with colonialism) would overlook the possibility of the eventual development of many poor countries.* At present, Western interests require mass impoverishment around the globe both for cheap labor and for cheap products. But for this situation to continue would mean the loss of an extensive market for Western goods. It is quite likely that Western needs will eventually demand development and consumerism rather than poverty and misery. The multinational corporation would appear to be admirably equipped to bring this about. By integrating the international bourgeoisie into the great companies and thus going "beyond nationalism" they will be able to avoid the two major problems that plague contemporary imperialism: development will make national uprisings unnecessary, and internationalism will preclude destabilizing competition from purely national companies. In such a way the multinational corporation exists to bring the world market under control.† What we have to look forward to, then, is a "technocratic vision of a planetary economy controlled by a unified elite of scientifically trained managers who have left the national state behind and merged their separate identities in the formation of a global cartel linking all the industrially advanced centers of the world."[49]

Imperialism would be exercised more in terms of power, control, and domination than through sustained material impoverishment. Thus, the development of an international bourgeois class limits alternative conceptions of social structure and social reality, until the Western need and reward system can be implemented throughout the world. At that time the desire for material prosperity could be met in general if uneven ways, and in return the masses would give up their own visions of political or social life.‡ Clearly the more enlightened elements of Western capitalistic leadership look forward to such a world. However, apart from the spectre of socialist revolution which would upset these plans, there is also the possibility that a shortage of world resources would make impossible such a general material advance and force

---

*The absence of development is caused by other factors besides imperialism. Such matters as a primitive social structure, overpopulation, poor agricultural resources, are very much involved. Nor is the absence of foreign capital a necessary impediment to development. In the early 1900's Japan developed without extensive foreign capital.

†Whatever the future prospects, the United States is hardly sacrificing present national needs. U. S. foreign policy outside of Europe still focuses on client centers (Brazil, Japan, Southern Africa) in various hemispheres. These serve not only as economic outposts but as imperial police agents. However, because it is still a time of national feeling these countries are also our competitors economically. The multinational corporations hope to mesh all world interests together and transcend such crude competition.[48]

‡The central contradiction remains, however. Production for private profit—even on an international scale—inevitably clashes with social need.

liberal capitalists to join hands with conservatives in stabilizing the world, by whatever means, to the absolute advantage of the American-led West.

In the whole process of controlling world capitalism, the United States reaps a large reward. Its burgeoning economy, fed by enormous profits drawn from throughout the world, is the most affluent in world history. But as the Indians, Mexicans, blacks, and other poor people paid the price of America's first industrial advance, the third world now pays the price of our continued prosperity. The human cloth is of a piece; the prosperous are always sustained by the misery of the weak. Thus the United States makes up only six percent of the world's population and yet controls thirty percent of the world's markets, thirty-three percent of the world's natural resources, and sixty percent of the world's goods and services.

Through the multinational corporation, the United States hopes to fashion a world in its own image. At home, the general advance of the working class has made it unlikely that there will be any massive challenge to the rule of the big capitalists or any desire to move toward an equalitarian society. Radical activists are too small to pose much of a threat and can be easily crushed by repressive moves when the occasion warrants it. Meanwhile, the resentments and occasional outbursts which are part of a society foundationed on imbalances and inequities are diverted or controlled by the increasingly hierarchical form of life and the intensification of manipulation. Likewise, abroad, the security of the world capitalist class is guaranteed by the promise of gradual development (which only the multinational corporation can finance) and the control of insurgency, either by military intervention or by the extended use of paramilitary and police tactics, bolstered by new technological devices which can be employed against radical outbreaks. In this sense the nation-state is still useful; it has the police. The result is a world society dominated by large capitalists in which inequality and exploitation are institutionalized even as world misery decreases. There is nothing in capitalism that points to equality; surely the world capitalist class, either now or in the future, sees no particular advantage to dividing equally the resources of the world or the power they now have. Capitalism is a system that guarantees power to ruling groups, and they are not likely to act differently from any previous ruling class. They will maintain their power until it is taken from them.

The prospects for the demise of world capitalism, it must be admitted, are quite slim. In the heartland of capitalist power, the United States, one is hard put to discover the outlines of a successful mass movement against capitalism. The incredible affluence of the nation, the docility and confusion of the people, the power of the ruling group, the general satisfaction with a certain degree of comfort, the absence of an anti-capitalist tradition of any significance and size—all combine to suggest that the American system is stable enough to pursue its imperialist adventures indefinitely. Further, the European socialist bloc, led to a large degree by the Soviet Union, appears so intent upon economic development (and cooperation with capitalist corporations) that they have given no sign that they are part of a concerted world effort to destroy capitalism. They demonstrate only a concern to prosper economically.

And yet from a Christian standpoint one could hardly think of an uglier configuration than the institutionalization of inequality and a world dominated by a small capitalist class. The equality of all people and their common destiny in the kingdom of God contradict this. Thus it is that the signs of God's power must be anticipated. After looking at the ideology of the bourgeois order, we shall examine those signs of hope which are appearing in the present, signs that point to the implacable will of God to establish his kingdom of love, peace, and justice.

Chapter Three

The TRAVAIL of FREEDOM in the AMERICAN CORPORATE STATE

Our conception of history depends on our ability to expound the real process of production, starting out from the simple material production of life, and to comprehend the form of intercourse connected with this and created by this (i.e. civil society in its various stages), as the basis of all history; further to show it in its action as State; and so, from this starting point, to explain the whole mass of different theoretical products and forms of consciousness, religion, philosophy, ethics, etc., etc., and trace their origins and growth, by which means, of course, the whole thing can be shown in its totality (and therefore, too, the reciprocal action of these various sides on one another). —Karl Marx

The laws of commerce are the laws of nature and consequently the laws of God. —Edmund Burke

An empty sock can't stand up. —Benjamin Franklin

The possibility of regulation is a dream. As long as the control of the necessities of life and, thus, wealth remain private with individuals, it is they who will regulate and not we. —Henry Demarest Lloyd

1

"Business," wrote Francis Grund over a century ago, "is the very soul of an American: he pursues it, not as a means of procuring for himself and his family the necessities of life, but as the fountain of all human felicity."[1] This was as fitting a description of America in the nineteenth century as it would be in the twentieth century. The capitalist business system is at the heart of the American experience, and men and women have been compelled to find direction more from it than from abstract ideas of freedom and peace. In this

America has hardly been unique. She has always been a part of the growth and development of Western bourgeois society. Bourgeois society grew up within the old feudal order and then, in country after country, established itself at the expense of the old epoch. In each place the contours of a nation's particular traditions and history altered the form of the new bourgeois age, but everywhere the rising order exalted private property, guaranteed the sanctity of capital, extolled the free market, and deferred to the new class of proprietors who rode the capitalist wave to power. And everywhere the new bourgeois elite celebrated the life of business as its central activity. The business of America, noted Calvin Coolidge, is business.

Business capitalism took firm root in America in the early nineteenth century. It was a kind of golden age. The previous century had been marked by one or another form of mercantilism which had placed the development of American enterprise within some frame of colonial commitment and quasi-planning. But by the time of Andrew Jackson's Presidency, the American business system had generally burst free of the old mercantile fetters and was well on the way toward what has been accurately called laissez faire capitalism.

The economic landscape was dominated by farmers, shopkeepers, small bankers, mechanics, craftsmen, and traders, each moving about on a relatively unspoiled continent, striving and competing for their place in the economic sun. It was the time of small-unit entrepreneurs, characterized by widespread economic independence and direct ownership and control of the means of production. It was fertile soil for the development of capitalism.* Most appropriately this economy of private, small-unit ownership invited a corresponding political ideology. The sanctity of private property (and consequently of capital) seemed to Americans (and to those overseas soon to come to these shores) to be the surest vehicle to independence, success, and security. Individualism, and the guarantee of certain personal and political liberties, fostered and strengthened women and men in their pursuit of gain. The doctrine of equal opportunity (to be distinguished from the doctrine of equality) provided for the removal of artificial restraints for energetic entrepreneurs. Similarly, the possibility of government interference in personal or economic life seemed less a betrayal of abstract theory than a potential brake on individual acquisition and advance. It was opposed with characteristic vigor. "Let us alone," noted a nineteenth-century Methodist circuit rider, "is, generally speaking, the language of the merchant, the manufacturer, and the farmer; or, at least, do no more than remove impediments."[2] This was a time when it appeared as if Thomas Jefferson's nation of small farmers and

---

*In 1830, land was selling for $1.25 per acre, and during Jackson's Presidency over 63 million acres of the public domain was distributed.

mechanics, placidly practicing what were called republican virtues, would emerge triumphant in a new historical epoch of peace and freedom. The young nation exhibited an economic system dedicated to independent ownership of the means of production; fashioned a political system which featured individual liberty and democratic participation; and prescribed personal values of ambition, self-restraint, thrift, honesty, independence, initiative, and hard work. It was the golden age of American laissez faire capitalism.

In Europe, the new capitalist class had implanted its system on the remains of feudal society. The results were devastating, particularly in England. Old traditions were upset, occupations altered or destroyed, villages transformed by "dark, satanic mills" (Blake), ancient privileges denied, and human rights ignored.[3] But such was not the case in America. Here aggressive entrepreneurs met an open, rich continent. Instead of implanting a new industrial order upon a farm and shop economy, restless, ambitious individuals installed a farm and shop economy which slowly produced the capital that would eventually finance an industrial order. Americans did not destroy old feudal customs and traditions, they built new traditions. Instead of altering a well-defined continent, these "new men," as Hector St. John Crevecoer called them, proceeded to construct a new continent. The formative years of American capitalism and the political and social ideology dependent upon it preceded the horrors, tensions, and instabilities of industrialization. In America, the separation in time between the first exuberance of capitalist growth and the dismay of the industrial age has fostered a nostalgia for early capitalism and its associated ideology which has virtually precluded any full-scale questioning of its basic merit. Americans seem to recall their early days with something approaching edenic awe.

The American conception of freedom has been particularly exempt from critical examination. Whatever the soaring rhetoric about freedom, the content of this notion has always been limited by economic and individualistic presuppositions. The medieval term *libertas* suggested the right to exclude others from one's property. It contained the idea of privacy and exclusion based on privileges arising from ownership in which those who did not own property did not share. Safety in private ownership implied independence and the absence of restraint on the individual. Hence individualism, independence, and proprietary prerogatives were bound together in a comprehensive scheme. C. B. Macpherson brilliantly sums up the doctrine of freedom:

The individual . . . is free inasmuch as he is proprietor of his person and capacities. The human essence is freedom from dependence on the will of others, and freedom is a function of possession. Society becomes a lot of free equal individuals related to each other as proprietors of their own capacities and of what they acquired by their exercise. Society consists of relations of exchange between proprietors. Political society becomes a calculated device for the protection of this property and for the maintenance of an orderly relation of exchange.[4]

Clearly, the fullest realization of this idea followed the decline of the aristocratic order with its interrelated duties and communal responsibilities. It was in the struggle with the old aristocratic order that the bourgeois conception of freedom came to be most clearly articulated in terms of economic individualism. Indeed, much of the struggle for freedom in Anglo-American history is set within the context of the fight of the rising bourgeois class to escape the economic restraints of the monopolistic economic practices of royal governments.[5] The freedom of man, i.e. the freedom of the individual, was the political expression of freedom of property, just as royal absolutism was the expression of royal monopolies. The struggle against tyranny, which young America proclaimed to the world, was but the echo of the intention of bourgeois interests all over Europe to throw off the fetters of the feudal order.

In America there was no feudal aristocracy to struggle against, though often enough inflated rhetoric cast the federal government as tyrannous oppressor. However, the federal government was in no way similar to the old aristocracy; governmental restraints were never of the same magnitude or character as those imposed by royalist policies. Freedom in America was divorced from any large struggle which could have provided it with grandeur. Instead, freedom in America became associated with the exercise of untrammeled economic individualism. It was reduced to the elaboration of individual safety and proprietary exclusiveness. This development required no commitment to collective responsibility, embodied no common struggle, and possessed no conception of social reality. It was related only to economic expansion and the promise of ever larger shares in the apparently unlimited resources and wealth of the continent. Thus, freedom became the working out of individual economic enterprise apart from any consistent social emphasis or communal responsibility. "Few men can doubt," Martin Van Buren observed with candor, that "A system founded on private interest, enterprise, and competition, without the aid of legislative grants or regulations by law, would rapidly prosper."[6]

American apologists continued to draw upon appellatives from the golden past and apply them to the American experiment, and they continued to see America as the last great experiment in the history of freedom.

> Humanity with all its fears,
> with all the hopes of future years,
> is hanging breathless on thy fate.

But the rhetoric that depicted human destiny as the unfolding of republican liberty on this soil kept the nation from seeing that its conception of freedom was exceedingly narrow, that it was essentially devoid of any social dimension, and that, most important, it was very much related to a particular stage in the development of capitalism. These weaknesses would become all the more apparent when the form of capitalism changed in America.

Capitalism, Joseph A. Schumpeter noted, "is by nature a form or method of economic change and not only never is, but never can be, stationary. . . ."[7] The profit-seeking, energetic, acquisitive, ruthless and expanding nature of capitalism meant that inevitably it would accumulate more capital, organize more and more resources, and grow in inordinate fashion. Early nineteenth-century thinkers did not fear this development so long as the essential small-unit nature of American economic life was preserved. James Madison, for example, devoted Federalist Paper Number Ten to this problem. He hoped that the vast space of the continent would preclude concentrations of economic and political power. This proved to be wishful thinking. The central capitalist drive for profit and growth is not consistent with an economy of small enterprises. Growth in America has, instead, led to the removal of direct ownership of the means of production from large numbers of Americans. In time fewer and fewer people controlled the means of production. Insofar as capitalism is an honest creed, it has always exalted self-interest above the common good and has, therefore, invited the use of unchecked power for individual gain. The outcome was predictable: the concentration of ownership and power in fewer and fewer hands.

The corporation proved to be the major unit embodying this extraordinary change in American economic life. Big business had always been a part of the economic scene; but with the extension of railroad and communication facilities and with the development of large urban centers in the 1880's and 1890's, the era of the corporation truly began.[8] The growth of the corporation provoked strife and contention at every turn. Of course, the form of the corporation and its relationship to society changed from time to time, but nothing deterred the drive of the corporation to become the central economic unit in America. Today, the corporation is hedged in on one side by the power of the federal government, which has consistently intervened in the operation of the so-called free market for over seventy years, and on the other side by the power of organized labor. But neither the power of the workers nor the force of state intervention in the economy has altered the fact of corporate dominance. It is the health of the corporation—which means the health of the profit system—that determines the health of the whole economy. And it is the influence of the corporations, either as employers or producers, that most directly forms and shapes the habits, customs, needs, and thoughts of the American people. The needs and prerogatives of the corporation, the central economic unit in America, essentially shape the life of America.[9]

The rise of the corporation affected American life in two major ways. First, by destroying competition, resorting to centralized decision-making, engaging in excessive profit-making, and centering economic control in only a few hands, the corporation ended an economic era in which large numbers of farmers, traders, mechanics, and shopkeepers exercised independent and direct control over their economic life. In 1849, for example, approximately one of every twelve workers was a wage-earner; by 1910 that ratio had narrowed to one in every six. In 1880, thirty-seven percent of the American work force were classified as entrepreneurs while sixty-two percent were listed as employees. By 1965, eighty-six percent were employees while the number of entrepreneurs had dropped to twelve percent.[10] At the same time, moreover, the growth of the corporation rendered obsolete the political and social ideology of individualism, equal opportunity, property rights, and political liberty which had been moored to the laissez faire economy of the early days of the republic. The great neutral arbiter of economic destiny, the free market, was destroyed because the corporations advanced on the market with considerably more power than did individuals. Competition was destroyed by various means of corporate collusion and control, which arose in order to ensure economic stability and sustained monopolistic growth. In 1839, the Supreme Court defined the corporation as a person in law. This decision meant that the corporation secured additional advantages over against individuals in law (and soon in custom and practice). Further, the decision symbolized the transfer of the doctrine of freedom from its base in individual activity to that of corporate privilege and prerogative. Traditionally, the possession of private property had been the means of economic advance as well as the expression of individual freedom. With the concentration of ownership in fewer hands, however, private property became a stumbling block to individual progress. The concentration of property and capital in great corporate centers meant, simply, the loss of power for the great mass of the American people. Equal opportunity was transformed from the possibility of individual entrepreneurship to competition for limited employee openings, or to increased material acquisition divorced from the exercise of power.

Private enterprise leads to a measure of dignity when it manifests itself in widespread, direct ownership of the means of production and command over the results of personal labor. The dignity of the system arises from the fact that work and activity are extensions of the person's being. In early America, ownership of farms or shops or closeness to trade and merchandise produced a direct personal relationship with the means and results of production. This guaranteed pride and made freedom a meaningful concept. But the corporation severed the relationship between people and the means of production. As a result, work became selling one's labor to large conglomerates. Gradually, the worker was separated from ownership and control, and in a most profound sense alienated from and in the economic process. In the corporate age the person possessed no control over personal labor or over the results of labor. This became the province of the owning class. The connection between life and work, which had been maintained through private ownership and which had given a measure of dignity to early capitalism, was broken by the rise of corporate power. The wage relationship came to replace the former connection between life and work. It was cash that summed up man's hopes for dignity, freedom, and meaning. Individual rights were linked with the right to spend and own goods. Equal opportunity came to be the opportunity to have possessions. And, most important, the connection between freedom and productive property was broken and freedom became associated with consumerism.*

When the growth of the corporation caused the political ideology of republicanism to collapse, the most blatantly materialistic aspects of capitalism came to the fore. Hopes for dignity and freedom based on popular control, or on social democracy, were effaced. Instead, women and men found themselves allied with the national goals of growth and material accumulation. The creed of material gain had replaced the older ideologies, thus confirming Karl Marx's description:

> Accumulation for accumulation's sake, production for production's sake: by this formula classical economy expressed the historical mission of the bourgeoisie.[11]

The crude materialism that emerged with the collapse of early American capitalism has found expression as consumerism. The corporations first arose as a means of more efficiently organizing the productive process. In this they differed only in intensity and organization from the small-unit enterprises that preceded them. Both were concerned with production. However, in order to protect the growth, stability, and regularity of production, the corporation was soon forced to attend to the matter of extended and continuous consumption. (It needs to be emphasized, contrary to much present-day mythology, that consumption is not a reality which has replaced production; rather it is a means of safeguarding production. Production remains the central reality of capitalist society. Consumption is a shift to a new dimension of the production process which serves to guarantee the continued primacy of capitalist production.)† Consumerism has signalled a

---

*It can be argued that freedom is widespread throughout contemporary America. This is true to a degree. But the freedom that is experienced is essentially private. Personal mobility (travel) and consumer opportunities (cars and homes) have replaced any larger understanding of freedom which would link people to public activity or communal destiny.

†Marx noted, "Production furnishes consumption not only with its object. It also gives consumption its definition, its character, its finish. . . . The object is not an object as such, but a specific object, which must be consumed in a specific way, a way which is

shift from the asceticism, organization, and discipline needed in order to accumulate the necessary capital for an efficient production machine, to the profligacy and exuberance needed to sustain capitalist production in its more advanced phase. This change has been important and far-reaching for American capitalism and the social institutions and values that depend on it. " . . . The most critical point in the functioning of society shifts from production to consumption, and, as it does so, the culture must be reoriented to convert the producer's culture into a consumer's culture."[13] In a consumer society the criterion of social value changes. The traditional virtues of frugality, work, and self-restraint are forced to give place to a "new set of drives and values in which consumption is paramount," where "the consumption attitudes of emulation, ostentation and sheer wastefulness" become prominent.[14] Spending replaces saving and profligacy supplants discipline in the new order of personal priorities. In 1870 it was possible to be jailed for indebtedness, but in 1929 almost seventy percent of the American public was in debt and yet safely at large. Extensive and long-term credit buying becomes the mark of a society dedicated to endless consumption.

As a result of the new emphases of the consumer society, people are conditioned to feel that individual value is bound up with the items they own. Increasingly the possession of consumer items has come to signify status and worth. Consequently, capitalist society is building upon ordinary pecuniary tendencies a system of almost biological need for items and possessions. As Herbert Marcuse has noted:

> The so-called consumer economy and the politics of corporate capitalism have created a second nature of man which ties him libidinally and aggressively to the commodity form. The need for possessing, consuming, handling, and constantly renewing the gadgets, devices, instruments, engines, offered to and imposed upon the people, for using these wares even at the danger of one's own destruction, has become a "biological" need in the sense just defined. The second nature of man thus militates against any change that would disrupt and perhaps even abolish this dependence of man on a market ever more densely filled with merchandise—abolish his existence as a consumer consuming himself in buying and selling.[15]

Advertising becomes a central adjunct to the corporate system. Its responsibility is promoting conformity to material values and educating people to the absolute necessity of consuming. The average American is assaulted with fifty thousand advertising spots, signs, or commercials each year, all designed to adjust attitudes to the necessity of consumption and to lead toward " . . . the

---

again determined by production itself. . . . production produces . . . not only objectively, but subjectively. Production thus creates the consumer. Production not only furnishes the object of a need, but it also furnishes the need for an object."[12]

stimulation or even the exploitation of materialistic drives and emulative anxieties . . . and the standardization of these drives and anxieties. . . ."[16]

In addition, consumerism has become the device through which class conflict is worked out. The opposition between the owning class and the working class has given way to intra-class rivalry for goods and services, just as the scramble for prestige through mounting acquisition has replaced the idea of democratic ownership of the means of production. Working class, and even middle class resentment over the inequities and instabilities of American life have been diverted in the mad rush for consumer items. Endless consumption is the goal of man in the corporate state. Ralph Nader is not celebrated for his efforts to expose corruption in government and business, he is touted as "the consumer advocate." The public puts up with inequity, manipulation, public fraud and deceit, and any narrowing of the dream of an egalitarian republic, so long as the possibility of the massive accumulation of goods and services remains intact.* As Jürgen Habermas has noted, the class struggle has become latent. In return for a degree of economic security and a set of consumption possibilities, working men and women temper their discontent and narrow their vision of economic and social democracy. This trade-off characterizes the consumer phase of advanced capitalism.

The growth of the corporation and the development of the consumer society significantly altered the American conception of freedom and exposed its inherent limitations. Proprietary exclusiveness in a small-unit economy was a force for personal freedom, even in economic and social realms, because it limited the exercise of absolute power. However, by building up property and capital, the corporation transferred to itself the prerogatives and options that had rested with the individual or small-group property holder. Corporate property led to the exercise of corporate power at the expense of small property holders. The realm of free action open to the individual was narrowed to the extent that his or her property could command power. Since the corporations had most of the property and capital, individuals found themselves without the power to exercise freedom in the realm of public life. And since the American doctrine of freedom lacked any societal emphasis, individuals were without doctrinal resources that could help them regain power in the public sphere. Only some form of collective action could reverse the trend started by the corporations, but the individualistic basis of the American conception of freedom militated against this. Without any larger sense of responsibility, freedom will either turn into anarchistic expression or else collapse altogether. The corporate state ensured that no ennobling sense of community would exist and, at the same time, encouraged the privatistic tendency toward consumerism among individuals. It is a tragedy, but no

*In late summer of 1973, when Watergate revelations were at a peak, Congress learned that their constituents' primary concern was inflation.

surprise, therefore, that instead of moving to gain democratic control of economic and social life in the name of freedom, Americans have fallen back to the point where individual and proprietary considerations form their sole definition of freedom, as evidenced by the American mania for personal mobility, consumerism, and home ownership. Lacking any direction, object, or purpose, freedom in America has been confined to the idea of personal relationships, individual expression, and self-directing activity, including accumulation, that is, to highly individualistic efforts unrelated to anything but the glorification of the self in its private capacities.

There is now a common American commitment, not to freedom, justice, or equality, but to the values of growth, expansion, personal acquisition and consumption, and to the techniques of efficiency and planning necessary to ensure the safety and progress of corporate capitalism. The traditional republican ideology has been rendered obsolete. As a result, the victory of the corporation is complete. With the characteristic wit of the cynical aristocrat, John Kenneth Galbraith writes,

> The state is strongly concerned with the stability of the economy. And with its expansion or growth. And with education. And with technical and scientific advance. And, most notably, with the national defense. These are *the* national goals; they are sufficiently trite so that one has a reassuring sense of the obvious in articulating them.... these goals reflect adaptation of public goals to the goals of the technostructure [Galbraith's term for the corporation].[17]

The corporate state may be without any ennobling political ideology, but nevertheless it engenders a set of values quite in accord with its own needs. Thus, cooperation, deference to authority, conformity to institutional prerogatives, ultimate respect for technical skill, a preference for stability and order over initiative and risk, and the priority of planning and predictability over competition have come to supplant the traditional values long associated with individualism, ambition, and daring enterprise.[18],* As a result, the corporation has prepared the ground for centralized, hierarchical control, a control now evident in all institutional behavior throughout America. This accounts for the widespread sense of powerlessness among Americans at every level of life. In addition, the public is in a state of bewilderment because, while the masses of people tend to proclaim loyalty to traditional values, the government, corporations, and social institutions are acting on the basis of the

---

*I find nothing wrong with cooperation and teamwork as values. However, the imposition of these values has not only destroyed the older individualism, but it has done so for the sake of nothing more ennobling than economic growth and consumerism. The counter to this situation is not the espousal of more individual freedom; that only serves to strengthen the status quo. Rather discipline, cooperation, and sacrifice should go toward the construction of a socialist commonwealth. Then, and only then, can true individuality flourish.

newer values and needs of the corporate state. The government and its corporate allies are charged with the responsibility of rule. They have few choices. Unlike liberals, they cannot afford to carp at this or that policy. No present-day American administration (and this would go for liberals were they in power) can afford to engage in the naivete of anti-corporation politics.* Nor, for that matter, can they afford to take seriously the old ideology of frontier America.† The public, of course, remains perplexed and confused because the older ideology, while still proclaimed at hallowed national festivals, is no longer adhered to in practice. Too much is at stake for the corporate elite either to return to the old days or to observe the old values in our present world (as Senator Barry Goldwater found out in his 1964 campaign). Hence, the government presses for Congressional guarantees of loans to Lockheed Corporation, aid to overseas investors, support for the Anti-Ballistic Missile system, extended military activity throughout the world, stringent law enforcement, and greater social conformity. A bewildered public either looks on passively or else immerses itself in privatistic activities.

It would be a mistake to conclude from this, however, that America is without an ideology. The end of the old republican ideology does not mean that the society is without a legitimating socio-political scheme. Technology has become the legitimating power of the American corporate state. Since the highest reaches of corporate power now exercise political control through the machinery of state, but can find no justification for this in the old ideology which had pointed to the autonomous "law of the market" (Burke's law of commerce which was also the law of God), they have been forced to find their legitimization in the operations and concepts of technology itself. Thus, technology (and most particularly technology combined with science) now acts as the official ideology of the system.

Unfortunately, this ideology remains, for the most part, hidden. It does not emerge as a positive, evangelizing tool. It is unable to be this because, unlike older ideologies, it is not directly related to such normative issues as the "good society" (which early capitalism had claimed to ensure because it identified societal freedom with individual opportunity) or to the "classless society." Instead, technology functions only to legitimate present political,

---

*The necessity for liberals to hoe the corporate ground once assuming the responsibilities of power is not new. In 1816, President James Madison approved the second United States National Bank he had vigorously opposed twenty-five years earlier. President James Monroe reversed himself on internal improvements. Woodrow Wilson ended up adopting the business-government entente formulated earlier by Theodore Roosevelt.

†See James MacGregor Burns' shrewd assessment of Richard Nixon: "His prime goal is not some grand ideology such as liberty or equality. Nor is it some program or policy. It is the conversion of crisis and tumult into management and control." "The Nixon Tightrope," *Life*, April 2, 1971, p. 48D.

social, and economic processes by rendering them *inevitable*. Since it is so closely allied to the dynamic operations of the business state, its actual purpose is to prevent the dysfunctioning of the system as a whole. It functions to keep the system going and to preclude operational breakdowns. This essentially negative purpose, which maintains the status quo, is not just a simple device, for in the process of guarding current processes, technology also takes on a wider significance. The cloak of scientism which has been thrown around present economic and social practices has also blocked out questions which could pose important alternatives to the given corporate order. This is why technology is so closely related to the manipulation of the public: depoliticizing and immunizing the masses precludes the raising of normative questions. But further, the whole process of economic growth and stabilization, which is underwritten by technology as *instrument*, becomes (under the influence of technology as *ideology*) quasi-autonomous, now imbued with the inevitability of objective fact, the law of life. As Jürgen Habermas has written:

> It is true that social interests still determine the direction, function, and pace of technical progress. But these interests define the social system so much as a whole that they coincide with the interest in maintaining the system. *As such* the private form of capital utilization and a distribution mechanism for social rewards that guarantees the loyalty of the masses are removed from discussion. The quasi-autonomous progress of science and technology then appears as an independent variable on which the most important single system variable, namely economic growth depends. Thus arises a perspective in which the development of the social system *seems* to be determined by the logic of scientific-technical progress. The immanent law of this progress seems to produce objective exigencies, which must be obeyed by any politics oriented toward functional needs. But when this semblance has taken root effectively, then propaganda can refer to the role of technology and science in order to explain and legitimate why in modern societies the process of decision-making about practical problems loses its function and "must" be replaced by plebiscitary decisions about alternative sets of leaders of administrative personnel.[19]

Increasingly, business and state officials are coming under the sway of technology as ideology. The possibility exists that eventually the public will internalize this situation, thus ensuring further docility. In the meantime there is tremendous confusion. Sections of the working class and other Americans enamored with the old republican ideology continue to react to contemporary changes by lashing out against those who *seem* to be responsible for change: blacks, students, or criminals. The old ideology is defended with great vehemence against these groups (and sometimes against left-leaning liberals as well). But, of course, the anger is misplaced. These groups have not been responsible for the massive economic and ideological changes which have taken place in the last hundred years, and thus any defense of initiative, small government, and the like can serve no purpose save that of self-glorification. The discussion is not central to the change society has been undergoing.

Others condemn the technological society outright. They envision a return to a simpler, personal world uncluttered by machines or technical manipulation. These groups forget that history cannot be turned back. The romanticism associated with another age cannot serve as a guide through the maze of our present confusion. Besides, this nostalgic casting back only diverts attention from the real needs of the present. The questions remain: How can we create a true, mass democracy? How can the people use technology for human ends? There is nothing inevitable about the present direction of political life, even though technology is used to convince us of this. Technology should be seen for what it is: a tool of the rulers of the new corporate state. The tool has become an ideology in which "the laws of domination appear as the objective laws of technology."[20] But this need not be so.

In the nineteenth century Karl Marx exposed the so-called objective workings of the "law" of the free market as, in fact, the working of social classes. Similarly, the so-called neutrality of modern technology reveals, on closer inspection, social groups using science as a cloak for their own designs on power. The opportunity exists now, as always, to fashion a true democracy. It is neither fate nor science that condemns men and women to impotence and despair; it is the workings of other men and women, operating, as have others before them, in the interest of greed and power.

Chapter Four

The TRIUMPH of FACTICITY
in the BOURGEOIS EPOCH

Solve the identity crisis with the Marine BankAmericard.
Wisconsin Radio Advertisement

Social facts are things.
Emile Durkheim

Each new class is compelled to represent its interest as the common interest of all members of society.
Karl Marx

A certain way of life and thought is dominant, in which one concept of reality is diffused throughout.
Antonio Gramsci

But how can I explain, how can I explain to *you?*
You will understand less after I have explained it.
All that I can hope to make you understand
Is only events: not what happened.
And people to whom nothing has ever happened
Cannot understand the unimportance of events.
T. S. Eliot

Perhaps a new law—or anti-law—of history will have to be invented: the law of surprises. Whenever anything important happens in history it is always by surprise.
Regis Debray

1

In order to live with some degree of creativity and joy women and men must have some confidence in the world.[1] Every culture tries to establish the basis for such confidence because without it the terror of time threatens to overcome human life and drive people to ennui, madness, or death. And yet the search for such confidence is plagued by uncertainty and confusion. The reason for this is that beneath every attempt to construct a reason for worldly confidence lies the created order, which is nothing but sheer existence. Neither natural life nor human life, regarded by themselves, demonstrate an ultimate base or goal. The world is basically without value, a self-contained, simple, brute presence. In itself it has no purpose, nor is it ultimately intelligible. It has come from nowhere and is going nowhere, the words "come" and "go" being human constructs impressed on a world that simply exists. And yet, men and women are forever searching for ultimate value and purpose in the world and the life it encompasses. This search acknowledges that people cannot live in the world without confidence in it.

For many centuries in the West confidence in the world (actually a better phrase would be confidence for the world) was established by Christian thought. Theologically, Christianity asserted that the basis and end of the world lay in God, who is outside the world of space and time. Christianity recognized the emptiness of the mere facticity of existence, and asserted that only that which is outside the world can confer meaning to the world. This solution, however, pointed to a paradox: while all attempts to assert meaning based on the facticity of the world are doomed to failure, those who attempt to vest the world with significance from outside are not able to point to immanent, empirical evidence to demonstrate their contention. This obviously can lessen rather than strengthen confidence in the world. Be that as it may, for believers, God and Christianity provide the coordinates, as it were, for locating value in the world. In the first place, Christianity asserts that God created the world by a gracious miracle (*creatio ex nihilo*), that is, he brought into being and sustains that which, by any other reckoning, need not exist at all. Further, by promising security to men and women beyond the limits of space and time, Christianity gives significance to human life which it hitherto did not possess and otherwise could not possess. For if life beyond the grave is guaranteed, its earthly expression is of incalculable importance. Life cannot be given importance simply because it is or because we have it. Only the promise of a sacred destiny beyond the sheer facticity of earthly appearance (Rom. 8:18-39) could serve as the basis for viewing existence as ultimately valuable and meaningful.

Having proclaimed that the ultimate significance of the world and the life it sustains does not lie in the simple fact of existence or in the given appearance of things, Christianity proceeded to articulate this faith with reference to an endless variety of myths and superstitions. It asserted that the simple facts of the world were not to be mistaken for the essence of things. But in elaborating this it proceeded to fill the world with demons, angels, ghosts, and a variety of other spiritual forces which it argued for in the most literal fashion. Thus in laying the basis for confidence in (for) the world, Christianity was vulnerable to the charge of gross superstition.

In the sixteenth, seventeenth, and eighteenth centuries Christianity was attacked by another world-view which also attempted to establish confidence in the world. In its protracted struggle with the feudal aristocracy, the rising bourgeoisie destroyed the medieval conception of history and life which had become shrouded in mystery, dogma, and superstition. Needless to say, the commercial classes were not primarily engaging in an intellectual contest. Their major concern was to remove any and all barriers to their own ambitions. Articulating a new world-view served bourgeois interests. Feudal society had possessed an elusive concept of reality which included not only external appearances but internal mysteries and essences as well. These mysteries, interpreted by the church and guarded by the upper ranks of the landed aristocracy, served as levers of power for these groups. Characteristically, the eighteenth-century *philosophes* (the first to give extensive expression to a predominantly bourgeois world-view) played a central role in exposing how contemporary aristocrats and ecclesiastical hierarchs used superstition and mystery, not as a means of furthering faith, but as a means of maintaining power.[2]

The bourgeoisie, in their turn, elaborated a view of reality that concentrated on the explicit, outward, and self-evident. They dominated an epoch in which the idea of reality was increasingly narrowed so that it became associated almost totally with external phenomena. In that fashion they created a world amenable to the pursuit of their own ambitions. It is also important to note that science was responsible for the most precise formulation of this world-view, namely, that reality was equivalent to fact and appearance; but while the influence of scientific discovery and methodology was important among the higher ranks of the bourgeoisie it was not central to the change in societal views.

What was important was the introduction of a new economic instrumentality. In the case of the bourgeois class, the growth of capitalism accounted for a new view which reordered human sensibilities toward the world, and which tried to establish a new basis of worldly confidence. In capitalism the free market is the central symbol of the new world-view. On the free market women and men are subjected to the pivotal test of their being. It is there that success or failure, winning or losing, is openly acknowledged. Open competition draws people toward material activity and toward potential rewards which then determine their standing in life. For the bourgeois man or woman to come to the market he or she must come as a self-consistent individual and not with social ties or responsibilities. Further, they must come armed with the virtues of acquisitiveness, ambition, aggressiveness, and competitiveness—the outward traits of the commercial person bent on conquest. They must forego activities which may be more leisurely or playful, which stress interior, implicit, mysterious, or immeasurable aspects of reality.

The bourgeois woman or man must be prepared for a struggle in which worth and personal standing are determined by outward signs. The free market can measure only in terms of wealth, accumulation, or size. Hence all relationships based on being, blood, station, or belief (immeasurable, inward, or immaterial relations) are subordinated to relationships dependent upon and defined by the market. "The bourgeois," Marx noted, "whenever it has got the upper hand, has put an end to all feudal, patriarchical, idyllic relations. It has piteously torn asunder the motley feudal ties that bound man to his 'natural superiors' and has left remaining no other nexus between man and man than naked self-interest, than callous 'cash payment.' "[3] In such a world dominated by the increased "thingification" of reality, money—capital or property—increasingly became the final referent.* It was, after all, the most basic, measurable, and self-evident fact. All reality could be subordinated to it. Thus, for the bourgeoisie, worth became a matter of commercial or monetary dealings, determined by a person's acquisitive stance in relation to the world. All of social reality gradually came to embody extrinsic characteristics, and the external world of comparative growth, size, accumulation, possession, accomplishment, wealth, and power dominated the consciousness of bourgeois society.

But there was still a basic ambiguity in the bourgeois revolution. Though capitalism pointed clearly to the identification of reality with external, material facticity, and though the growth of empirical science gave theoretical support to this position, the bourgeoisie insisted upon legitimatizing its rule by imbedding facts within a wider significance. They, too, felt it necessary to relate facts to some larger, if hidden or mysterious, purpose or meaning. While the new world-view focused on externalities, it was claimed that these facts or events were not pointless. A hidden hand was said to be at work in the economic sphere, guaranteeing eventual harmony (the outer world clearly demonstrating strife and misery), while the laws of inevitable progress promised security and peace for society as a whole. Indeed, the doctrine of progress, sometimes buttressed by a vague or immanentist Christianity, flourished and tended to give overall meaning to the strivings of the new epoch.

---

*Recall Karl Marx's description of the role of money in bourgeois society: "That which exists for me by means of money, that which can be paid for, that is to say, that which money can bring about, I am that very thing. I, the owner of money. My force is as great as the force of money. The virtues of money are my virtues and my power: the virtues of him who possesses it. What I am and what I can do is in no way determined by my person. I am ugly, but I can buy myself the most beautiful women: thus I am no more ugly, for the effect, the abhorrence of ugliness is made void by money. . . . Money is the greatest good, and so he who owns it is also good. . . . I who, thanks to money, am capable of attaining all that to which man's heart aspires, am I not in possession of all human values? My money, does it not transform all my insufficiencies into their opposite? If money is the link which attaches me to human life, to society, to nature and man, is it not the link of all links. . . ?"[4]

Thus the new external world growing up under capitalism was held to be in ultimate accord with the laws of history. Lord Macaulay, in 1837, expressed accurately the confidence of the bourgeoisie in the historical destiny of their new ideology:

It has lengthened life; it has mitigated pain; it has extinguished diseases; it has increased the fertility of the soil; it has given new securities to the mariner; it has furnished new arms to the warrior; it has spanned great rivers and estuaries with bridges of form unknown to our fathers . . . it has extended the range of human vision; it has multiplied the power of human muscles; it has accelerated motion; it has annihilated distance; it has facilitated intercourse, correspondence, all friendly offices, all dispatch of business; it has enabled man to descend the depths of the sea, to soar into the air, to penetrate securely into the noxious recesses of the earth, to traverse the land in cars which whirl along without horses, to cross the ocean in ships which run ten knots an hour against the wind. These are but a part of its fruits, and of its firstfruits; for it is a philosophy which never rests, which has never attained, which is never perfect. Its law is progress.[5]

Thus the bourgeoisie appealed to the hidden laws of the market and to the friendship of history to legitimate and vindicate an otherwise narrow and restricted view of reality and life. But the contradiction of this position is plain. The establishment and delineation of fact does not in itself lead to anything. The doctrine of progress—the notion of the "unfolding excellence of fact" (George Steiner)—does not and cannot be derived from the world itself, as the bourgeoisie had so desperately hoped, but is rather a philosophical imposition of meaning and, therefore, subject to the same radical criticism the *philosophes* had levelled against medieval Christianity. The bourgeoisie had risen to power by challenging the metaphysics of feudalism. But, in turn, they proceeded to establish their own metaphysic by associating meaning with the facticity of the products of the economic order. In so doing they consigned their own historical project to confusion.

When, therefore, the confidence concerning the regularity, harmony, and ultimate beneficence of the sustaining laws of nature, society, and history collapsed in the twentieth century under the impact of persistent and implacable moral evil (world wars and genocide), and the irregularity of nature or the relativity of all things (modern physics), confidence in the world was fatally undermined. Consequently, the life of the twentieth century has exhibited an ever increasing failure of nerve and hope. The world now confronts man in its most primitive and basic form, as arbitrary fact and valueless existence. The failure of immanentist, naturalistic, or progressivist schemes to account for the course of the world's life and to establish value in the world has been of singular importance. The world has been reduced to self-evident being, devoid of meaning, purpose, or goal. In like fashion history has been reduced to the manipulation and projection of the brute facticity of life itself, the endless rearrangement and alignment of events, experiences, and facts without purpose, still carried on with the rhetoric of confidence that inspired an earlier age, but shorn of any substance. In short order, confidence in the world and life has given place to busyness (business), and underneath busyness lies the spectre of impotence and fate, of material tasks repeated endlessly without meaning or hope.

Yet even if confidence in the world has waned, and even though confusion and loss of nerve characterize so much of the Western human enterprise, the engine of capitalist development proceeds. And it still requires the objectification of existence. This project now advances without a consistent or compelling metaphysic, but it continues, nonetheless, with a kind of crude imperative, fashioning a society given over to facticity, exploitation, and alienation. With frightening speed bourgeois society externalizes all meaning into measurable facts.

The needs of capitalist development continue to shape social reality. Increased rationalization and stepped-up planning now characterize the capitalist epoch; but far from altering the view of reality first created by the emerging bourgeoisie, the new face of capitalism has intensified its development. The very need for massive control over political and economic life has fostered a concept of reality in which people are ineluctably reduced to their outward activities as wage-earners or consumers. Life is narrowed down to the quantifiable phenomena which become the measure of prosperity and the means of manipulation. Clearly, the key to the continued power of the capitalist elite lies in the ability of the highest ranks of the bourgeoisie to produce an unlimited array of goods and services for a population enamored with, and accustomed to, the externalization of meaning.

At the level of everyday existence reality has become appearance. Life is beauty, youth, expensive clothes, the various perfumes and deodorants which cover the body, the style one possesses in relation to others. At once pandering to this and shaping it, advertising concentrates on appearances, on packaging and external images, rather than on the actual substance or performance of the product or service put forward for consideration. Political campaigns have become the manipulation of "images," and the practitioners of this "new politics" astonish us by engaging in their endeavor without the slightest regret or apology. Women remain ornaments, things to be dispatched in a society used to treating people as things. In New York City, for example, a recent campaign to rid Times Square and the surrounding area of prostitutes was undertaken—if we are to believe the news reports—not for medical reasons nor out of concern for the women involved (i.e., because of a threat to their health or because prostitution is a form of social slavery), but simply because their presence made the area look bad.

On the intellectual level reality is likewise narrowed. In the ancient world knowledge was conceived of in terms of internal or spiritual enlightenment. In bourgeois society knowledge is utilitarian; it is the study of facts that can be used for commerce or personal advance. Increasingly it is technical and functional and related to the use and extension of power, to the building of the state, or to securing a better job. Within the humanities in academia the various fields are increasingly subject to the most limited understanding. Economics is dominated by an interest in constructing abstract mathematical models directed toward explicating the factors of economic growth, wages, and development, with almost no consideration of the interrelatedness of economics with politics and class power. Economists fail to see, writes Robert Heilbroner, "that the social universe that they are attempting to reproduce . . . is not and cannot be adequately described by functional relationships alone, but must also . . . be described as a system of privilege."[6] Philosophy has, by and large, surrendered the study of metaphysics and now concentrates on a discussion of human language, in terms either of its verifiability or of its functional rules. Sociology continues to be dominated by a system of research that assumes a given, self-evident (and hence functionally stable) social order needing only the description of its various parts. Thus it tends to blunt critical impulses that suggest the viability of alternative social systems. The study of history threatens to become journalism in which the past is objectified, and the elusive but inescapable relationship between investigation, ideology, and writing is all too often denied. As Martin Heidegger has observed: "Because history, as research, outlines and objectifies the past as an explainable and observable nexus of effects, it requires source criticism as an instrument of this objectification. The standards of this criticism change to the degree in which history approximates to journalism."[7] Freudian psychology, which had established the doctrine that man's consciousness does not correspond exactly to what he or she is, because of a deeper level of mental activity not readily available to complete rational control, is slowly giving place to one or another school of "personal relationships" which exalt simplistic views of understanding, feelings, or personal honesty; or to behaviorism, which sees men and women acting in simple patterns amenable to change through elaborate conditioning mechanisms.

Finally, politically and socially, issues are understood only in the most restricted fashion. Protest movements, for example, are comprehended in terms of their most superficial demands. The labor movement is stripped of its socialist component, the populist movement is separated from its egalitarian mystique, the black liberation movement is divorced from its cultural and revolutionary radicalism, and women's liberation is divided from its hope for a radical change in female and male consciousness and societal roles. These movements end up being represented in the media (the final censor, interpreter, and representative of bourgeois sensibility) in terms of higher wages, additional political institutions, extended civil rights, or increased economic or representational opportunities, that is, in terms of changes which not only are politically and socially possible (and not dangerous) but which also conform to the bourgeois conception of reality, which pictures progress and change as the growth or extension of already given material facts or institutions. Progress is equated with building upon what already exists; it amounts to selecting issues that can conform to given reality. All else, i.e. all that suggests a new vision of reality, is screened, blunted, diverted, or crushed.

And so appearance is confused with reality and, more specifically, facts are mistaken for essences. The thrust of the bourgeois epoch (now divorced from any compelling metaphysic) is to establish the facts that appear to common sense or to investigation as the positive index of truth. "Raised to the status of an autonomous idol," writes Tito Perlini, "the *fact* is an absolute tyrant before whom thought can do nothing but bow down in silent worship."[8] The free market reduced differences of quality to differences of quantity so that every relationship could be essentially measurable. Having used facts to destroy the superstition and dogma which undergirded the power of the feudal aristocracy, the bourgeoisie use facts to establish and guard their own power. Of course, it is admitted that bias or lack of knowledge occasionally hinders the search for facts, but it is nonetheless maintained that once facts are established they have authority. But the concept of fact that prevails assumes that outward reality is basically unrelated to implicit personal factors[9] which might render it less than certain, or to social relations or ideologies which might cast doubt on any notion of pure objectivity. Outward reality is measurable and capable of being established as self-evident, as binding, as truth. "The world is doomed," Margaret Mead would have us believe, "if we can't reach a point where everyone can understand facts."[10] When economists, for example, discuss wages and profits apart from their setting in a structure of social privilege, that is, in relation to their built-in bias for or against certain social classes, they may be establishing facts, but they are doing so only in the most limited sense. Yet, having passed off these facts as truth, they can proceed to obtain obedience in the face of their discovery. Facts become tools in the hands of those who use them. They are established on the basis of so-called neutral observation and hence possess ultimate authority. It is presumed that facts and not their presenters have authority, when in reality it is the investigators and reporters of facts who possess authority, and use this authority through the medium of so-called objective and neutral facts.

Authority rests with people and not with facts. In this sense the otherwise extravagant Marxist notion that all truth is class truth is a sound observation.

Yet bourgeois society persists in the elaboration of facticity and in claiming that facticity in itself determines all reality.

Biblical theology, much like critical philosophy, presumes that all human activity takes place within the context of history as process. But history is forever characterized by the contrast between the present situation and future possibilities: by the incompleteness of the present when viewed from the standpoint of the future, and by the promise of the future viewed from the present.

Because of its concentration on the facticity of existence, bourgeois positivism ignores history as process and overlooks the creative tension between the present and the future. Its attention to facticity implicitly assumes the static quality of the space or time investigated or recorded, and looses it from any processional context. For that reason positivism is the faith of the status quo: it is forced to identify that which is, not with that which could be or will be, but simply with that which is.

At any time what is empirically perceived in the world can only be an imperfect realization of the world's true destiny. Hence, the challenge to thought offered by Biblical faith is not to elaborate material facticity and thus sanctify the status quo, but to comprehend the course of human history; to discover in the events or facts of the present how they are related to the future freedom of man.

2

The collapse of optimism in the twentieth century has left the age without a compelling purpose or a widely held sense of historical meaning. Yet out of a desperation that underlies both the implacably barren soul of modern bourgeois life and the intense need of all systems to inspire confidence by identifying their rule with some ultimacy beyond the appearance of things, capitalism struggles to vest itself with a great purpose. Therefore it continues to profess faith in progress. But now, modern technology is the major force in attempting to restore this doctrine to capitalism.

Until late in the nineteenth century empirical science did not contribute significantly to the articulation of society and culture. At best its contribution was indirect. Empirical methodology remained a fascinating subject for various intellectuals who otherwise were drawn to productive activity on a traditional basis. But in the latter half of the nineteenth century science and technology became interdependent. At that point it became possible to extend the full force of empirical science, now in the form of technical control, not only to all of nature but to social institutions as well. "The power of technical control over nature made possible by science is extended today directly to society: for every isolatable social system, for every cultural area that has become a separate, closed system whose relations can be analyzed immanently in terms of presupposed system goals, a new discipline emerges in the social sciences . . . the problems of technical control solved by science are transformed into life problems."[11] In America the rise of scientific technology accompanied the rise of corporate capitalism. As a consequence, as the doctrine of laissez faire capitalism lost its authority, technology became the handmaiden of the new corporate-political elite as that elite proceeded to order the economy and political and social life. As they did so, however, they could only proceed on the basis of the fundamental assumptions of bourgeois capitalism: facticity and the "thingification" of reality. Technology now serves to gird the capitalist system.

Apologists for technology insist, of course, that they are scientists. They would deny that technology is essentially related to capitalism or to the issue of class power which has always been at the heart of capitalist development. Instead they point to the application of their work to the problems of mankind, and decry the notion that technology is linked to any particular ideology.[12] After all, they argue, are not material abundance, the end to disease and poverty, and the orderly functioning of society universal goals which exist beyond ideology? Technology simply applies a certain methodology to these problems. Basic research and the application of factual knowledge are neutral endeavors, it is argued. But this is disingenuous. Technology is essentially a methodology and as such it is employed toward reaching certain goals. But all goals are political goals; all goals involve the use, gain, or dispersal of power, and the allocation of resources in a certain fashion. Bourgeois technology is dissembling when it tries to extend the net of neutrality beyond research to the application of research, or when it tries to suggest that the goal of scientific activity is of the same character as the means. Quietly the so-called neutrality surrounding the methodology of technology is extended to cover the goals for which technology strives: the goals of American capitalism. The upshot of the process is that the total endeavor, both technique and goals, claims the twin ascriptions of scientific neutrality and facticity. In this way capitalism promotes the very conception of reality that it uses in turn to suggest its own benevolence, omnipotence, and inevitability.

This is an ingenious device for preserving power, and, not so incidentally, it allows the new group of technologists and their academic camp followers to nudge their way into the courts of power as allies of the capital-owning class. Hence a new business-scientific-educational elite has emerged in America, speaking not only about the future but as the future. Characteristically, opposition to the new elite is described not in political categories but in scientific terminology, in the neutral language of science itself. This is a predictable move on the part of those who confuse power with destiny. Thus, those at home or abroad who oppose the technological extension of American interests are not seen so much as political opponents, but rather are described as unstable, irrational, dysfunctional, or unpredictable. Since facts carry their own authority, those who act contrary to facts, that is, contrary to the self-evident progress that comes with technology, are not simply political opponents, but are in a deeper sense mad, unstable, or irrational. Thus in 1969 during the struggle for "People's Park" in Berkeley, California, when a National Guardsman threw down his rifle and openly went over to the students shouting "I can't stand this any more," he was immediately taken to a hospital, given a psychiatric examination, and diagnosed as suffering from suppressed aggressions.[13] In similar fashion Zbigniew Brzezinski has characterized anti-war demonstrators as people who manifest signs of a " . . . psychological crisis [for which] Viet Nam provides an outlet. . . ."[14] Congressional committees have likewise heard testimony from psychiatrists like Bruno Bettelheim who suggest that the behavior of radical students can best be explained by reference to psychological problems. And so it goes. The language of neutral facticity is used against political opposition, and the externalization of meaning so characteristic of the bourgeois epoch is now carried to another extreme in the interest of power and control. But technology serves not only to protect the functioning of the capitalist system (that is, to prevent dysfunctions) but also to ensure that the material externality of bourgeois capitalism is commended as the goal of human history.

Coupled with the dogma of inevitable progress, the mandate and authority of outward fact and appearance are imbued with a dynamic quality. The future is the time of guaranteed progress which can be predicted and controlled. Routine processes of investigation and projection become tools for extending material abundance. The future unfolds as a matter of course. The future is determined, and hence the present (as simple prelude) exercises a peculiar tyranny over criticism and dissent. It is no longer a time of utopian possibilities, that is, of alternatives conceived in terms of qualitative difference. As the extension of the regular and benevolent facts of the present, the future is plain for all to behold: a self-evident time in which the quantitative and outward reality of growth, expansion, and material accumulation enrich one and all. Technological calculation and implementation guarantee such a future by blocking out the consideration of alternatives. The shape and content of society and the many relations within society have become quantifiable data, imbedded in calculations and projections leading automatically to an abundant future. By this means the bourgeois epoch, which began so heroically by destroying a civilization based on fate, now introduces its own civilization of fate, for in the hands of the technological planners history is not progress but fated occurrence. The inevitability of events and relationships is firmly established beyond gainsaying. Progress turned into fate means that the future and its promises are but extensions of the present into the future, that is, they are the elaboration of facticity under the cloak of progressive rhetoric. For capitalist society has no great goals and is not constituted on the basis of any great change in human relationships or any hope for a new freedom on this earth. The technologists would have us believe that the apparatus surrounding the mechanism of investigation and application is somehow bound up with great dreams. But it is not. In capitalism it is inseparably linked to a crude materialism which, if we are to believe the futurologists, is to be man's inevitable fate. Such a conception of progress does not inspire optimism, it provokes resignation and despair. Hannah Arendt brilliantly describes the whole process and deserves to be quoted at length.

> The logical flaw in these hypothetical constructions of future events is always the same: what first appears as a hypothesis ... turns immediately ... into a "fact," which then gives birth to a whole string of similar non-facts, with the result that the purely speculative character of the whole enterprise is forgotten. ...
>
> Events, by definition, are occurrences that interrupt routine processes and routine procedures; only in a world in which nothing of importance ever happens could the futurologists' dream come true. Predictions of the future are never anything but projections of present automatic processes and procedures, that is, of occurrences that are likely to come to pass if men do not act and if nothing unexpected happens; every action, for better or worse, and every accident necessarily destroys the whole pattern in whose frame the prediction moves and where it finds its evidence. (Proudhon's passing remark, "the fecundity of the unexpected far exceeds the statesman's prudence," is fortunately still true. It exceeds even more obviously the expert's calculations.) To call such unexpected, unpredicted and unpredictable happenings "random events" or "the last gasps of the past," condemning them to irrelevance or the famous "dustbin of history," is the oldest trick in the trade; the trick, no doubt, helps in clearing up the theory, but at the price of removing it further and further from reality. The danger is that these theories are not only plausible, because they take their evidence from actually discernible present trends, but that, because of their inner consistency, they have a hypnotic effect; they put to sleep our common sense, which is nothing else but our mental organ for perceiving, understanding and dealing with reality and factuality.[15]

The highest reaches of the capital-owning class continue to cling to this new doctrine of progress in the vain hope that it will provide for society the basis of a new confidence in the world. Such has not been the case. This faith exists (if at all) only among the elite. It has not permeated the society at large save in the most vapid, and hence immaterial way. One need only notice the degree of national boredom (or anger) in the face of the extraordinary accomplishments of the American space program, surely the greatest product of contemporary technological effort. Gallantly every effort has been made to fill these adventures with cosmic purpose (note the prayers of the astronauts), but to little avail. The basic malaise of bourgeois life continues, as does the captivity to pointless facticity.

Consequently the bourgeois epoch is increasingly characterized by a lack of confidence in the world, an absence of any sense of history, a mistrust of the technical forces that exercise greater control over life, and a growing impotence in the face of a meaningless life. As Hannah Arendt has suggested, this has been implicit in the world-view of contemporary society.

> Modern man, when he lost the certainty of a world to come, was thrown back upon himself and not upon this world; far from believing that the world might be potentially immortal, he was not even sure that it was real. And in so far as he was to assume that it was real in the uncritical and apparently unbothered optimism of a steadily progressing science, he had removed himself from the earth to a much more distant point than any Christian otherworldliness had ever removed him. Whatever the word "secular" is meant to signify in current usage, historically it cannot possibly be equated with worldliness; modern man at any rate did not gain this world when he lost the other world, and he did not gain life, strictly speaking, either; he was thrust back upon it, thrown into the closed inwardness of introspection, where the highest he could experience were the empty processes of reckoning of the mind, its play with itself. . . . What was left was a "natural force," the force of the life process itself, to which all men and all human activities were equally submitted.[16]

Therefore, as a result of the dominance and control of public life by the operations and ideology of the bourgeois elite, it was natural that the sense of public impotence would lead to a concentration on the highly circumscribed area of "personal life." The self, either in its interior regions or in its limited expression among small groups, has become the final place where ultimate meaning is found in life.

Individualism had been one of the most useful values in the struggle of the bourgeoisie with the feudal aristocracy. It signalled the break from the stultifying corporatism of the middle ages and was intended as an active, aggressive virtue, contrasting with the sense of resignation characteristic of the preceding epoch. But whatever its original purpose, contemporary American individualism is by no means associated with the creative, active person in search of a new future; instead it represents a retreat from public life. It involves finding meaning in the restricted realm of personal expression or in the interior regions of intense subjectivity. Individualism means the retreat to privatism where the person can find meaning beyond that of objective facticity. For many of the young it is drugs or Eastern religion; for sections of the affluent middle class it is sensitivity training and the cult of "feelings"; for others it is the safe world of the tavern, the mania associated with professional sports, or escape through travel. The sense of resignation, ennui, and impotence that hangs over public life drives people to find meaning in the cult of privatism, in the supposed creativity of the self in its private capacities.

As a result seeing history as meaningful—resting basically on confidence in the world—has become impossible. Now the self has become the locus of meaning. And it operates with no essential connection either with public events or with the processes of history.

This helps to explain, it seems to me, the predominance of Freudianism and existentialism for so long in intellectual circles. Both these schools of thought are products of the bourgeois epoch in that while they are creative attempts to give meaning to the epoch, they do so operating from within the subjectivist presuppositions of the age. In short, they are anti-histories. Both systems, for example, in the final analysis commend adjustment to the outward features of the age on the basis that there is no escape from the grim reality of time itself, except, of course, within the self. With Freud, for example, personal

> control is to be sought in the privacy of therapy . . . not the arena of political . . . action. Persons do not meet one another politically in their dreams. Consequently, the private time and space of the therapeutic hour become the *polis*. The problem of how to connect personal history with communal history or personal selves with public institutions still remains.[17]

Freudianism and existentialism are essentially individualistic and subjective creeds which exalt the person or the self over history, without at the same time offering a challenge to the shape of history. Both movements are now in a state of exhaustion precisely because they built upon the weakest aspect of bourgeois ideology: the self in its ahistorical capacities. When, therefore, a large number of Christian thinkers linked up with these two schools of thought in the hope of providing a contemporary vehicle of interpretation for the Gospel, they succeeded only in arriving at the same dead-end at the same time.

The self divided from history leads not to freedom but to despair or blind rebellion. Human integrity is maintained not by exalting the self above history but by effecting a unification of public and private activities and thought. The collapse of a sense of history and the absence of confidence in the world, while inviting a retreat to the self as a means of liberation, cannot lead to that liberation; it can only prevent it. The self locked in on itself, continuously distorted by a commercial culture which moves blindly toward the thingification of existence, can only serve to facilitate the victory of bourgeois facticity. The cult of privatism assures the bourgeoisie that no challenge will be directed at its public order. Further, in the private sphere dominated by television (58 million American families watch television with the average family watching six hours per day), the screen is dominated by a pre-packaged reality conforming to the needs of bourgeois ideology, featuring consumerism and the presentation of an externalized world of meaning.* In the more occult worlds of drugs, mystical religions, and sensitivity training, virtues are often inculcated which expressly limit political action while encouraging concentration on the "inner" world of "true" meaning. Privatism cannot provide the basis for a new conception of the world or life precisely because the self exists in time and is as problematic as any other level of reality. Further, privatism presupposes a view of reality which must ignore what once was, for the bourgeoisie, the central arena of concern, namely the totality of human affairs. Only the transformation of the entire culture in all its aspects can lead to a new and humane future for women and men.

The great hope remains. The extraordinary accomplishment of man in the field of science and technology awaits a better setting than in advanced bourgeois capitalism. The great contribution of science and technology can be realized only when it is linked with the hope of human freedom. Indeed science was nurtured in the expectation that there was an inextricable bond between truth and human liberation. Such was the hope of Marx.[19] But technology has not led to this. Instead it has become a tool for the interests of the bourgeoisie and a force of domination in its own right. Surely the present de-politicized malaise characteristic of bourgeois society cannot produce a movement for a new future in which man controls technology for human ends. As a result the need to establish a basic confidence for the world and hence provide the basis for a new political surge toward humanization is as pressing as ever.

3

The ancient doctrines of creation and eternal life, reinstated within Christian consciousness so as to provide an understanding of history, would not inspire confidence for the world. Both ancient notions correctly pointed to the need for guaranteeing and securing life from outside the ordinary processes of the

*"These are reflected in ... the idiom of advertisement, wish-fulfillment and consensus-propaganda of consumer technocracies. We live under a constant wash of mendacity. Millions of words tide over us with no intent of clear meaning. Quiet is becoming the prerogative of a sheltered élite or the cage of the desolate."[18]

world. However, the former doctrine has too often led to a vague naturalism, while the latter has been altogether lost either in superstition or in its adherence to the substance of the discredited Greek body-soul dualism.

Biblically, man's life in time is inextricably bound up with the promises God makes for human liberation. Since, however, these promises are basically related to God and not to human potential, natural goodness, the rights of man, or the teleology of creation, the lives of women and men have potential fulfillment, not as they coordinate with the natural world or the regular progress of all things, but as they (individually and collectively) are related to the future of God. Consequently, the Biblical story posits the course of events—as they are dominated by God—not in terms of the regularity of nature but in terms of the surprises of history. The entrance into time of the new, the incalculable, the unexpected, particularly as they are related to God's power to create life from death and to overcome misery and slavery, was central to the Biblical understanding of reality. " . . . according to Paul," Ernst Käsemann notes, "discontinuity is the mark . . . of history. . . ."[20] The intractable appearance of the new dominates the consciousness of the New Testament writers. Those of us who live in another age quite naturally focus on the formal aspects of this kind of description of reality: visions, miracles, divine intrusions, spectacular fulfillments and predictions, demonology and cosmic struggles. In so doing, we tend to be blind to the main Biblical insights present in this view. In the New Testament the world is understood apocalyptically, that is, the present is understood not in terms of its current course, but in terms of the fulfillment of the promises of God as these have already been revealed in the raising of Jesus. Since these promises deal with the end to human misery, the conquest of death, and the overcoming of transitoriness, it is only in terms of miracle and resurrection that one can speak. The destiny of man is at stake, not the raising of the Gross National Product. The world is capped by misery and hence has no power of itself to promise or deliver liberation. The present bourgeois epoch considers talk such as this fanciful (or even mad) precisely because it has so closely identified its hegemony with the ultimate goal of history. If we live in the best of all possible worlds (needing, of course, a little reform here and there), if the present state of affairs, arrived at after a long progressive struggle against tyranny and superstition, is fundamentally sound, then it is only natural to view the Biblical story as at best quaint and at worst misguided. For the bourgeoisie it is but right to view the future in terms of the indefinite, if slightly reformed, extension of the present.

The New Testament does not know history primarily in terms of cause and effect, or in terms of the continuity of events, which leads to careful calculation and prediction. Clearly, there is a dimension of regularity and repetition in man's life in time, but the idea that the meaning of human existence is to be found in the regular and consistent development of the species is in error. It is possible to look back after a series of events have occurred and point to connections and to relationships and even to hazard opinions about causations and continuities. However, that is possible only because it is done from the vantage of hindsight. Even with the advantage of hindsight, it is clear that causal connections are tenuous, related closely to the process of selection and elimination which the investigator employs. For example, those who emerge victorious in the struggles of an epoch tend to write with a view toward suggesting that past events have led in a line of natural development to the point of victory. The winners in history write about the past to vindicate themselves and to establish the inevitability of their triumph. Whatever else the exposition of causality and continuity may mean in the study of past time, for the Christian it does not mean history. Regularity, causal linkage, natural development, "historical" laws cannot be elevated to mean history precisely because the most meaningful events in time are idiosyncratic, intractable, and surprising. Inevitably, the careful study of the past means shepherding the new and incalculable into the herd of simple (or complex) cause and effect. Whatever this helps to explain (and clearly it does not help to predict), it explains by sacrificing wonder and awe at the meaning revealed in the irruption of the new into time. The point of reading regularity from and in the events of time is to establish control over these events. But there can be no control over the future. Santayana's dictum, that those who don't know history are bound to repeat it, is a fashionable cliché among modern investigators; but it is wrong precisely because even if we knew the past (a highly dubious proposition), we would continue to live into the future with our characteristic confusion, because one cannot push the understanding of the past into the future. The future remains open, mysterious, and intractable.

In the Biblical understanding, particularly as it is influenced by apocalyptic thought, the present (every present) is full of misery and without any natural hope. Yet for that reason history is the relationship of the present to the future of God. This is not a natural, predictable, or calculable relationship. It is a relationship determined by the signs that point to eschatological fulfillment, by events related to the end of the world, by tendencies linked to the final promises of God. Thus the events of the past are significant, not because they lead causally to my present state or to the establishment and power of my nation or class, but because they are linked parabolically to the end of history, to the kingdom of God.

It is for this reason that the New Testament portrays the acts of Jesus as miraculous. Miracle is the primary category of history in that it most adequately describes both the substance and the effect of the irruption of the end of history in time itself. Miracles draw their significance not from their formal aspects (nor from their undoubted relationship to primitive magic) but because they present the substance of the coming end. The destiny of humankind is the conquest of death and the end of tyranny and misery; yet the present of this life reveals horror, ennui, and disgust. Not the illusory progress of life, but the reversal of life, is the true meaning of time; and when that occurs it is a miracle. The regular processes of life give way, intense struggle erupts, lives are transformed, time is transfigured into history. Ernst Bloch captures the sense of miracle best:

> ... the sign of the end, of the *basic miracle of the Apocalypse* that was believed and phenomenologically linked with the coming of the Messiah. Thus the miracle as exploding of the accustomed state of affairs attains in Jesus its most radical expression, for it is augmented by the *novum* itself. ... it is always meant to be a new heaven and a new earth already. ... it always occurred as an interruption, and a visible one at that; above all, it happened so as to advance the particular, substitutive visibility of a totally changed order. ...
> What all this makes clear is that no matter how far the miraculous has since been reduced to ... a banal occultism ... the miracle concept does, most significantly, contain a far from superstitious concept *derived from explosive faith: the concept of the leap* .... a purely mechanical, causal world, antithetical to miracles in any form, [has] no room for the idea of a leap. ...[21]

In Christian faith, therefore, it is the eventful interruption, the leap, the coming of the incalculable related to the end of time that makes time meaningful.

This means also that whatever unity there is in time is provided by God, not by progress or causality. It is he who brings about both past and future, and it is in relation to his kingdom which lies beyond time and death and which yearns to be established on earth that all earthly affairs find themselves and their destiny.

History is apocalypse. Time is meaningful only in relation to the final unveiling of the world's destiny. Yet in Christian remembrance, the resurrection of Jesus is a proleptic anticipation of the final destiny of all humanity. This is why the resurrection is central to the Christian understanding of time. It signals the dramatic quality of life at the end of time while it points to the presence and character of God in time: as the one who overcomes misery, death, and transitoriness.

But time and its disintegrating power still exist and subject man and nations to vulnerability and temptation. Time has not yet drawn to a close. It still exercises its pernicious influence over all the earth. It still struggles with God. Thus, schemes that posit a tragedyless present or future are illusions because they forget the corrosiveness of time. The entrance of the *novum* in time is inevitably met by corruption and decay as it is threatened by the forces of disintegration. In this manner the hope of the American Revolution gave way to brutal slavery and imperial expansion, the French Revolution degenerated into Robespierre's "terror" and Napoleon's dictatorship, the Paris Commune of 1871 gave way to acts of incredible savagery, and the Russian Revolution succumbed to the tyranny of Stalin. Every new event turns the enthusiasm and hope it represents into an attempt to secure itself from the temptation of time by identifying itself as the final stage of history. Instead of accepting its provisionality and its life as a *sign* of a new future, it represents *itself* as the future, styles itself as the victor over time, and proceeds by whatever means to extend its rule. Always, however, the transitoriness of time haunts an epoch. And always in its vain attempt to escape, deny, or overlook the transitoriness of time, each epoch succumbs to the temptation of idolatry. In this fashion it is clear that tragedy is not simple accident or unfortunate occurrence, it is rooted in the very life of time experienced by men and nations. In the New Testament Paul struggled against those who would identify Jesus' resurrection with the total victory over time, that is, with a victory that freed all people from adherence to earthly regulations or restraints. For Paul, the resurrection was a Christian possession only in anticipation. The future would reveal the full dimension of this reality. For the present, however, the Christian lived in the misery of time and would have to remain subject to the life of temptation and suffering. For Paul, hope is related to misery and decay, it is not a product of optimism. In this regard Christians are called to struggle against every present, to hail the new as it enters every regime or epoch, drawing that epoch away from the stasis of death to the light of a new dawn of freedom and equality.

Characteristically, nations forget the distinction between time and history. They are forever associating their moment on earth with the final meaning of time. They forget their inevitable provisionality. In so doing they fall prey to the temptation of equating justice with redemption. The final victory over time is not a matter of human effort or choice, it is solely a matter of the mystery of God's grace. The earthly form of redemption—symbolized by the fact that Jesus is the righteousness of God, that is, the one who is right with God and establishes in his deeds the world's rightness with God—is human justice. Indeed, justice is the earthly destiny of all people. But while we live in time we are still subject to its limiting power. Christian faith in the resurrection of Jesus drives hope past time to the very heart of God, to a mystery beyond human knowing. That hope encompasses the world, but since it is rooted in the God who is beyond the conflict of time, it is beyond all imagining and all projection; it is the hope beyond hope which God has prepared with himself for all people.

4

In the New Testament Jesus is the ultimate sign of the end of the world. Hence, from within the world a sign of the world's true destiny arises. This Jesus is God's word, but in more than the literary sense which the phrase implies. He is the embodied word. As such the preliminary advance of the kingdom is not simply announced, it is implanted in time. Thus the present, every present, is potentially the bearer of the sign of new life. Every present is linked to the eschatological destiny of all people. The kingdom of God is not an explosion on the earth which suddenly reduces all things to flames or dust. The kingdom is in continual tension with the present, revealing tendencies or possibilities in the present that point to the end of death and misery. But no present contains such signs by virtue of its own goodness, potential, or natural movement. These signs exist as miracles related to God's grace.

As a consequence, any person or institution can find itself linked with the end of the world. Confidence for the world is possible and natural, and not simply a matter of optimism or positive thinking. Surely it is not related to the bourgeois concept of progress. The world remains locked in misery and grief and on its own leads to nothing new. Confidence for the world's life is established only on the basis of the revealed destiny of all people. This has occurred proleptically in Jesus, and has occurred in time, giving to all human events the potential to link up with their eschatological destiny. Indeed, insofar as Jesus appeared as a sign on the earth and also rose from the dead to the earth, it means that the affairs of the earth can be trusted one day to burst forth to reveal the fulness of God. When the destiny of man is limited to material advance or the regularity of oppressive fate, as has happened in the age of bourgeois hegemony, the basis for confidence has been destroyed. People are compelled to exhibit allegiance to the world in terms of a material facticity which is pointless and not fulfilling, and which further drives men and women in despair and distrust to the inner world of subjectivity. This latter world is no more a basis for confidence, because it is cut off from history itself. The question of confidence is seen most properly as the question of man's destiny of freedom and equality. This is an eschatological not an immanent possibility. But insofar as it happened to Jesus, it can happen to us. This provides us with confidence for the world. It also enables us to work with the structures of the world, always with an eye to emergent possibilities which may break the spell of death and decay. Since God has embodied this victory, the earth and all its life stand in parabolic relation to this new moment of hope and transfiguration.

And yet as Dostoyevsky has written, trust in God is accompanied by disdain for the world. The world cannot on its own produce or signify anything. Only when the earth is seen as a place of continual eschatological struggle (and not as a place of the elaboration of fact) is it possible truly to understand the world. We love the world and have confidence in it on the basis of trust and hope in God. We love the world for his sake. It is from him that the world's true life and freedom will one day come.

PART THREE

THE SIGNS
OF THE END

Chapter Five

The POOR
and the KINGDOM of GOD

A man in America is not despised for being poor at the outset ... but every year which passes without adding to his prosperity is a reproach to his understanding or industry.   **Francis Grund**

Christianity displays a certain inclination to side with those who are immature, sullen and depressed, with those who "come off badly" and are, in consequence, ready for revolution. There is, for this reason, much in the cause of socialism which evokes Christian approval. . . . It sees in the lowly at least a parable of life. This is because it cannot forget the Resurrection.
                                                            Karl Barth

He sets on high those who are lowly,
and those who mourn are lifted to safety.
He frustrates the devices of the crafty,
so that their hands achieve no success.
He takes the wise in their own craftiness;
and the schemes of the wily are brought to a quick end.
They meet with darkness in the daytime,
and grope at noonday as in the night.
But he saves the fatherless from their mouth,
the needy from the hand of the mighty.
So the poor have hope,
and injustice shuts her mouth.   **Job 5:11-16**

It is easier for a camel to go through the eye of a needle than for a rich man to enter the kingdom of God.   **Mark 10:25**

So the last will be first, and the first last.   **Matthew 20:16**

1

The basic core of the New Testament message is that Jesus preached salvation to the outcasts.[1] Peel back layer after layer of theological excursus and dogmatic formulation and you find Jesus announcing the coming of the kingdom of God to those who, by virtue of moral deportment or occupational choice, were viewed as sinners by the society in which they lived. That is, Jesus preached salvation to those whom the most sacred traditions of Israel considered unworthy of the promises of God. When Jesus shared community with sinners (particularly at meals—which had the effect of prefiguring the eschatological feast of the world to come), he was demonstrating that the forsaken and despised were the central elements in the kingdom of God. Thus, by linking the most fundamental of Israel's hopes—safety and joy in the world to come—with the ungodly and rejected, rather than with the righteous, Jesus reversed traditional expectations, directly challenged religious authority, and endangered cultural and social stability. For this reason, and not because of a dispute over messianic claims, Jesus was branded a blasphemer of the law, handed over to the Roman authorities, and summarily executed for sedition.[2]

Clearly, Jesus was guilty as charged. The New Testament writers, particularly Luke, tried to establish Jesus' innocence by suggesting that malice and unfounded jealousy among the Jews forced reluctant Roman authorities to act against a man they knew to be guiltless (Luke 23:1-25). In fact, Jesus was a blasphemer of the Jewish law and a political troublemaker. His notorious friendship with known revolutionaries (Zealots) cannot be ignored, and his culpability before both Jewish and Roman officials cannot be excused by reading back into it modern conceptions of jurisprudence. Nor can Jesus' guilt be hidden by the theological smokescreen that he was innocent in the eyes of God. The political and legal fate of Jesus cannot be reduced to the matter of a martyr who suffered unjust punishment for a crime which in the sight of God he did not commit. Jesus was neither Mahatma Gandhi nor Joe Hill. Whatever the standing of Jesus in the sight of God, he was guilty in the sight of men.

It was logical, therefore, that Jesus' fate on the cross would be viewed by his religious contemporaries as apt: "Cursed be every one who hangs on a tree" (Gal. 3:13). And the shame of crucifixion was a fitting end for a political rebel. The fate of Jesus matched his crime.

For his earliest followers, the resurrection of Jesus confirmed the correctness of his announcement of salvation for the outcasts, and at the same time justified his life as an accursed criminal. Whatever else can be said theologically about Jesus—his exaltation, triumph, and glorification—it cannot serve to eradicate or bypass the reality of his status as a guilty outlaw. Hence

Christianity is wedded to the belief—quite unique among all religions—that the work of God has come to definitive fruition, not simply in the life of a man, but in the life of this particular man, Jesus, a despised malefactor. This central insight was picked up by Paul, who testified that the meaning of Jesus' crucifixion and resurrection was to give standing to the ungodly.[3] Paul applied this by preaching salvation to the hated Gentiles, an extraordinary action because it both contradicted Jesus' injunction against going to the Gentiles (Matt. 10:5-7) and offended Jewish belief which saw the Gentile as a godless outsider. Paul, however, had a wider sense of history and went to the Gentiles precisely because they were outsiders. For Paul the resurrection confirmed the logic of salvation: the kingdom of God was for the outcasts.[4]

By going to the Gentiles, however, early Christianity lost the edge of offense which was rooted in Jesus' basic preaching. The original proclamation of Jesus (and his status) meant that universal salvation was available to all through the dialectic of God's primary friendship toward those abandoned to hopelessness. In relation to Israel the Gentiles were outcasts; but as preaching spread throughout the Gentile world, the dialectic which was such a central part of the earliest tradition was dropped. Instead salvation was made universally available through the repentance of sins.* This was undoubtedly an important move on the part of the church. By emphasizing the universal nature of salvation the way was paved for successful missionary activity. In the process, however, the poor and downtrodden were dislodged from their central place in the scheme of salvation. At best, the way was open for treating the poor as objects of charity or moral concern.†

This development reflected a further shift in the Christian understanding of history. In the earliest sections of the New Testament, salvation was inextricably bound up with the expectation of a transformed history. In this expectation, hope for the coming kingdom of God was tied up with the fate of the poor and oppressed. The Lucan story of Dives and Lazarus, for example, builds upon the notion of a reversal of fortunes of the rich and the poor in the coming kingdom (Luke 16:19-31). In Matthew's Gospel Jesus

---

*Matt. 22:1-14 combines two stories which neatly indicate this shift. In the first parable we find the host at a feast demanding that outcasts be invited to the event as replacements for those originally designated to attend. In the second story a guest without a garment is deemed improperly attired and thrown out of the celebration. The first story clearly refers to the reversal of roles in God's plan for history—a sociological point. The second story, however, bears an ontological explanation with universal applicability: repentance and preparation, and not social role, are central to safety in the kingdom.

†There is all the difference in the world between treating, for example, the concern expressed for the poor and destitute in Matt. 25:31-46 as a general ethical principle and seeing it as a story which has as its primary referent that the castaways and forgotten are to be at the center of the approaching kingdom of God.

says that in the coming kingdom, "The last will be first, and the first last" (Matt. 20:16). However, when the church moved out of Palestine and lost contact with Jewish thought and experience, salvation became associated not with expectations about the future of the world and the special role played by the outcasts in historical transformation, but with mass conversion and the triumphant growth of the church itself. Thus, the history of the world increasingly became the history of the church.

As a result of these developments, the fate of the poor and oppressed was separated from any central place in Christian preaching. That the church's preaching originally found greatest acceptance among the lower ranks of society attests, perhaps, to the retention of some of the earliest insights of the Gospel. Surely, the church's early adherence to the principle of equality was rooted as much in the message of and about Jesus as it was in the strivings and hopes of the oppressed urban proletariat of the Mediterranean world. Still, the fate of the outcasts was no longer related in any special way to the hope of worldly transformation. Therefore, as a class the poor became, at best, deserving of special pity and concern. They became one among many groups to whom the grace of God was available even while their material abjection qualified them for charity.

Even though the stage was set for relegating the outcasts to the margins of Christian thought, it was a long time before the process was completed. Monastic communities insisted on poverty as a virtue. In addition, medieval society held that the poor were entitled, by virtue of (and not in spite of) their status, to monetary support from the rich and from the church. Clearly, for a long period of time the poor were seen as rather special objects of pity or charity. "The poor man," noted a medieval catechism, "is the most beloved son of the father . . . the very image of Christ . . . and almsgiving is the pre-eminent good work."

The rise of the bourgeois class, however, brought to an end any notion that the poor enjoyed an exalted status in the eyes of God. The bourgeoisie elevated work and production as primary virtues and attacked both the poor and the rich as sinful because they were slothful and lazy.[5] At best the poor might deserve handouts, but this only in relation to the charitable instincts and good feeling of the bourgeois donor and not because of any inherent right the poor might have. Edmund Burke argued that it was not "within the competence of the government, taken as government, or even of the rich, as rich, to supply to the poor those necessaries which it has pleased the Divine Providence for awhile to withhold from them."[6] The separation of the oppressed from any central place in the proclamation of the Gospel, or in any hope for a transformed world, was complete.

Meanwhile, understanding history in terms of triumphalism predominated in the West. As far back as the New Testament (particularly in Luke) the ground had been prepared for understanding history in terms of the successful extension of the church. And, as has been mentioned, the loss of apocalyptic expectations coupled with the subsequent omission of the central role of the outcasts in a transformed history further paved the way for Christian triumphalism. These impulses were propelled forward to a position of dominance when in the fourth century Christianity forged an alliance with the forces of triumph (Constantine). This ensured the loss of the Pauline insight that the meaning of history is wrapped up with the future of the outcasts. Instead, the Constantinian alliance meant a shift to concern for the apparatus of triumph: order, stability, reason, and measured progress. Having then combined ecclesiastical history with civil history (that is, with those who dominate the civil order), a course was set in which history would be seen as the growth of Christian civilization and the stabilization of that order, not only by world-wide conversion (and sometimes force), but also by the spread of the accoutrements of culture which served to control and domesticate alien groups who might otherwise upset the stasis of dominance. Later, with the ascendancy of the Western bourgeois class, the church, by now accustomed to associate the meaning of history with the domination of triumphant groups, gradually shifted loyalties to this new victorious class. By this time, however, the last traces of Biblical dialectics and medieval otherworldliness had been removed, and nothing stood in the way of the church celebrating history in terms of the prevailing bourgeois hegemony. One is tempted to argue, nonetheless, that God did not leave himself without a witness. For just as Christianity was justifying bourgeois dominance as the new goal of human history, Marxism was picking up on Biblical themes and connecting the future of world history with the fate of the oppressed and despised masses of the world.

It remains a fundamental mistake to tie Christianity so closely to victorious classes, and the culture they elaborate, to ensure their dominance. Christianity is basically a faith that is wedded to the outcast. Others may insist upon identifying world history with the history of the triumph of the Christian West (and the decline of Christianity with the decline of Western civilization), but an authentic Christianity must assert once more that world history is the history of the destiny of all people, as that destiny is first worked out among the oppressed. Further, Old Testament prophetic iconoclasm and New Testament apocalypticism, with their suspicion of "culture," remain live options for Christians, not because they are manifestations of demonic barbarism, as was assumed by those stricken with horror at the anti-cultural outbursts of the Reformation, but because the articulation of culture tends to be but another way of ensuring the dominance of some classes over others. The focus of Christian activity is with the oppressed and in solidarity with their struggle for a new future.* The collapse of Western bourgeois hegemony and the instability of American-led Western capitalism should not, therefore, be viewed with alarm. The fall of the victors is always the first sign of hope. It provides the opportunity for a new history.

2

Amidst all the splendor and self-congratulation surrounding the achievements of America's corporate, technological age stands the spectre of poverty. The older generation of working poor have, by now, generally scrambled up a notch or two on the income ladder; but in their wake a new generation has arisen threatening to establish through its children a permanent community of the poor. Some of the poor are unemployed, living off friends or relatives, while others receive public assistance. The greater number exist as transient farmers and laborers, small, rural farmers, odd-jobbers, domestics, retired people, or employees of restaurants, hospitals, cleaning establishments and other small businesses. The poor are visible because they exist outside the major economy of corporate capitalism in the small-unit, low-profit-margin, non-union world which J. K. Galbraith has called the second economy of "cockroach capitalism." Here, low wages, protected by law, help marginal economic establishments survive. It must serve as one of the cruelest ironies of America's corporate age that the small-unit shop, the very backbone of traditional American economic independence and freedom, has now become the guarantor of wage slavery and human poverty.

Presently, close to thirty million Americans live in poverty. In addition, large numbers live close enough to the poverty line to suffer insecurities and frustrations similar to the poor. These are people who, in the words of Michael Harrington, live "only an illness, an accident or a recession away from the other America."[7] One estimate of those in or around the bleak circle of poverty places the number at fifty million.[8] This in the richest and most technologically advanced nation in the history of the world.

Regard, if you will, the world of the poor:

*It should be noted that while I hold the poor and despised to be, theologically, the harbingers of a new epoch, I do not translate that hope directly into politics. That is to say, I do not hold the world's despised masses to be the sole revolutionary force and hence the world's only hope. Such romanticism, often found in the American left, completely overlooks the crucial role to be played by other social and economic strata. Nonetheless, it is out of the desperate reality of the life of the poor that radical hope arises. Even if at times that hope is given political expression by others, the generative role of the outcasts is secure.

In 1970 over sixty percent of Navaho Indians were unemployed. Their average educational level was the fifth grade. They possessed the highest birth rate in the nation and an equally high mortality rate. Their life expectancy was forty-five years. Eighty percent lived in one-room hogans. Ninety percent had incomes below the poverty level.

Fourteen million Americans are presently suffering from hunger.

In 1970, according to the Columbia Broadcasting System, there were 200,000 migrant farm workers in Florida with an average yearly income of $891. They were excluded from the protection of child labor and minimum wage laws. They were without strike protection and excluded from Workman's Compensation laws. They earned the lowest wages of any group in America. In ten years their wages had not changed. Only twenty percent of their children went to high school while only fifty percent went as far as the seventh grade in school. The average life expectancy of the migrant worker was forty-nine years.

One of every three black persons in America lives in poverty.

Families headed by women account for forty-four percent of the poverty population.

Of the twenty million Americans who are over sixty-five years of age, 4,800,000 live in poverty. Most of the elderly poor live in substandard housing while large numbers are cared for in ill-equipped, under-staffed, and under-financed institutions. In many of these institutions the elderly are often drugged or otherwise reduced to an automaton state in order to ensure order.

In 1970, 12,200,000 Americans were receiving welfare benefits.

Predictably, the matter of poverty is treated by the American government and by the public as a regrettable fact of our common life. "The poor you will always have with you." Yet we are assured that everything is being done and that progress is being made. This is a reassuring doctrine in a nation that cannot bear to have its cruelties elevated beyond the status of incidentals. Yet poverty is no passing phenomenon: it has been with us since the earliest days of the republic.[9] Nor is it in any way incidental, a kind of unpleasant after-effect of material advance. The gratuitous starvation, the fear and cold, the militant insecurity of close to one-seventh of our population stand, not as an unfortunate accident, nor as the necessary price one pays for progress, but as a blasphemy which confutes the American experience. All this in a nation that is, and has always been, racked with gross inequities of wealth and power; a nation that has treated as alien any doctrine of economic equality; a nation that, whatever its claims about social mobility, has continued to maintain a pervasive class system. By virtue of the dynamic imbalances of American life, millions of people remain perpetually at the bottom of the social and economic ladder, resigned there in the midst of patronizing protestations and official regret, held there because the system demands that someone be at the bottom. It is well to remember that the materially fortunate live in suburbs and eat well and move with ease only at the sufferance and the suffering of the poor. There is no more lucid, tragic, and contemptuous demonstration of the interdependency of people and the calamitous reality of sin.

The working poor are caught in a variety of economic squeezes. The firms for which most of them work are generally marginal enterprises which fix wages at a low level (twelve million Americans work for less than $1.90 per hour) and which press for exemptions from minimum wage and other state and federal laws designed to protect workers. Consequently, these workers provide a cheap labor pool. And while the proprietors of these establishments do not have the political clout of the big corporate leaders, they still manage to wield more influence with legislators, police, and other officials than do their unorganized employees, thus guaranteeing the maintenance of the status quo. The bedrock of the business position has always been that the rights of property and capital are more secure than the rights of labor. After all, it is still true that if a man starves to death, no one need be charged with a crime; however, let the window of a store be broken and if the culprit is found an arrest will surely be made. "The law in its majestic equality," wrote Anatole France, "forbids the rich as well as the poor to sleep under bridges, to beg in the streets and to steal bread."

The economic problem is further complicated in that federal plans for extensive minimum wage coverage or for a high guaranteed annual income threaten regions like the South and Southeast. Here a cheap and bountiful labor force is needed precisely in order to attract Northern industry. Hence these areas are among the most vociferous opponents of measures that would raise wages. Higher income for workers would hurt the local economy. Indeed, since American business in general welcomes the opportunity to move to cheap labor areas, some of the most powerful forces in American life have an interest in maintaining poverty.

Because of the economics of small or large enterprises that operate on a very narrow profit margin and are unable, because of competition, quickly to pass on wage costs to the consumer in higher prices, it is difficult for millions of workers to receive decent wages. Many such businesses have failed precisely because they could not meet higher wage costs. Of course, such a situation could have led to a discussion about the nature of a business system that sacrifices workers to the god of profit. But such has not been the case.

Neither big business nor big labor (nor the general public) seems disposed to move beyond general regret about economic injustice to the fundamental question of the basic nature of the whole capitalist economy. And the poor remain the losers.

Similarly, the economics of large agricultural enterprises are such that they cannot raise wages without at the same time provoking a rise in food prices. And in a consumer-oriented economy any significant rise in food prices invites public outrage. A public that is concerned more with the price of consumer goods than with fair wages finds the prospect of inflation far more distasteful than the fact of wage slavery. The consumer acts as the enemy of the poor, and the working poor suffer.

Tragically, the working poor are prisoners of an increasingly sophisticated technological age in which the degree of skill required for meaningful and well-paying work steadily rises, leaving behind pockets of unskilled workers who cannot acquire training fast enough to keep pace. They remain locked in the unskilled world of low pay and economic humiliation. The encomiums rising from the lips of politicians, corporate managers, and technologists about the new technological age serve only to obscure the truth that whatever the contribution of technology, it is still set within the framework of capitalism and is thus bound to place profit before the welfare of people. Hence to sing the praises of technology without talking at the same time about a major overhaul of the American economic system is to propose eradicating economic inequality by building on it.

Finally, there is an even more ominous reality imbedded in the economics of poverty. Whereas in the past the impoverishment of the great mass of American workers meant that the capital-owning class was living directly off their labor, the present situation shows only a minority of people to be utterly impoverished. The great majority of workers suffer impoverishment only relative to the wealth of the capital-owning class; that is, they suffer impoverishment but not misery. Only a fraction, about fifteen percent, is subject to abject poverty. And this fifteen percent, with some exceptions (particularly among farm workers), is no longer necessary either for the enrichment of the American ruling class or for the smooth and efficient functioning of the economy. For the first time pauperization is not coincident with exploitation (as it has been traditionally known). The workers who are poor are exploited, but not in such a way that they are central to the economy. *The system does not need their labor.* In large measure they are an impediment to the economy as a whole and could be eliminated without the economy suffering to any significant degree. When, therefore, the poor talk of genocide, it should not be taken as simple rhetoric; it is grounded in the reality that, unlike their sisters and brothers of a generation ago, the poor of our day are ultimately expendable.[10]

3

Commentators have long noted that the prevailing attitude of the public toward poor people (and particularly those on welfare) involves the conviction that the poor are shiftless and lazy, lacking in initiative, and personally responsible for their fate. Out of such a welter of convenient myths comes the view that welfare or public assistance is a dole to otherwise lazy schemers. In regard specifically to welfare, it apparently does not matter that in 1972, for example, ninety percent of welfare money was going to old people, the disabled, and dependent children; that all the federal job-training programs were oversubscribed; or that those who came out of these programs were unable to find work because the jobs were not available. It does not matter because there remains a persistent national desire to make the poor and those on welfare (the two are not the same: only about thirty percent of the poor are on welfare) scapegoats for the failure of the American economic system to provide equity and justice.

It is not that Americans lack a sense of charity. As a predominantly middle class nation, Americans possess a very strong sense of morality and have demonstrated a strong willingness to give voluntarily to "good" causes. But Americans steadfastly refuse to acknowledge that there is any endemic inequity in our system which would require systematic, institutional overhaul. Failing this, Americans fall back on prolific individual giving. Traditional notions of individual charity leave aside larger issues and instead focus on the fulfilling experience of direct giving, thus re-creating a kind of personal, pre-industrial world in which problems are understood in the most individualistic way. But the tragedy of this mode of giving (beyond the humiliation it visits on the recipients of personal charity) is that it only serves to highlight the absence of any larger sense of institutional analysis and social responsibility. Thus, by its very haphazard, infrequent, sentiment-filled nature, personal giving as a response to large social need only succeeds in reinforcing the very system responsible for poverty in the first place. In truth the poor are at the mercy of myth and misguided charity, buried in the hopelessness perpetuated by bourgeois kindness.

4

In 1860, when Abraham Lincoln campaigned for the Presidency, he denounced slavery as a moral evil when speaking in northern Illinois, but when he stumped in southern Illinois, he simply opposed the extension of slavery. Lincoln was no fool; there were votes to be had in southern Illinois, not for moral pronouncements, but by acknowledging that black people might come and compete for jobs held by white people. Today, competition between elements of the poor still exists. This blocks the kind of organizing that could make a significant economic difference for the poor. Then, too, there is the resistance of the more economically unstable elements of the working class who exist only one notch above the poor on the economic ladder and are continually in fear for their jobs. The $5000 per year they make does not lead them to cooperate with the poor in an effort to restructure the whole economic system. Instead, they remain in bitter competition with the poor. And all the while the real winners remain safely ensconced in the corporate board rooms of this country. Further, when the poor try to organize among themselves they are often thwarted by the federal government. The government sees its job in terms of charity. It is generally hostile to organizing efforts among the poor. For this reason the Nixon administration killed large portions of the Johnson poverty program. The government does not wish to function as an organizer of the poor. Instead, it prefers to dispense just enough funds to the poor to prevent them from becoming an unassimilated, independent, frustrated, explosive mass. Public assistance, therefore, represents the effort on the part of government to create that kind of dependency which makes for social order. Welfare is social control, as are practically all organized forms of charity. Thus, on the one side, the anxiety and anger of the middle and lower-middle classes (the former because they pay the highest percentage of taxes; the latter because of economic competition with the poor) set a boundary against too much aid to the poor, while on the other side the corporate elite and their political spokesmen, out of fear of revolution, ensure that just enough help is given— without it leading to organizing—to provide effective social control. The poor are caught in the middle and forced to pay in misery for the fear and machinations of others.

Thwarted and victimized at every turn, manipulated and betrayed, it is no wonder that so many of the poor fall back on the explanation of personal failure. During the Depression, Studs Terkel has noted,

The suddenly-idle hands blamed themselves, rather than society. True, there were hunger marches and protestations to City Hall and Washington, but the millions experienced a private kind of shame when the pink slip came. No matter that others suffered the same fate, the inner voice whispered, "I'm a failure."[11]

Much of this is true of today's poor. It is a tragedy that all people, in some fashion, buy the stories that are sold to them about their fate. The poor often become the shame and humiliation which is their condition. And proudly, the owners and managers of their fate point to them as passive, lazy, untrustworthy. Despair, death, and misery are triumphant.

Of course, it is part of the official condescension of the haves that they provide an ideology by which the have-nots may take comfort in their pitiful state. The poor are exhorted to believe that a person's ultimate worth is not determined by his or her material standing. According to this view a person's worth is determined either by the fact of his or her simple humanity or by their relation to God. This doctrine is delivered and sanctioned from the porticos of the White House, from countless wealthy pulpits, and by the most respected of our national media commentators. It suggests a common brotherhood apart from money or status. This is indeed a reassuring notion for the advantaged classes who apply it to the poor while steadfastly refusing to apply it to themselves. After all, there could hardly be a more demonstrably false doctrine in regard to the standing of the dominant classes. They have always operated on the basis that a man or woman is what he or she makes or owns. Indeed, if a person is not what he or she possesses, then some of the most prized and accepted values of bourgeois society would have to be scrapped—such values as initiative, success, ambition, efficiency, work, competition, ownership. Yet, with perfect sincerity the aphorism that worth is related to being, and not to having, is conscientiously applied to the poor by the advantaged, but it is not allowed to interfere with the pursuit of pecuniary status by the wealthy. Such is the power of good will in America.

Some persons become sentimental about the poor, ascribing to them the acceptable virtues of humility and longsuffering. In this manner the poor are more manageable. This is not surprising, for in a bourgeois society help is always conditional: only the worthy receive rewards. One of the most cherished beliefs of bourgeois culture is that all people reach their appropriate station in life in accord with their moral character. Thus, if the poor are to have any regard shown them, they must first be endowed with some redeeming virtue.

But the behavior of some of the American poor clearly contradicts popular notions about their patience and courageous humility. Many of the urban black poor, for example, refuse to exhibit humility and, instead, engage in acts of rebellion or violence as signs of their desperation; and sections of the white and brown poor sometimes break out in rage against the constraints of their condition. When this happens these people are immediately denounced as criminals and removed from the category of "poor." In that fashion they are no longer viewed as deserving help or sympathy, such being the bourgeois theory of moral station. These "violators" invariably find their way into the prisons of this land, where they encounter the rewards due to those who exhibit no redeeming moral virtues: vicious social control, humiliation, official contempt. In prison, the wrath of officials combines with the heedless indifference of a middle class public, thus making direct the fury and hatred that in the outside world is only indirect and symbolic. It is in prison that society can at once vent its rage on those who refuse to conform to the theory of moral station and also exhibit its belief in the absolute sanctity of the doctrine of individual responsibility. There in the barbaric underworld of official "rehabilitation," the poor-become-criminals reside forgotten and banished as a possible reminder of society's responsibility for the material welfare of all its citizens, as a possible reminder, that is, of the crime of society itself. The ultimate tragedy of the Attica prison revolt of 1971 was that the issue articulated by the prisoners—the hated, black underclass—namely, that society continues to assign people to poverty and misery, was buried under the official liberal interpretation that the major issues were the violence of the prisoners and the need for prison reform (which, incidentally, has not come). At no point, it appears, will the poor who bear the brunt of society's injustice be allowed to articulate either the reasons for that injustice or the hope for its end.

5

The New Testament is clearly biased toward the poor. In fact, one is hard-pressed to find in it a good word about the rich. In story after story the poor are either the inheritors of promises or the recipients of favor (for example, Matt. 19:16-30; Luke 16:19-31; Mark 10:23-27). It is correct to conclude, therefore, with Nicolas Berdyaev that "Only Christians who have lost their conscience are capable of defending the rich against the poor."[12]

And yet the New Testament bias toward the poor is not to be taken in any romantic fashion, nor should it be seen as an exhortation to plead the cause of the poor with the rich. It is hardly a plea for the welfare state. The New Testament stories of the poor are not isolated moral tales told with the intent of persuading women and men to be moral or good. Instead, they are announcements concerning the shape and content of the coming kingdom of God as that kingdom mysteriously and arbitrarily breaks in upon mankind.

The poor do not exist to prod the conscience of the well-to-do. They do not exist to call forth extended charity or moral concern. Nor do they exist to provoke guilt. The poor do not exist as a problem that must be solved. In the New Testament the poor are none of these things because they are not primarily regarded from the point of view of this age, that is, in terms of the system that holds them in chains. After all, the advantaged tend to act toward the poor in charity, concern, or sympathy primarily with an eye to the safety of their own systems, their own priorities, their own sensibilities. The advantaged always caution "go slow"; they always contend that the "system" cannot be endangered just to help the poor. They argue, that is, from within, and for the safety of their own lives. They have no perspective but their own well-being. In relation to the poor the advantaged wish only to save themselves. Hence, in the New Testament the poor are related, not to the world and the systems of man, but to the kingdom of God. Only from this perspective can the cruelty and blindness of man be exposed and judged. The poor possess the secret of the kingdom, for they are the judgment of the present age. And further, by the grace of God, they exist as a sign of the promise of God's saving activity. When Jesus asserts that the poor will always be with us (Matt. 26:11), he is not substantiating political conservatism, but is referring to the basic apocalyptic insight that the poor exist as a sign of promise. In the New Testament God acts precisely through those who have nothing to expect from the world, and for whom the structure and life of the world have become enemies. God acts through the outcast, the despised, through those without possibilities, without any future, through those who, in possessing nothing on the earth, bear the promise of a new age in which all people can possess everything equally.

This was Paul's understanding of Jesus Christ. God had acted through, from, and in death. That is, he had acted from the other side of life itself. He brought out of the nothingness of death a new creation: Jesus, the risen one, *creatio ex nihilo*.

> ... God chose what is weak in the world to shame the strong, God chose what is low and despised in the world, even things that are not, to bring to nothing things that are... (I Cor. 1:27-28).

Because Jesus himself was poor, in that he associated with the dispossessed, since he proclaimed a new age in which the last would be first, and because he was crucified as a despised agitator, we are forced to attend to the poor and the outcast. This is not so that they might be treated more "fairly," but because, in the dramatic reversal of their fate, which shatters the form of this present age of misery, lies the dawn of an age of freedom for all people. No one is free until the poor are free. Hence, God acts from the end of time in the future of the poor in order to provide life for all. In the promise of a new fate for the poor lies the content and shape of the new age for mankind.

The presence of the poor, locked in their stations by bourgeois prejudice and economic capitalism, stands as a reminder to the Christian of the deep and unyielding power of the forces of darkness and death at work in worldly systems. As Paul said, we wrestle not against flesh and blood but against principalities and powers. To welcome the kingdom of God is the Christian's pleasure and task. But that kingdom is thwarted by the poverty of some people and the stubbornness of others. The matter of Christian faith is the exaltation of the poor as the sign of the end of the world. For our common life that does not mean the reform of the welfare system—however necessary that may be—nor should it lead to increased charity or the hope for purer hearts among all people. It means the end of this society and the establishment of true equality in a new democratic socialism.

Chapter Six

AMERICAN YOUTH
and the AMBIGUITIES of HOPE

Every age, every culture, every custom and tradition has its own character, its own weakness and its own strength, its beauties and ugliness, accepts certain sufferings as a matter of course, puts up potentially with certain evils. Human life is reduced to real suffering, to hell when two ages overlap. Now there are times when a whole generation is caught in this way between two ages, two modes of life, with the consequence that it loses all power to understand itself and has no standard, no security, no simple acquiescence.   **Herman Hesse**

We of the first post-industrial generation are natural communists. For us property is not a thing to keep men apart and at war, but rather a medium by which men can come together to play . . . and learn the importance of communal fellowship and cooperation. . . . the future is ours as a matter of course. . . . We were born to build a cooperative commonwealth upon the wreckage of this class-ridden barbarism. Only one thing could go wrong—there might not be a future.   **Mario Savio**

1

One of the astonishing ironies of contemporary history has been the growth of a dissident, stubborn, and rebellious youth within the heart of American technological capitalism.* The most advanced industrial nation in the history

---

*In the following discussion it should be noted that I am referring primarily to white youth. This does not mean that the activities and thought of black, brown, or red young people have been without significance. On the contrary, in many ways minority youth have been in the vanguard of the whole youth movement. I omit extended references to them, however, for two reasons. First, I feel less confident in describing their activities. Second, I believe their activities very often represent less the insurgence of youth than the rebellion of a deprived and exploited underclass.

of the world, with a degree of prosperity heretofore unknown and seeming to possess an extraordinarily high degree of cultural and ideological unity,[1] has witnessed the irruption of a youth culture dedicated to a set of values and hopes almost contrary to those on which this country was built and on which it so desperately depends. There could hardly be a better example of the intractable and unpredictable character of history.

Apologists for technological capitalism did not greet the rise of the youth movement with sympathy. It was hardly to be expected that they would. For them the form of technological capitalism was the new age itself. It combined material progress with the absence of ideological discord. In the new age there was something for everyone. Consequently when young dissidents rose to protest the form of technological capitalism, the defenders of the new age were quick to react. Unwilling to consider the substance of the youth complaint—to wit, that advanced capitalism was cruel and repressive—the defenders of the system dismissed the youth protest out of hand. They claimed that youthful dissidence represented the natural lag in any system undergoing rapid change. The young, they argued, were clinging to outmoded concepts of reality and humanity which were now in the process of rapid transformation, and thus represented a last-ditch stand against modernity. Since the young protesters represented a past stage of development, their activities and beliefs were but "the death rattle of the historical irrelevants" (Zbigniew Brzezinski).[2]

It was, of course, in the interest of technological apologists to halt their investigation into the rise and significance of the youth movement at such a point. To ascribe a deeper meaning to the claims of youth would be to question the whole techno-capitalist system and to cast doubt upon it as the next inevitable stage in human development. Nonetheless the youth movement itself succeeded in casting such a shadow of doubt over the present capitalist system.

Whatever its mistakes and confusion, the youth protest pointed to an enormous contradiction in modern advanced capitalism. The young were the unmistakable product of the system. They arose at the point where prosperity and cultural uniformity, so carefully engendered in order to ensure progress, became widespread. To the degree, therefore, that the system "succeeded," it witnessed a commensurate growth in dissent. In large part this was probably due to widespread affluence. Prosperity freed many young people from the compulsive struggle for existence which had tied people to the system in the past. Freed from this bond, and somehow not at all worried about sustaining the affluence they enjoyed, they proceeded to question the meaningfulness of affluence itself. As a result many young people existed at the point where the questions of quantity, on which the system rested, gave way to questions of quality, for which the system had no answer whatsoever.

The horizon of questioning and expectation had widened past the point where the system could supply meaningful answers or hopes.[3]

This meant that the young were probing the question of the ultimate legitimacy of industrial capitalism itself. Not only were they horrified at the war in Indo-China, the hypocrisy of the educational system, and the existence of racism and poverty at home, but they found unbearable the absence of any meaningfulness in society itself, save the importance placed on the endless repetition of already existing forms and goals.

The protest of the young represented a unique and powerful negative witness in the heart of American capitalism. They were a sign of the kingdom of God, a pointer to the power of God's majesty on the face of the earth. Yet even though the young were an unmistakable sign of hope, their activities and values were not without ambiguity. The surprises of history always occur in time and, hence, partake of the dilemmas of time. The actions, ideology, and hopes of the youth movement were, therefore, very much subject to the fragility that limits all new events in history.

Thus, more than they cared to realize, the American youth movement was closely linked to many of the basic predicates of the American experience and quite vulnerable to the same kinds of problems. Specifically, this meant that the emergence and growth of the youth movement, for all its marvelous, new, and refreshing power, was characterized by the same loss of confidence in the world that has been such a central feature of the ongoing life of America.

American history has been dominated by the desperate attempt to fashion a new Eden by breaking away from outmoded, corrupt, and stultifying institutions and traditions. The Puritan break with England and the continent, the Colonial revolt against England, the westward move to the frontier and the Pacific shore, the great wave of foreign immigration to America all represent, in varying ways, the desire to find or build a new society free from the forms and restraints of the old. On one level this hope looked toward new institutions; but since so much of the pioneer or rebel energy was directed against old institutions and structures, it is more accurate to posit individual freedom as the generating ideology behind the American experience. Thus, each breakaway movement, each uprooting, was accompanied by greater and greater hopes of individual freedom and a concomitant mistrust of traditions, institutions, and long-standing habits. As a result, not only did the falling away of restraints on the individual become the central hope of American life, but, in addition, the growing suspicion of institutions and structures meant that what was taken as most real was not the historical process but the limited sphere of the individual.

The close of the frontier and filling-out of the American continent seriously altered edenic hopes. It foreclosed the possibility of working out future libertarian dreams in terms of a new breakaway culture. Further, the growth of the corporation added to frustrations by re-ordering life in terms of extensive institutional control and hierarchical dominance. Consequently, feelings concerning the need for individual freedom in a world dominated by corrupt and oppressive forms were intensified. But now there was nowhere for women and men to go. As a result, disdain for the structures of society this time did not take the form of a new breakaway move but instead dissolved into occupational docility and consumer obedience. Yet the ideological dream of individual freedom from corrupt institutions and enslaving structures continued to linger in popular mythology, even as the possibility of its realization faded. When the young began their assault on the oppressive political and social forms of the nation, they picked up on this old dream, but with a difference. They deepened the contrast between the untrustworthy worldly structures and the individual by making the inner aspects of the self the true vantage point from which to comprehend the world. Thus, some of the more culturally oriented young posited inward liberation as the goal of life, while the politically minded young, even though they espoused social and political change beyond the inward liberation of the self, nevertheless based these hopes, not on the movement of history or on the possibilities or tendencies inherent in worldly structures, but on the apocalyptic projections of the self. In the case of the political young the self had become the basic prism through which outward reality was measured, tactics planned, and the future anticipated. Both groups of young people, however, viewed history, traditions, and structures as essentially untrustworthy. As a result, loss of confidence in the world was even more profound. In the course of this development the young were simply linking up with an already present tendency in American life and culture. In this sense the youth movement, for all its astonishing vigor and insight into the failings of American society, remained a prisoner of that same society. Inevitably this meant a limitation and corruption of the sign of hope.

Theologically speaking, the young were quite right to lose confidence in the world, for there is nothing inherent in the structure or process of the world to inspire confidence or invite hope. Neither a naive scientism nor a stoical optimism can convince anyone that the world process can establish itself as trustworthy. The revival of apocalyptic dismay on the part of the young has contributed mightily to tearing away the veil from liberal ideology which had so confidently spoken of the best of all possible worlds or of the inevitability of progress. Yet it does not follow, after all this has been said, that history has completely fallen away. It is one thing to lose confidence in the world's ability to guarantee or manifest meaning on the basis of its own self-contained life; it is quite another thing to re-establish worldly confidence on the basis of trust in God. Christian faith confesses confidence in the world because God is the world's final referent. As such He guarantees the safety and meaning of the world. The world is the locus of God's promises. Thus history and the processes of institutions and structures become organs through which the signs of God's victorious purposes appear. For that reason the Christian upholds the importance and trustworthiness of the world while refusing to grant it any inherent strength or meaning. But this can be maintained only on the basis of trust in God who lies beyond time and history. Anything else entails a futile attempt to discover meaning in the world, or it leads to a despairing resignation from all earthly activity when such activity becomes, as it must under the conditions of time, problematic. The dialectical relation the Christian has with the world overcomes these alternatives precisely because the God who raised Jesus from the dead has moved from beyond death and time, into time, in order to give men and women the meaning and hope they would not otherwise possess.

2

The political young have been moved for almost a decade by the gap between political promise and political performance. In a sense, political radicalism has always been forged on the crucible of hypocrisy. Thus when the rhetoric of democracy came to be seen not as a description of, but a veil over, reality, political radicalism among the young was born. Whether suddenly or gradual-ly, alone or with others, the political young perceived the fraudulent charac-ter of a society which preached freedom and justice but practiced war, racism, and oppression. Society celebrated stability, control, and consensus as the marks of progress and success. But when the young worked among the poor or against the war in Indo-China, they found that the stability which the society proclaimed served to cover the reality of conflict, deprivation, dissen-sion, and repression. Indeed, they were the first to question the theory of the eternal benevolence of the integrated state and its handmaiden, technology. Where the dominant order boasted of gradual material progress in the new, integrated, technological state, the young saw that the poor, at home and abroad, were continually asked to pay the price for this progress. And as the technologists planned for a future utopia, the young saw the bombs, sensors, computers, and napalm in Vietnam as the fruit of such planning. The political young were appalled that freedom had come to mean the unchallengeable right of American cultural and economic expansion. They were tutored by the black liberation movement and matriculated during the American inter-vention in Vietnam. As a result, the political young, whatever their tactics, came to espouse the values of sharing, democratic planning, and direct, popular control of institutions and enterprises, in short, values long associated with decentralized, democratic socialism.* Thus, whatever their deeper, inward emotions or projections, the political young raised the question of the ultimate benevolence of American capitalism.

The political young did not mount a traditional campaign of opposition. They did not use the electoral process. Instead they employed direct and immediate tactics which were intended not only to draw attention to present injustices, but also to force an apocalyptic choice between the present and a new future. Thus, demonstrations, confrontations, sporadic acts of violence, and a variety of other direct challenges to American domestic and foreign policies characterized the activities of the young during the 1960's. They quickly moved from reformism to radicalism in the face of the intransigence of the established order. Hence, by the end of the 1960's the direct challenge of the political young appeared as the challenge of a quasi-revolutionary force. Quite naturally this frightened and bewildered a public long accustomed to believe both in the sanctity of national goals and the unassailability of traditional politics. By 1970 the Gallup Poll revealed that student unrest was the number one national concern.

This concern turned into hysteria under the prompting of national leaders who announced that the nation was in danger. This claim was made more plausible when young radicals, especially the Weatherman faction of the Students for a Democratic Society, engaged in a sustained campaign of destruction in order to create the very crisis national leaders said already existed. As a result, increased police repression and harassment was instituted all over the country. Colleges and universities were singled out for humiliation. The elections of 1968 and 1970 continued a long-standing American electoral tradition when Republicans and Democrats diverted attention away from the economic, structural, and foreign policy dilemmas of the nation to false issues, in this case the issue of student radicalism and law and order. The national hysteria associated with this policy of scapegoating was blunted only because an economic recession in 1969-1970 made it difficult for the voters to shift their attention completely from pocketbook issues to the admittedly spectacular but nonetheless somewhat removed issue of young radicalism.

As we look back now from some distance it is quite clear that the nation was never in any kind of danger and that, despite the voices of alarm, the republic was hardly shaken by the activities of the young leftists; much less was it about to lose its sacred traditions. Indeed the political effect of the

*At first the political youth appeared as popular democrats urging wider participation in the political process. As such they fit within the left-wing of the Democratic party. With time, however, the young extended their critique to economic affairs. By the end of the decade most of the young political leaders were espousing one or another form of socialism.[4]

radical attack was minimal.* What then accounted for the public hysteria? In part the fear which was maintained at such a high pitch was a product of the political opportunism of men like Spiro Agnew, John Mitchell, and Richard Nixon. But when a nation terms a crisis that which is not a crisis; when it thinks there is a mortal danger when there is none; when instead of meeting opposition with the tact and persuasion that underlie strength and confidence, it moves toward the barricades in anxiety and trepidation, then it is apparent that more is at work than political expediency.

In fact, the political young posed no real threat to the established order. It only seemed as if they did. They were, however, provoking a crisis. In my judgment the young exposed an already existing crisis in the American system.[5] The reason for the excessive reaction to the activities of the political young was that these activities showed the American system to be without any full, internal support beyond that of habit and grudging acquiescence. What numerous social critics had said about post-World War Two America—its conformity, confusion, escapism, boredom, and unhappiness with work— proved to be significant when the challenge of the young forced the issue of internal support for the goals and policies of the American government.† For many decades the de-politicizing of America had taken its toll. The young leftists, for their part, thought they were attacking the established order itself, that they were engaged in a political struggle with the heart of the system. But whatever their intentions and hopes, the actions of the political radicals had an altogether different effect. What the young succeeded in doing was laying bare the lack of commitment and enthusiasm Americans had for their own system. The ideological confusion, the systemic alienation, the burden of inequality, the widespread exploitation, and the bewilderment arising from technological manipulation had all taken their toll—but in the

---

*The student movement had its greatest political impact in the Civil Rights movement. Even there, however, the pro-forma gains registered in national legislation served to strengthen and further the advance of the black middle class while leaving unresolved the economic plight of the black masses. And the students were never able to apply the same tactics against the Vietnamese war with similar effectiveness. The anti-war movement was, therefore, consistently outmaneuvered by successive Administrations so that by the middle of 1972 American policy in Indo-China was domestically as secure as at any previous time.

†David Riesman, William Whyte, and Vance Packard, each in a different way and from a different perspective, were pointing to significant changes in American life in the 1950's. While these writers mostly focused on the growing boredom and alienation of the middle and upper-middle classes, studies concerned with the working class tended to show that "most production-line jobs do not produce the kind of occupational involvement or identification necessary to make work a satisfying experience."[6] In short what we have here is a kind of systemic malaise which prepared the ground for the insurgency of the 1960's. The film, The Last Picture Show, nicely captures the vacuity of the 1950's.

only way possible: people had gradually withdrawn consent from the system itself. What remained was a de-politicized, grudging participation through habit. If political power rests on sturdy and widespread public support, then it was clear that the American political system had been functioning for some time without effective power. In the absence of this power, in effect the power of legitimacy, it was natural that, confronted with a direct challenge to authority, the established order would respond in the only way authority could respond without power, namely in terms of violence. The overreaction of the authorities was related, not so much to the challenge of the young, but to the absence of public support. The national hysteria provoked (but not caused) by the young radicals revealed a nation with no confidence in itself and an established authority given to camouflaging their impotence with violence and repression.

Large numbers of young radicals, however, perceived the situation in a different way. They saw the nation in the throes of a revolutionary crisis. They believed that the old capitalist society was collapsing and that a new world would soon emerge out of the ashes. Their apocalyptic fervor was matched by an apocalyptic analysis: the last days were here. This romanticism made for interesting theology but rather bad politics. The country was in no such crisis. Widespread societal disenchantment is not to be confused with a political crisis. A political crisis is about who will have power, and this is precisely what was not at stake in the 1960's. "The sad truth," Mary McCarthy noted, "seems to be that whatever else the protest movement can accomplish . . . what it cannot accomplish is the very purpose that brought it into being."[7] The appearance of discontent in the form of confusion and fear may precede a political crisis, but it is markedly different from such a crisis.

The inability of the young to make such a distinction was due in large part to their fascination with action as the substance of politics. "Act first. Analyze later. Impulse not theory makes the great leaps forward," proclaimed Jerry Rubin.[8] Since societal confusion, rage, and cruelty inevitably followed direct action, the young radicals came to the conclusion that action was the key ingredient in the whole political process. Invariably they overlooked, ignored, or played down the presence and operation of other less exciting or more elusive structural and historical factors. Social and political reality increasingly appeared to be in crisis as long as fervor, excitement, and tension were present in the political act. The political environment soon became the projection of the exhilaration of the political act.

This led to further difficulties. Excessive concentration on the cult of action led to the equation of action with power. In this regard, direct action was seen as power that brings about revolutionary crisis. The appeal was made to "put your body on the line." The fact is, however, that action is not the same thing as power. Power is related to widespread support, that is, to public support of programs, values, and goals. Action is a tactic that facilitates the building of support, or can contribute to tearing down support given to opposing systems, but action is not a substitute for support. Thus, political power was precisely what the young did not have and action could not possibly secure. Some means of translating widespread public discontent into cohesive support for alternative systems was needed, but the cult of direct action consistently disregarded this option. Even if the political young had focused attention on building power in this way, direct action could hardly suffice as a primary instrument.

Some of the strongest supporters of the cult of direct action were those young people who used this strategy, not for a particular political ideology, but for the politics of conscience.* An intense moralism had been a significant if not crucial part of political activity ever since the days of the Civil Rights movement. Many young people endeavored to establish it as the basis of politics in their direct confrontations with the system. In some ways this effort was manifestly successful. Discontent among large numbers of young people over war, racism, poverty, and technological manipulation was often based on a sense of moral outrage. This proved to be fertile ground for the radicalization of young people on the campuses. There was an enormous positive response when young radicals claimed that the overreaction of campus authorities to confrontations symbolized American cruelty throughout the world. Both the claim and the heroic action of radicals appealed to moral conscience and the long-standing belief that the witness of personal integrity or the exercise of courage carries with it political effect. But the politics of conscience was also vulnerable. It continued to assume that the key factor in political change was direct action, and that radicalization was related to the moral bankruptcy revealed in the brutal overreaction of established authority. The truth was, however, that the frightened reaction of

*Some of the strongest support for the politics of conscience has come from the left-wing of the religious community. However, the religious (mostly Roman Catholic) left seemed to be energized less by concern for political strategy than by horror at worldly evil and individual complicity in that evil. Continually drawing parallels between American society and Nazi Germany (and seemingly forgetting all the differences), they produced action in response to conscience and outrage. But if America were Nazi Germany, then more drastic actions than burning or defiling draft files would be called for. Yet, fear of participation in violent or de-humanizing deeds precluded this. As a result there was little purposeful release for mounting guilt save senseless and basically a-political acts leading toward civil arrests. This only made it appear that action was related to the meritorious work of lessening guilt and ensuring salvation rather than to political strategy or effect. This "salvation by works" was all the more cruelly ironic since the religious left possessed a keen sense of ecclesiastical corruption and remained cut off from the traditional source of release from guilt, namely, worship, confession, or the sacraments. Vainly, quasi-religious services of "celebration" were pieced together to provide for this need, but the banality, forced enthusiasm, and maudlin sentimentality of these occasions could pass for profundity and healing only to the most deceived.

campus officials was related less to the attacks of the radicals than to the prior disenchantment of the masses of students. Like the American public the students felt no need to invest legitimacy in existing authority. Had they wished to do so it would have been simple for them to demonstrate their loyalty by isolating and neutralizing the young radicals. But they did not do this. Instead their disenchantment had the effect of removing legitimating power from officials and bringing about the use of official violence and student radicalization. However, this prior withdrawal of legitimating consent had its limits. Direct action based on moral outrage can draw only so much water from the well of disenchantment, and in time the well went dry. Since the radicals had so closely associated organizing with the power of moral example, they could do little else but assume that the drop in support for their cause was due to their own lack of will. Consequently they urged even more heroic deeds from their people, all to no avail.

The cult of action was an understandable phenomenon. What with the expansion of corporate power and the intensification of technological manipulation, meaningful public action has been difficult for some time in America. In the face of growing public impotence and the gradual de-politicizing of the masses, one could expect some attempt to revive the ancient faculty of action. But the revival was closely related to the beginning and end point of all American experience: the self. Having been cornered, as it were, by corporate and societal power at the point of the self, the cult of direct action assumed it could create a politics on that basis. The young would create a new future by action and will. "The assumption of all Movement political analysis," writes Michael Miles, "was that . . . social change could be effected through a collective act of will."[9] Direct action, sustained by the desire for personal integrity, fed by the excitement of a moral crusade, undergirded by the intensity of the self, and propelled forward by apocalyptic fantasies was quite within the American tradition. Naturally, it repeated all the old errors. It confused the enthusiasm of personal action with political effect, characterized the lack of will and heroism as the reason for the demise of radical influence, substituted action for careful political analysis, and mistook action for power. Any politics based on the self—its desires, pains, moral outrage, or will—that is divorced from history, thought, tradition, and the structures of existence is bound to lead nowhere.

The cult of action seemed all too often motivated by a profound disgust for the world. The desire for a new social order was admirable, but the excessive reliance on the energy or moral outrage of the self and the fervent application of will to bring about the new world shows a loss of confidence in the processes of history. The desire to "end the war now" or "bring Washington to a halt" (May Day, 1971) reveals a commitment to a rhetoric which sees the structures of existence in only the most questionable light. The reliance on sheer will to replace the old order without any serious consideration of intermediate steps or recognition of the necessity of long-range political planning indicates an inordinate disgust with the world. Only the intensification of personal vision or the exercise of moral outrage could be relied on in such a case. To embody hope in the ordinary structures of life, or to acknowledge the intricate character of advanced industrial capitalism, was considered corrupt. The loss of confidence in the world was almost complete.* As Ernst Bloch notes:

> Social utopias in particular [are] liable to be abstract because their designs [are] not mediated with the existing social tendency and possibility. . . . Hence the utopians all too frequently construct the outlines of a brave new world out of their own hearts and heads—or as Engels says "for the basic plan of their new edifice they could appeal only to reason, just because they could not as yet appeal to history."

In large measure the confusion of the political young could be traced back to their ambiguous socio-economic position. Most of them came from middle or upper-middle class homes where there was a strong tendency to view the world in highly moral categories, and to identify one's role in social change not with expanding self-interest, but with "helping the oppressed." As a result, the young were prone to forego the necessity for careful and intense political and structural analysis in favor either of apocalyptic moral judgments or (and this was often the same thing) sweeping identification with

---

*The attitude of many radicals to Marxism was characteristic. It was turned into a vehicle of apocalyptic anarchism. Marxist thought was turned into a world-negating system. The apocalyptic elements were stressed while those aspects dealing with the use of ordinary political processes or with the notion of the development of socialism out of capitalism were overlooked. Further, since so much of Western Marxism had participated in the political life of the West and had produced not a new world but rather a tired, bureaucratic copy of the old one, the radical young turned their gaze to China. Not wishing to deal with the dull problems of East European socialism (which, however, were far more relevant to industrialized America), attention was given to China in general and the Cultural Revolution in particular. Here the basic anarchism of American youth could combine with political apocalypticism. The Chinese experiment signified the attempt to erase stubborn economic and technological problems by sheer will and collective enthusiasm. In addition the asceticism of the People's Republic (very much related to its primitive stage of economic development) seemed to allow for a greater focus on personal and ideological concerns and thus provided a welcome alternative to the material corruption of the West. Finally the totalism of revolutionary thought associated with Maoism seemed a positive replacement to the loss of confidence in the world that the American youth had so bitterly experienced. In plain language it offered something to believe in.[10]

"the struggle of third world peoples against American imperialism." But this was a sure recipe for domestic isolation and irrelevance. Further, since the political young were drawn from the schools and universities of America, they suffered from an unclear position in the productive order. At once consumers of education as a product (Ivan Illich), and also workers being trained by the "knowledge industry" for future jobs in the economy, the young never quite found a secure niche for themselves. As a result American institutional reality was increasingly problem-filled. The laxity and confusion of the university is hardly a model of American institutional life, but the young tended to overlook the coherence and stability of most American institutions, branded them (as they had branded the university) essentially corrupt, and insisted that social change would result from direct revolutionary challenge of institutional authority. No one who has held a job in capitalist America could have come to such a conclusion; those who hold jobs in the American productive order know full well the stubborn reality of institutional life. Moreover, in proposing change, workers do so on a basis the young could not, namely, self-interest. Except for the abolition of the draft (which when accomplished by Richard Nixon practically crippled the protest movement), the political young acted without any clear concept of self-interest. Indeed the idea often seemed blasphemous to them. As a consequence, they continued to identify with the great themes of anti-imperialism and third world liberation, all the while at a loss to understand the structural and institutional reality of domestic capitalism, and not knowing how to build upon self-interest in order to change that reality. Instead, the young insisted that reality was essentially comprehended under the category of morality and that it was changed by fervor and will. But since there was no evidence for this in human history, the political young were doomed to wander throughout the corridors of "pop" revolution and end in failure.

By ignoring the process of power-building—the conversion of disenchantment into support for alternative political and economic systems—and by foregoing the hard work of political organizing, the study of advanced capitalism, and the careful planning involved in the exercise of power, large segments of the political young opened themselves to the madness, despair, and ennui that accompany misplaced optimism and attend action that is divorced from the tendencies and possibilities of history. As a consequence, many young radicals have since gone back into the main political system while others have foresworn politics altogether. Nonetheless, many other young radicals (for example, those in the newly formed New American Movement) have not succumbed to the manifold temptations and difficulties of their comrades and remain dedicated to constructing a new political order. As such they remain an unmistakable sign of hope.

3

There is yet another way in which the clash of values has occurred in American life. I refer to the phenomenon loosely designated as the counter-culture. The growth of the youth counter-culture has created a crisis at the level of cultural values. These young people have not merely exposed societal and cultural disenchantment, they have embodied it. Youth-culturists make up a group whose very style and sensibility is a threat to the dominant order at the level of cultural consent. Whereas the political young directed their activities against the state, the cultural young attacked society. Society, in the distinction employed here, refers to the level at which men and women consent to certain basic values and goals. These reflect views about human-kind, life, and reality and come to be embedded in institutions. The state, on the other hand, is the political expression of societal consensus; it is society organized in terms of power and authority. In this regard it is possible to have crises of state, namely crises dealing with the shift of power, without having civil crises precisely because shifts in power relationships are not necessarily accompanied by changes in societal goals or values. This has invariably been the case in American history. Political changes have generally been simple instrumental shifts of power which have left virtually untouched the societal consensus underlying American life.* Perhaps only during the War for Southern Independence did a clash of societal values accompany a political struggle. Apart from this epic conflict, however, and in spite of periodic political upheaval, there has been a consensus of basic cultural values throughout American history.

This means that disenchantment, disaffection, or confusion at the societal level is a potentially dangerous matter. And indeed, the ideological bewilder-ment and increased boredom which have been so prevalent in American life do seem to indicate a breakdown in societal cohesiveness. But disenchant-ment is not alienation, confusion is not hostility, and social paralysis is not outright opposition. In general, society may be shaken, but it is still secure. Only among the youth counter-culture has disaffection given place to the rejection of cultural values. The very life of the counter-culture is a rejection of the goals and values of a consumer and technological age. Unlike the demoralized general public, the counter-culture pursues hopes and embodies

*Writers like Daniel Boorstin and Louis Hartz have pointed to continuity in American life. Contemporary radicals, on the other hand, see the American experience as dominated by dissent, instability, and class insurgency. In fact, both perspectives are correct. At the level of political power there has been constant turmoil in American life. However, it is difficult to see when (with the exception of the War for Southern Independence, 1861-1865) there has been any significant difference at the societal level of values and goals.

dreams quite unlike the materialistic, work-oriented, disciplined culture it seeks to overthrow. It stands for the transvaluation of values. Thus, the counter-culture is a threat because it affects the cultural consensus needed to sustain a civilization. It is not a political force and seeks no political power. It is insidious, and if it were to grow the dominant culture would not survive. In this regard Charles Reich is perfectly correct in picturing a silent, non-violent revolution which spreads within the heart of America, slowly affecting the vital organs of values and consent.[11] Without some form of agreement on basic values no society can survive. Thus, the counter-culture is a direct threat to the nation because of its power both to undermine confidence in traditional values and, more importantly, to convert women and men to an entirely different way of life.

Except for the issue of the American intervention in Vietnam—in which the counter-cultural youth have consistently aligned themselves with their political counterparts—the counter-culture has generally avoided political activity. Instead it has expressed itself in terms of style and behavior embodying a different set of cultural assumptions. The major concern of the counter-culture appears to be the loss of personal identity, individual freedom, and integrity in an increasingly hierarchical and mechanized world. In addition, these youth fear the increasing loss of personal space due to the encroachments of the technocratic state. Since society seems to possess the ability to continue present trends into the future without substantial change, the youth-culturists fear the future. As a result their despair has been matched by a strikingly totalistic rejection of the form and substance of culture. Having lost the world and the future as trustworthy and having been relentlessly assaulted by the valueless present, the young have retreated into the self in the hope of creating both a new culture and a new future.

> The foundation of Consciousness III [writes Charles Reich] is liberation. It comes into being the moment the individual frees himself from the automatic acceptance of the imperatives of society and the false consciousness which society imposes. . . . The meaning of liberation is that the individual is free to build his own culture from a new beginning. . . . Consciousness III starts with the self.[12]

The counter-cultural youth find society in all its grand plans—capitalist or Marxist—bankrupt. The rigidity, oppression, and stultification of the modern technological state know no political or geographic boundaries. They crush the human spirit everywhere. As an alternative, the counter-culture envisions a time of freedom—freedom gained for the self. This accounts for the widespread interest in music, mysticism, and drugs. Here the self meets reality without the aid of mediating structures. Wild, flappy clothes and the natural state of the human body (long hair and unwashed skin) testify to the freedom of the self. It is with the self and the body that one begins anew the creation of a moral and humane culture.

The values of the counter-culture reflect their orientation. Possessing a sense of the unity of all things and a strong commitment to reality as essentially inward, they espouse simplicity, equality, physicality, and community.* Instead of production they value pleasure; in place of the necessity of deferred gratification (long associated with a society pledged to achievement and work), they prefer the sensuousness of present experience. Instead of intellectuality and rationality, they value mystery and mysticism. For the cynicism of the realist, they exchange the naivete of the innocent. They substitute passivity for careerist aggressiveness. In place of consumption they put meditation and enjoying each other. And instead of having goals for which they sacrifice all things, they sacrifice all things to possess the moment.

At present the counter-culture remains a relatively small and insignificant phenomenon. Despite the publicity surrounding its activities—mostly because so many people in the counter-culture come from the upper-middle class, the traditional newsmaking class—it is clear that these youth have had no significant effect on the occupational, productive, or consumption patterns of the nation.† In the first place they have been unable to convert large numbers of people to their life-style. But more important they have been unable to convert what is a societal challenge into a political challenge.

This set of failures is directly related to the way the counter-cultural youth conceive of change. Is it true, as Reich and others have suggested, that it is possible to have a revolution by consciousness? Can there be a successful, non-violent revolution in which personal liberation and conversion spread silently, inevitably, and peacefully through the institutions and structures of the land until "the power of the corporate state will be ended as miraculously as a kiss breaks a witch's evil enchantment" (Reich)? I think not. In the first place the structures of society are products of a long history. This makes

*Counter-cultural youth are somewhat ambiguous about communality. On the one hand they espouse personal freedom ("do your own thing"); yet, on the other hand, they emphasize comradeship and mutuality. What seems to underlie both tendencies is a way of viewing life from the interior perspective of the self. This provides the possibility for individual expression and the basis for a mystical egalitarianism leading toward community.

†Despite talk about the possible decline in qualified personnel available to fill management positions, no such drop has occurred. The general disapproval of careers in business by young people was noted far back in the early 1960's, but the supposed disenchantment was never converted into effective action. The low level of productivity among American workers during the 1966-1970 period cannot be attributed to the counter-culture. Neither can the upheavals in such businesses as watchmaking, suitmaking, and coffee be assigned to causes outside of normal market fluctuations. Consumption patterns may have altered but consumption levels remain very high. It is only for a very tiny minority that the incentives of money and status have lost their appeal.

them resistant to change of any kind, much less to a change that comes through the alteration of consciousness. It is quite possible to undermine or weaken structures by a shift in consciousness, but these structures will not fall or turn into their opposite automatically. More often, they will try to save themselves by accommodation (which is currently happening in America). This means that change occurs only when societal disaffection is accompanied by the seizure of political power. To imagine otherwise is to suppose that society is but the collection of independent individuals and that historical change happens when individuals, by some mysterious process, reach a new state of consciousness or perfection. But society is more than this and so are the dynamics of change. Society is the composite of habits, traditions, and beliefs that have extended in time beyond their identification with the individual. These become implanted in structures, operations, processes, and institutions not amenable to change by virtue of individual good will or the force of personal liberation. Society, writes Peter Berger,

> ... is a product of man, rooted in the phenomenon of externalization, which in turn is grounded in the very biological constitution of man. As soon as one speaks of externalized products, however, one is implying that the latter attains a degree of distinction as against their producer. This transformation of man's products into a world that not only derives from man, but that comes to confront him as a facticity outside of himself, is intended in the concept of objectification. The humanly produced world becomes something "out there." It consists of objects, both material and non-material, that are capable of resisting the desires of their producer. Once produced, this world cannot simply be wished away. Although all culture originates and is rooted in the subjective consciousness of human beings, once formed it cannot be re-absorbed into consciousness at will. It stands outside the subjectivity of the individual as, indeed, a world. In other words, the humanly produced world attains the character of objective reality.[13]

Thus, change requires not only individual perfection but collective political action. While it is true that the structures of society are undergirded by common consent, they are also, more importantly, sustained by the exercise of power. And until society is confronted at the level of power all disenchantment and demoralization arising from the loss of confidence in traditional values will have no effect.

To fall back on the myth of the transforming power of the liberated individual may be just what the established order needs to secure the status quo. The search for individual freedom takes one away from, rather than into, society; it fragments rather than unites men and women. Reichian hopes concerning the inevitability of the transformation of society are no substitute for actual political work. Indeed, Reichian determinism underlies the inability of the counter-culture to confront the incredibly complex matters of society, the state, power, and change. What, after all, is to prevent the dominant order from simply making space for the practice of different life styles? Why shouldn't a highly organized and still flexible order save itself by allowing the search for personal liberation to take place in times and places that are apart from the major productive and consumptive operations of the land? Would this not divert attention from the issues of power and political control? Significantly, the much publicized alternative institutions of the counter-culture are only alternatives, not replacements. And it is very much to the advantage of the dominant order to tolerate these experiments, particularly if they make no effort to convert a societal and cultural challenge into a political or economic challenge. Writing several years ago, Donald Michael was prescient:

> The very fact that society will be so big, so complex and tending to be more rationalized also means it will be able to tolerate groups living at different paces and styles, if they show no deliberate intent to alter significantly the drive or direction of the prevailing social processes. . . . Isolated and insulated from the major and majority preoccupations of the society, and thereby offering no threat to the *status quo,* these enclaves will provide opportunities for more whimsical, personally paced styles of life. [14]

Another major question remains. Can an essentially moral or metaphysical revolution truly be the vehicle for radical social change? The counter-culture is clearly related to the boredom, drudgery, and frustration of the affluent class. Its protest and anger is a product of disaffection with a grossly materialistic and manipulative culture. But only those accustomed to wealth and privilege can afford the luxury of boredom and disillusion. None of that would be a drawback if this sentiment were directed toward transforming material reality. But in too large a measure the youth of the counter-culture lean toward an escape from materiality and the construction of a primitive, tribal commonwealth quite apart from the major political and economic struggles of life. Their vision is not centrally concerned with the democratic control of state power or with the equal division of wealth. Thus, their hopes are completely irrelevant to the needs of almost two-thirds of the globe. As children of the elite, their anguish is more closely related to their sense of personal loss than to the concrete misery of the rest of the world. Hence they are untrustworthy agents of change. The metaphysical revolt of the enraged elite will fail to the extent it divorces itself from the material realities of worldly existence. Moral visions that function as substitutes for reality instead of prods to alter reality are dangerous. As Henry Adams once remarked, "Masses of men are always prompted by interest rather than conscience. Morality is a private and costly luxury."

Finally, notions of the perfection of a new consciousness leading to the inevitable fall of the corporate state overlook the tragic dimensions of human history and human personality. It is pure myth to suggest that a new commonwealth can be constructed on the basis of the inherent goodness and creativity of the self if only the inhibiting structures and institutions of life could be escaped. This presumes a goodness to human nature for which there is absolutely no evidence. But, the youth-culturists are heirs of the American dream. Like past generations, the young believe in the perfectibility of the self and consequently in their own exemption from human tragedy. Their hope is that the self can be recovered, free from the limitations and corruptions imposed upon it by a materialistic society. The liberated self is the cornerstone of a new existence. As Michael Novak suggests, this is a repetition of traditional American optimism.

> ... the children repeat the illusions of the parents. No more than their parents have they attained a tragic view of life. They remain optimistic, innocent, Adamic Americans to the end. And thus they prepare yet another cycle of American irrationality and violence. For the truly overwhelming innocence and optimism of [these] Americans ... cannot easily sustain the inevitable defeats and ... limited victories which life ... allows.[15]

The youth culture sees the processes and structures of history as problematic. But it is prevented from viewing life as tragic because it tends to exempt the self in its supposed integrity from the ambiguous quality of life. To isolate the self from its connections with the conditions and structures of time is to burden it with hopes that its essential fragility cannot sustain. The self is part of reality, not separate from it; as such it is vulnerable to weakness, negativity, corruption, and evil. This corruption does not come from the material structures of life, it is part of the warp and woof of every aspect and level of reality. Thus, naive views about the tragedyless potential of the self serve only to build up optimistic hopes which the fragility and vulnerability of the self cannot sustain and which will eventually lead to frustration and despair. Any hopes for a new society must recognize the essential ambiguity of the self. This is precisely what the youth culture has not done.

The self is not some mysterious essence awaiting recovery or release apart from the structures of existence.[16] It shares in the ambiguity and tragedy of time because it is related not simply to itself but to the social, political, and historical aspects of life. Indeed, the mystery of self lies not in its essential goodness or in its anticipated perfection or in its potential freedom, but in its relationship to the processes of history. It is part of misguided American optimism to separate the self from the drama of history in order to find the final point of freedom and integrity. The self is inherently related to the structures and course of history and in constant interplay with social and political life. Therefore, the destiny of the self is not to be found in the inner recesses or visions of the self, but in the course and end of history. Theories of self-determination or individual liberation are myths based on the notion of the isolated self possessing inherent potential. The self possesses no such grand possibilities. Instead its destiny is found outside itself.

Because it is essentially related to the drama of history, the self is always in continuous construction. It is continually acting at the behest of some claim made on it by history; it is constantly being determined outside itself by the loyalties it gives to one or another set of claims. Since the self responds to demands made upon it and does not create history by its own goodness or perfection, the major question for the self is, What is the appropriate historical destiny placed before it? The self is known only in terms of the destiny given it by history and thus should not attempt to discover its own so-called health, but should focus instead on the various claims made upon it. By searching for the liberated self, the youth culture is dangerously vulnerable to claims that allow for a measure of freedom but proceed to fortify oppressive rule. This overlooks the question of destiny that encompasses the hope for the transformation of material reality. It also ignores the social and historical conditions that determine the future reality of the life of the self.

4

The self possesses no inherent freedom. Hence, it is futile to posit a social reconstruction on the basis of this non-existent possibility. The freedom of man comes through communality in which equality and personalism are evident. Freedom is, therefore, less a process than a goal. But to realize this goal the self must actively seek to create a new world in which social and economic conditions are transformed. This is man's earthly destiny. Thus, when speaking of man, it is less appropriate to use the word "freedom"— which is best applied to man's communal destiny—than the word "capacity." Man possesses a limited capacity to respond to events and to claims that various systems, ideologies, or theologies make on his destiny. The capacities of the self (including the ability, in the ultimate sense, to say "no" to slavery or to destiny) are securely related to the projects that confront the self out of the many emergent possibilities of history. Inevitably, this means the self is drawn to the construction of material and historical conditions. It does not mean the self can operate apart from these conditions. The true place of man relates to the future kingdom of equality and justice which is man's earthly destiny.

Theologically, neither the so-called recovery of the self nor the overthrow of oppressive material and social conditions signals the final freedom of man. The former cannot happen because the self is never free in itself. The latter cannot happen because the final and complete freedom of the self does not lie in earthly reconstruction (though it is man's great *earthly* destiny), but in the future of Christ, which lies beyond every present man can experience.

The self, as the apostle Paul knew, can never be fully known at any point in time. God alone knows the self (I Cor. 13:2). The gnostics in the church at Corinth thought the self could be discovered in mystical ecstasy, in a transcendence that left the world behind. Paul contradicted them because their belief divorced them from history and neighborly solidarity. He argued that while the self had its final safety with God beyond death (Rom. 8), the substance of that condition still awaited man in the future. For the present, on earth, the self found proximate fulfillment only in the midst of the historical process. Women and men participate in final freedom, not by mystical escape, but by suffering hope and a commitment to the transformation of the earth.

Hence, man's life in time is full and complete, not in terms of some ecstatic form of personal liberation, but in terms of hope and expectation. The self is driven beyond itself to history and to the final end of history in order to find its true destiny. And it is Christ who is the destiny of man. But the future of Christ is always to be found beyond any present moment of experience. Only from the vantage point beyond the present can judgment break in on the misery and corrosion inherent in every present, and only from that point can men and women be beckoned out of every stasis. " . . . In the world there is always an exodus that leads out of a particular stasis, and a hope that is linked to dismay," says Ernst Bloch. That exodus and that hope, however, are not located in the recesses of the self, but in the future of history guaranteed by the power of the God who raised Jesus from the dead and who conquers sin, misery, and death. The power of this God comes from the other side of time and death. It guarantees the safety of the self, even as the self is locked in its present state of uncertainty and fragility. It is the power of God that holds secure the future of history, even though it is continually threatened by stasis on the one hand, and by the identification of some present moment with man's final hope on the other. It is to that God that both man and history are consecrated.

Chapter Seven

The VIETCONG
as a SIGN of JUDGMENT

To many of us the enemy had seemed all-powerful. The strong can afford to be wrong at times without loss of prestige, because even the most powerful are, after all, only human—yes their mistakes make them all the more human—but he who claims omnipotence must never be wrong because there can be no alternative to omnipotence except insignificance. If one stroke, no matter how tiny, proved successful against the enemy's alleged omnipotence, everything was won.   **Anna Seghers**

And now, go, write it before them on a tablet,
    inscribe it in a book,
that it may be for the time to come
    as a witness for ever.
For they are a rebellious people,
    lying sons,
sons who will not hear
    the instruction of the Lord;
who say to the seers, "See not";
    and to the prophets, "Prophesy not to us
        what is right;
speak to us smooth things,
    prophesy illusions,
leave the way, turn aside from the path,
    let us hear no more of the Holy One of Israel."
Therefore thus says the Holy One of Israel,
"Because you despise this word,
    and trust in oppression and perverseness,
    and rely on them;
therefore this iniquity shall be to you
    like a break in a high wall, bulging out
        and about to collapse,
    whose crash comes suddenly, in an instant. . . ."   Isaiah 30:8-13

1

History, said Karl Marx, is the history of tyranny. The dominant class articulates the values of each age, defines what is or is not oppression, and determines what can or cannot be done to alleviate that oppression. Behind every act of the oppressors lies the ultimate concern for their own power and privilege. Secure in their might and advantage they insist that the ease of *their* condition is proof of the beneficence of the total system. Because of this the dominant class is an untrustworthy interpreter of the true shape of an epoch. Only those who suffer under the pain and brutality of affliction can be trusted to signal the true nature of the age. The outcasts alone know the ultimate reality about any political, social, or ecclesiastical system. It is in the insurgency of the despised and maltreated that one can discover the buried secret of the epoch. Thus, in the most profound sense, revolution is apocalypse, the unveiling of misery and disquiet, the irruption of truth. It is not a gradual unveiling in which, at each step of the way, the elite can provide for their own self-justification by covering or re-interpreting the nature of what is revealed. Revolution points to the swift revelation of that which was heretofore inarticulate. It occurs before the dominant forces can corral it and shape it for purposes of extending the status quo. Revolution is violent, chaotic, and startling. It bursts the boundaries of understanding hitherto provided by the forces of domination. The oppressed are drawn to revolution because it is the uncluttered vehicle for the apocalypse, the unveiling of truth.

Revolution as apocalypse, however, is not to be confused with aimless destruction. It may entail the tearing down of old forms; but far beyond that apocalypse is fulfillment. The destiny of all people is not death but life. The oppressed bear the secret of fulfillment, which includes the ultimate liberation of the oppressors. The oppressors mistake the form of their present dominance with the true goal of history. They confuse present reality with wholeness. They forget that the stability of the present is bought with the blood of the poor and afflicted. The oppressed, on the other hand, by possessing nothing comprehend the whole. Their existence and insurgency contain an invitation to wholeness beyond the exploitation bound up in the oppressor's way of life. They promise freedom for the exploiters as well as for themselves. It is for this reason that Jesus did not consign the rich to perdition but instead pointed them to the activity of the poor. Together, the oppressed and the oppressors await a new heaven and a new earth (Rev. 21:1-5).

However, during the time of the apocalypse, as during the time of any shift between ages, the insurgent despair of the oppressed is rarely greeted as the prelude to freedom. It is not seen as the unveiling of truth. The militant anger of the poor and despised is not viewed simply as an attack on privilege but as an assault on the foundation and meaning of life itself. The oppressors consistently confuse privilege with destiny. Only the exploited outcasts can shatter the deception embodied in this ancient and evil mistake. And this shattering implies violence.

Some, therefore, renounce revolution out of hand because of the formal aspects of destruction and pain. Many regard the appearance of violence as that which sunders the unity between means and ends. This remains an important matter as do the more subtle forms of coercion and violence practiced by dominant groups (which provoke insurgency in the first place). But whatever the verdict on this issue, revolution is more than violence. It is the apocalyptic unveiling of the new in the midst of the old. How can that take place without turmoil? It is an eternal mystery. But the unveiling of truth by the action of the brutalized masses of poor and wretched is and will always be a sign of hope, a sign of the power of the end of history already revealed in the resurrection of Jesus. This sign will inevitably meet with resistance. Every attempt will be made to crush or divert insurgency. But whatever the outcome of the struggle, it still remains that the central role in history is reserved for the oppressed. And it is in their future that the true future of all men and women lie.

2

Property is theft, said Proudhon. By extension, all imperial nations exist by virtue of theft. Expansion and growth necessitate the conquest and control of others. The words "expansion" and "growth" themselves are but colorful euphemisms for theft. The property of one nation, group, or tribe is taken by another and empire begins. Quite naturally, such imperial ventures are explained in terms of the logic of necessity, the spread of progress, or even the will of God. More sophisticated apologists root imperial expansion in the necessary tragedy of history, suggesting that some must pay the unfortunate price for the advance of others.[1] But no manner of excuse or elaborate justification can hide the fact that, inevitably, the growth of empire means that some women and men live at the expense of others.

Despite the rhetoric of freedom and anti-colonialism the American imperial impulse has been active. America's conceiving herself to be the "new" world does not mean she has acted in a different fashion from the "old" world. The vast expanse of the North American continent which is now the United States of America was not originally ours by right or title. Nor was it gained by "manifest destiny." It was taken by conquest. That is, it was taken now by force, then by intimidation, here by occupation, there by enforced treaty. The present-day existence of Indians in the stark deserts and backwaters of this land is a sobering reminder of the bitter fruits of imperial conquest. And the bleak record of exploitation of Mexicans on this continent by generations of "settlers" mocks the so-called American dream.

The early conquest of the continent, accomplished in the seventeenth, eighteenth, and nineteenth centuries, resembled a form of piracy which soon gave way to the sophistication of modern imperialism. The search for territory receded in the wake of the search for markets.

The modern, Western imperial urge has been closely associated with the need of the bourgeois class to expand economically beyond the restrictive borders of the nation-state.* In America this phenomenon occurred only after the continent had been filled, that is, only after the continent could no longer be simply a territorial market but had to become a territorial base as well. Thus, in the last years of the nineteenth century the outlines of modern American imperialism became clear.† By that time American capitalism had acquired its contemporary corporate form and bourgeois hegemony exercised in the interests of American capital had been established. Both the economic sphere and the political apparatus of the state were firmly in their control. The search for overseas markets accelerated.‡

Imperial extension involved more than material penetration and gain. Western imperialism had long possessed a cultural dimension which was not simply a cover for economic exploitation. Thus, from the start, American imperialism was very much involved in extending the culture of the white, Western world to what were then thought of as benighted peoples. This involved, therefore, a total view of life which extended beyond economics. It implied the articulation of a whole culture. Clearly, free enterprise was at the heart of this system, but it was seen to be related to a whole way of life. Thus, the astonishing arrogance with which early imperialists tended to justify their economic activities should not be seen as mere hypocrisy, but as testimony to their belief in the ultimate benevolence and saving grace of Western culture itself, even as that culture was propelled forward and shaped by capitalist economic needs.

*"Imperialism was born when the ruling class in capitalist production came up against national limitations to its economic expansion."[2]

†American economic activities abroad date from the early years of the Republic. However, as Mira Wilkins has pointed out, "The extension of business abroad before 1893 was dwarfed by what followed. . . . At the turn of the century there was a veritable 'wave' of new U. S. corporations introducing operations beyond the American boundaries; . . . Between 1897 and 1902, Europeans pointed to the 'American invasion of Europe'. . . ."[3]

‡One of the main factors in the increased need for overseas markets in the middle 1890's was that in the depression of 1893 goods were being produced at home which could not be sold at home.[4]

The American imperial impulse was a part of the general Western movement toward foreign domination, except for the peculiar American reluctance to acquire a colonial empire. American control and occupation in the Philippines and Cuba seemed somehow out of keeping with the American commitment to self-determination and the American mission to serve the world, not as a conquering giant, but as a moral example. As a result the American imperial effort was never pure colonialism. Instead it proceeded as a commercial empire. Thus the characteristic American imperial form was that of economic expansion—particularly in Central and South America—very much dependent on the instruments of domestic and foreign state power to protect or redeem private investment.*

By the end of World War Two, American imperialism reached another stage. The devastation of Europe and much of Asia propelled the United States forward as the most powerful nation in the world. Consequently the temptation to exert world leadership was irresistible. No longer would America think simply in narrow terms of national protection or interest; instead, she would concentrate globally as the protector of the whole Western world and of the civilization upon which it rested. Of course, a core of economic interest lay at the heart of America's imperial ascendancy. American capital and products needed safe outlets while her industrial system demanded a steady supply of raw materials. The Marshall Plan took care of the former† while our continued hegemony over Latin America helped with regard to the latter.‡ But the extension of American economic and political power was bound up with more than simple monetary gain. It was part and parcel of an effort to convert the world to the Western (now primarily American) way of life. The time has come, asserted President Harry S. Truman, "when nearly every nation must choose between alternate ways of life." And just to make sure that everyone understood which nation stood at the center of the Western way of life, Mr. Truman went on to announce on

*Smedley Butler's oft-quoted boast is worth repeating: "I helped make Haiti and Cuba a decent place for the National City Bank boys to collect revenues. . . . I helped purify Nicaragua for the international banking house of Brown Brothers. . . . I helped make Honduras 'right' for American fruit companies."[5]

†"When we look at that problem, we may say it is a problem of markets. . . . We have got to see that what the country produces is used and is sold under financial arrangements which make its production possible. . . . You must look to foreign markets."[6] In 1947 Secretary of State Dean Acheson made these remarks in view of the fact that Europe did not possess the capital to absorb our products, hence forcing us toward serious economic instability.[7]

‡In 1945 Secretary of War Henry Stimson opposed the idea of a Russian sphere of interest. But he could also maintain that "it's not asking too much to have our little region over here which has never bothered anybody." Assistant Secretary of War John J. McCloy added, "We ought to have our cake and eat it too. . . . We ought to be free to operate under this regional arrangement in South America, at the same time intervene promptly in Europe. . . ."[8]

March 6, 1947: "The whole world should adopt the American system . . . the American system could survive in America only if it becomes a world system."[9] The combination of economic interests and an exaggerated messianism served to alert the world that America was to be understood no longer simply as a powerful nation intent upon protecting her own interests, but as an aggressive force, endeavoring to establish a world-wide hegemony in the name of a total socio-political system. The white man's burden had been transformed into apocalyptic messianism.

Her new situation inevitably led America to translate leadership into empire. And like empires before her, America began to identify the course of world history with her own history and to ascribe to her national deeds the import of destiny. Thus in 1947, when an exhausted Great Britain handed over to the United States the primary responsibility for the defense of Greece, the symbolism of the end of one empire and the beginning of another moved Joseph Jones, a State Department official, ecstatically to proclaim:

All barriers to bold action were *indeed* down. . . . A new chapter in world history had opened, and [we] were the most privileged of men, participants in a drama such as rarely occurs even in the long life of a great nation.[10]

But the messianic character of American foreign policy was destined to lead to deep frustrations. Even though the United States had emerged from the war as the most powerful nation on earth, there were limits to the exercise of this power for which her extravagant ideology had not prepared her. America possessed a booming economy and military superiority, but she could not always translate this into effective power in each and every foreign policy situation. Therefore, domestic hopes raised by a messianic ideology which coupled apparently unlimited military and economic power with absolute moral goodness would inevitably be dashed by the realities and limitations of international life.

America was unable to stop China from becoming a Marxist state and she could not prevent Eastern Europe from falling under the sway of the Soviet Union, because in each case she would have to risk nuclear war in order to secure her goal. Her messianic ideology allowed her to pay such a price, but humane, practical, and political considerations forbade it. The frustrations arising from these and other situations provided the emotional backdrop for the rise to considerable power of Senator Joseph McCarthy. McCarthyism spread throughout the land, and for over half a decade exerted an enormous and pernicious influence in American life. The Senator had given powerful expression to suspicion, fear, and frustration, natural by-products of a thwarted messianism. This ideology had been the legitimating force behind the drive to world hegemony and the instrument that had forged the anti-communist, cold-war consensus at home. McCarthy only asked that the ideology be taken seriously and followed to its logical conclusion. The reality of world politics, however, prevented the logical extension of absolute American power. She could not send an army anywhere and at any time she pleased, and she could not drop atomic bombs at the slightest policy setback. Further, and here McCarthy had his finger on an exposed nerve, the Eastern financial and manufacturing establishment, America's effective ruling class, while clearly supporting the drive for American world hegemony, did not wish to establish this hegemony at the risk of world disorder or conflagration. As time wore on it became clear that to them American messianism was more a device for holding and extending class economic power than an all-embracing ideology to be followed to its logical conclusion. The elite would risk war only when their material interests were at stake.

By the late 1950's it became clear that, whatever the fate of American messianism as an ideological force, foreign policy difficulties had not affected the core of interests at the center of American policy. The issues surrounding McCarthyism were largely symbolic.* They were related to the limits of power which an apocalyptic messianism could not acknowledge, and to the anger that accompanies frustration. But these issues did not touch on the matter of the growing American commercial empire. Whatever else transpired in the 1940's and 1950's, there had been no meaningful setback to American commercial aspirations.

In time the obvious immunity of these economic concerns from foreign assault provided the basis for a shift in American foreign policy. When it became clear that, rhetoric aside, the Soviet Union had neither the intention nor the power to threaten our commercial interests, an opportunity immediately presented itself for American liberals (for example, Reinhold Niebuhr, Walter Lippmann, George Kennan) to argue that messianism be dropped from our foreign policy. They argued for a pragmatic rather than an ideological approach to foreign affairs. Liberals suggested that the needs of our principal adversary were primarily those of security and economic growth.† They pointed to the fact that Soviet society was very much like our own, given over to material interests, consumerism, industrial growth, and technical efficiency. Liberals urged an accommodation with the Soviet Union on the practical matters of economic growth and security in which spheres of

---

*This is not to belittle the terrible effect McCarthyism had on the lives of those who suffered the loss of civil liberties. It is only to say that, as with most nostalgic attempts to install an ideology of an earlier day, the issues addressed are usually symbolic and have little to do with major economic or political matters. At no time during the McCarthy period was economic or political stability really threatened.

†As a recent article has expressed it, "Soviet ideology is at the minimum only propaganda or window-dressing, and at most but the ritualistic justification of policies arrived at by calculating men doing business in much the same way as non-communist planners."[11]

interest were acknowledged and vital interests preserved. Pragmatic academic liberals were joined by practical businessmen in opposing any notion of an apocalyptic world struggle between incompatible ideologies. Instead they insisted on treating world problems as matters of practical adjustments. They preferred to extend technical rather than ideological solutions to the very mundane problems of poverty, hunger, illiteracy, and industrial growth. It was this shift in understanding that helped lead to the rapprochement between the Soviet Union and the United States in the late 1950's[12] and which continues to motivate common understandings between the two great powers.

So long as American commercial interests were secure and so long as the shape and concerns of Soviet society mirrored our own, it seemed safe to discard the messianic dimensions of our foreign policy. However, in arguing for the acceptance of pragmatic realism as the standard content of our policy, liberals only begged the question of whether American commercial expansion could forever be treated so benignly; that is, whether the economic core of our system would ever find itself in basic conflict with different social systems or national aspirations. It was one thing for liberals to argue that American messianism was irrational, it was quite another to ignore the question of the effect of American economic expansion on the rest of the world. Could the question of American commercial expansion be so easily subsumed under the heading of technical and pragmatic responses to world problems? A concern for technical matters might have seemed to liberals a rather simple and progressive way to view the world; however, the question remained open as to whether this world-view did not in itself contain elements quite consonant with the traditional, expansionist hopes of bourgeois capitalism, hopes that could lead to basic conflict with other nations. In short, liberals overlooked the possibility that an excessive concern with practical and technical matters was but another way of baptizing the basic imperial impulses of bourgeois America.

It remained for the conflict in Indo-China to expose the full implications and dilemmas of American imperial policy. The American intervention in Indo-China, in clear violation of the Geneva Accords of 1954,* indicated the lengths this country would go in order to maintain world hegemony. American policy goals in Indo-China have always been clear. We have sought to install and secure a government in the southern half of Vietnam (and in Laos)

---

*It is well to remember that our violation of these accords is basic to an understanding of the Indo-China war. American officials are quick to dismiss mention of the accords as irrelevant to present reality or as an "exercise in dull history." The Laotians and Vietnamese fighting for liberation, however, see the American violation as a blatant attempt to interfere in the natural course of their national histories. And, of course, they are perfectly correct.

which would act as a client for our interests. The reasons put forward for this were the need to provide a rim of containment against so-called communist expansion, to frustrate guerilla activity (and prevent it from becoming an example to others), and to stabilize the region economically both for our commercial needs and for those of Japan, our foremost Asian ally.* Messianic embellishment accompanied our intervention in Southeast Asia as public officials trod the well-worn cold-war path of apocalyptic warning and struggle. Once into the war, successive administrations felt compelled to proceed with ever greater involvement so as not to be responsible for "losing" Vietnam and unleashing the vitriol of the American right-wing, whose adherence to a strict cold-war ideology had ill-prepared them for defeat.[14]

The plight of American liberals was most pathetic. They were seriously compromised by the intervention in Indo-China. On the one hand they argued for pragmatism in our relations with the Soviet Union, but on the other hand they had to resort to cold-war messianism in order to build a domestic consensus of support for our military adventure in Asia. The Indo-China war, while supported by five administrations, received its most militant defense from liberal administrations.

By 1968 it had become abundantly clear that American military efforts could not secure a client government in southern Vietnam without continuing to pay an enormous price in loss of American lives and domestic discontent. Consequently, beginning with President Lyndon Johnson and continuing with President Richard Nixon, there was a shift in tactics: the military land effort was replaced by a stepped-up air war and increased aid to the military and police activities of our Asian allies.[15] The air war and the use of ever more complex electronic devices brought horror, destruction, and disruption to Indo-China that are beyond description and morality.† The concentration on electronic weapons marks a distinct stage in the development of warfare and is the natural product of a society given to the worship of technological efficiency as somehow both the inevitable outcome of history and free of ideological content. In the impersonal, automated war electronic sensors

---

*Dwight Eisenhower pointed to the fact that a communist success in Indo-China "takes away in its economic aspects, that region that Japan must have as a trading area or Japan, in turn, will have only one place in the world to go—that is toward the communist areas in order to live. So the possible consequences of the loss are just incalculable to the free world."[13] The State Department noted in 1951 that the loss of Indo-China "would be taken by many as a sign that the force of communism is irresistible and would lead to an attitude of defeatism."

†"It is a policy of indiscriminate aerial warfare and blind firepower on the ground that means death and destruction wholesale, not just body counts of enemy dead, but a slaughter of innocents—women and children and old people—villages destroyed, the earth ravaged, refugees in their miserable thousands wandering homeless and hungry ... war ... like a holocaust."[16]

implanted throughout war zones radio messages to planes (soon to be pilot-less), which relay information to huge computers, which in turn map out complete details for bomber raids; the human element is almost completely eliminated. As a result the mystique of technical efficiency has taken over.* Those humans who remain on the job carry on their work with almost no reference either to feelings of guilt at the possible loss of life or to loyalty to the government prosecuting the war. These distant issues are overridden by the primary questions concerning professional competency and technical performance. The "problems" of war are seen in purely technical terms. As two experts in counterinsurgency put it: "all the dilemmas [of counterinsur-gency] are practical and as neutral in an ethical sense as the laws of physics."[18] Consequently, the United States was able to conduct a cruel and unjust war in Indo-China without domestic protest, that is, in the face of a public mesmerized and overpowered by the complexity and horror of events.

With the shift in tactics in Indo-China, American liberals took the oppor-tunity to open the case against messianism. By 1970 liberals had sufficiently diverted attention from their original messianic support for the war to suggest that the war had been a gigantic error. They contended that the primary problem lay with policy-makers who responded to the pulse of messianic longings rather than to a careful reading of what exactly were American interests in Southeast Asia. Since America possessed no significant interests in Vietnam or Indo-China, liberals argued that we had erred in exercising power without any relationship to our interests.[19] Rabid anti-communism was the reason we acted as we did. Messianism led us to the quagmire in Indo-China. The full horror of Indo-China lay in our having expended so much in the way of lives, money, and morale in a country that was of no significant interest to us. The Indo-China adventure was madness because it was fought over nothing. But once again liberals glided over the question of what our core interests were by assuming that they were minimally present in Vietnam, Laos, and Cambodia. Followed to its logical conclusion this suggests that for eighteen years American policy-makers had been insane, or at least terribly stupid.

Liberals now argued that the situation in Indo-China and the rest of the

---

*Apropos of the battlefield of the future is William Westmoreland's technological vision:
  I see battlefields and combat areas that are under 24 hour real or near real time surveillance of all types.
  I see battlefields on which we can destroy anything we locate through instant communication and the most instantaneous application of highly lethal firepower.
  In summary, I see an army built around an integrated area control system that exploits the advanced technology of communications, sensors, fire direction, and the required automatic data processing.[17]

third world should be treated pragmatically.* Recalling the accommodations reached earlier with the Soviet Union, liberals pressed for a foreign policy in the East that would focus solely on the matter of technical issues.†

But the reality of the conflict in Indo-China continues to elude liberal realists. They persistently overlook the question of America's true interest‡ because they are unable to make some crucial distinctions concerning Vietnam and Southeast Asia. Having accurately noted that our *original* intervention in Vietnam was due not to a threat to our economic interests but to a commitment to a blinding messianic ideology, liberals have continued to assume that this has remained the substance of the situation in Southeast Asia. But what liberals overlook is that the 1950's and 1960's were a time of nationalistic ferment throughout the globe, which still continues in most areas, and that in so many of these cases such nationalism has been decidedly anti-American. That is, in the midst of these nationalistic strivings is to be found the threat that guerilla warfare or other kinds of militancy would seriously affect American power and American commercial efforts. It remains true that Indo-China is not centrally important for our own economic empire.** But the insurgency of the Vietcong is, by example, very much a

---

*Henry Kissinger, a liberal Republican, has now become the symbol of and spokesman for technical pragmatism in American foreign policy. Kissinger believes that the basis for settling international problems lies in translating global, ideological struggles into pragmatic national negotiations. As a result, peace is reached in Indo-China on the basis of practical compromises (since the conflict there is not essentially rooted in irreconcilable or ideological matters). And with such a peace, Vietnam, according to Mr. Kissinger, will recede to a "footnote" in history.

†It is important to note the assumptions on which this realism rests. At base liberal realists assume women and men to be given over to greed, envy, and self-advantage. For this reason ideological formulations are seen as crude covers for more basic impulses. The way realists and their partners, the modern technocrats, propose to deal with man is through technical management and manipulation. In this way control combines with the promise of increased material bounty to give content to the contemporary notion of freedom.

‡A *Wall Street Journal* editorial (July 7, 1972) was quick to note this when it chided Senator George McGovern for claiming that the fall of nations like Brazil and India to communism would not "fundamentally damage our interests." The editorial wondered aloud if Mr. McGovern knew "just what our interests are." I would suggest that if the Senator does not understand the importance of friendly regimes for our expanding economy, he ask International Telephone and Telegraph. ITT did not make elaborate plans to overthrow the Chilean government of Dr. Salvadore Allende because it was in doubt about our fundamental interests. *The Wall Street Journal* is absolutely right when it speaks of a "political dynamic [which] affects international relations."

**However, this has not stopped American oil companies from securing leases for off-shore drilling in Vietnam. Nor has it prevented our government from sponsoring studies on how best to integrate the Vietnamese economy into our own. The future economic possibilities of the region are significant.

threat to our whole policy of global containment, a policy primarily given to the protection of an expanding economic network and to building a world capitalist culture. Any nation that receives $9.5 billion worth of dividends from foreign investments (1971) cannot afford to be diffident about militant nationalism in any form. The rhetoric of messianism which came from the lips of John F. Kennedy and Lyndon Johnson concerning the need to prevent dominoes from falling, was very much related to the need to protect important economic interests. It was not the insanity of men caught up in the illusion of messianic ideology. For in the increasingly integrated world economy, one far more complex in 1972 than in 1954, a challenge to one part of the empire could, in fact, trigger attacks on other parts.* Thus, by ignoring how rising nationalism poses a significant threat to American interests abroad, liberals have continued to misunderstand the extent to which real interests remain at stake in Indo-China even today.

By discounting the fact that real interests were at stake in Vietnam and believing that what is needed is only the deflation of the messianic balloon as the prerequisite for a more rational approach to our relations with Southeast Asia, liberals have come to view the efforts of the national liberation forces in the most restricted terms. They understand the struggle of these forces as one for national integrity against foreign (i.e. American) domination. In so doing they ignore the socialist content of various national movements as somehow irrelevant or insignificant. Liberals argued that the United States should withdraw from Indo-China in order to allow the people of that area to settle their own affairs. But this begged the question of what kind of governments would exist in Indo-China once the American involvement ceased. Since liberals treated this matter with diffidence, they have been vulnerable to conservative complaints that American withdrawal would simply pave the way for the victory of revolutionary socialism, an ideology manifestly hostile to American economic interests.

But if liberals are confused about basic interests, Richard Nixon is not. Mr. Nixon shares the same commitment to pragmatism, but has little doubt about how that pragmatism will serve the corporate interests of America. What Nixon has done in stealing the foreign policy thunder from liberals is to join our basic interests to a more flexible policy stance, something liberals were unable to do. Globally, Nixon is pursuing a policy of rapprochement with China and Russia on the basis of security and technological needs. As a result he has replaced cold-war hysteria with diplomatic reasonableness and ideological confrontation with technical accords. In defense matters he has substituted financing deputy peace-keeping forces (the Saigon Army) and

*Notice how difficult it has been to contain the war in Vietnam, which spread to involve four Southeast Asia nations.

counter-insurgency programs for massive American troop involvement. But this move from "ideology" to "pragmatism" is not a reversal of previous foreign policy.[20] It represents only a change in strategy. It is not a switch in basic orientation but rather provides a different framework for sustaining American dominance in world affairs and safeguarding American economic expansion.

Nor does it mean any great change in Indo-China. Nixon intends to secure friendly governments in southern Vietnam, Laos, and Cambodia. American interests in the Southeast Asian basin dictate this policy whatever the means used to implement it. At present Nixon has been forced to accede to the pressure of a public which will not support every tactic to pursue imperial goals. But no matter what the public wishes, the basic policy will not be surrendered. Thus, whether by means of American ground troops or American air power or a client military, the ruling class will not give up its hopes for a series of outpost states in Southeast Asia. In this there is no mystery and no insanity; it is the working of imperial power.

Despite the worst suffering the insurgency continues. It draws its strength from its promise of a new reality for the oppressed. It promises an end to crude materialism and the formalism of Western bourgeois democracy. It seeks a world of democratic participation and equality and the end to exploitation and privilege. In short, it offers a socialist vision. This vision is not a cover for simple material and technical needs, as pragmatic liberals would have it, but the opportunity for a life of sharing and communality. What the national liberation forces signal, in a way few other efforts have, is the end to Western capitalism and the world-view it has come to espouse. One need not be starry-eyed about the third world, nor need one overlook the enormous differences in these countries and the movements within their borders; one can even express sadness that so much of what is good in Western life is being challenged. But, above all, one should recognize what insurgency is. It is a sign of the kingdom of God.

3

Theologically, the judgment of God is derived from the belief that the Word of God is not bound by or to any nation, epoch, or institution. Rather, the Word of God is linked with the dynamic forces of history which expose every present as a time of hypocrisy and misery. However much women and men may wish to absolutize the provisional nature of their present social and political existence by associating the Word of God with contemporary earthly expressions, these efforts are ultimately vain because no present nation or institution contains within it either perfection or the resources to overcome its own failings. The form of the present stands under the verdict and judgment of the future. And that sentence is not carried out in disembodied verbalisms, but in and through the powerful currents of history.

No epoch or nation is complete. It contains within it powerful negative forces which drive the form of the present to judgment and transformation. As Herbert Marcuse notes, drawing from Hegel, " . . . the given facts that appear to common sense as the positive index of truth can only be established by their destruction. . . . all forms of being are permeated by an essential negativity, and . . . this negativity determines their content and movement."[21] The despised and maltreated are the sign of judgment and hope. They are the negative that is present in our common life. It is their apocalyptic and revolutionary anger that exposes the incompleteness and the inhumanity of present earthly forms. According to the Bible, the Word of God is linked with the oppressed and brutalized as the negative force of judgment and the parabolic sign of hope. It is not the church as the people of God, or America as the promised land, that corresponds to the future promises of God. The church or nation can be faithful to the honor of God only as they point to the future of God. But this entails submitting to the judgment of God. That is, it means recognizing the role of the oppressed as the bearers of hope and transformation.

It is for this reason that Christians should await the victory of the National Liberation Front and their socialist allies in Indo-China. It must be so. God's *Opus Alienum.* The appearance of our defeat and humiliation in which it is obvious that all has been lost must and will occur in Indo-China. The revolutionary forces will throw us out, our puppet governments will topple, our policy will be defeated, our efforts will be exposed as cruel and vain. The strange but purposeful judgment of God will emerge as from the end of time.

> Ah, Assyria, the rod of my anger,
>   the staff of my fury!
> Against a godless nation I send him,
>   and against the people of my wrath I command him,
> to take spoil and seize plunder,
>   and to tread them down like the mire of the streets.
>   (Isaiah 10:5-6)
>
> Thus says the Lord to his anointed, to Cyrus,
>   whose right hand I have grasped,
> to subdue nations before him
>   and ungird the loins of kings,
> to open doors before him
>   that gates may not be closed:

> "I will go before you
>   and level the mountains,
> I will break in pieces the doors of bronze
>   and cut asunder the bars of iron,
> I will give you the treasures of darkness
>   and the hoards in secret places. . . ."
>   (Isaiah 45:1-3)

The tragedy that is America's presence in Indo-China will not be amended until this nation suffers the apocalyptic judgment, that is, until the Indo-chinese liberation movements are victorious. That is the unpleasant truth Americans, particularly moderates, will not face. For any number of reasons men and women may find the concept of the judgment of God objectionable; however, one wonders whether it is more fitting to match the obstinacy and cruelty of privileged nations with reasoned excuses than with the stern and sobering spectre of apocalyptic judgment and defeat. Justifying reason turns into complicitous reason when it is unwilling to move to action. Apocalyptic defeat opens the way for a new future.

It is fitting that God should vindicate his majesty in the work of the liberation movements in Indo-China. What else will utterly shake our confidence in our benevolence but defeat? What else but the victory of a band of guerillas in Indo-China and elsewhere could convince us of the folly that has now become the sign of the American empire? As with Assyria, so now with the Vietcong and their allies, God appears from the end of time to disrupt the oppression of the world.

To those who are horrified that one can resign the lives of so many Americans to oblivion and that the majesty of God could be celebrated over the death of 50,000 Americans in the face of their grieving friends and relatives, let it be said that no one wants death or enjoys the futility of life in any form, much less in terms of a vain war. Nor does one take lightly human grief. But life is composed of tragedy and all people must die. It is ultimately defeating only when women and men assign a significance to their lives that is trifling, petty, or misguided. For that, one should blame the official agents and apologists of the extension of the American empire. As a Christian I persist in celebrating only the majesty of God; a majesty known in the vindication and resurrection of Jesus and in his ultimate desire to introduce the kingdom of love, equality, and justice. At present this desire is frustrated. And yet this is man's great hope; a hope to which, paradoxically, the death of men and women in a cruel and exploitative war contributes; a hope found not in the wars of imperial pride, but in the expectancy of and identification with God's ultimate triumph at the end of time, a foretaste of which man has had in the resurrection of Jesus. Toward this hope the Christian lives, in spite of war and death; and to this hope all people who have died, either in vain or heroically, and all who live, either in pain or glory, are consecrated by the power of God.

4

It is no doubt disturbing to the people of the West to contemplate the possibility that those outside of Europe and North America should be assigned such a crucial role in world history. Western parochialism continues to ignore any notion of world history that shifts the locus of primary concern and responsibility away from itself. This is evident in recent books. Charles Reich (*The Greening of America*) pictures the youth counter-culture leading America to a new deliverance. Jean Revel (*Without Marx and Jesus*) sings the praises of young American liberals and radicals who are, for him, harbingers of a new, peaceful revolution. Alvin Toffler (*Future Shock*) celebrates the wonders of American technology as precursive of a new future. George Steiner (*In Bluebeard's Castle*) broods over the end of traditional Western literary culture and reluctantly turns to Western science as the substance of a new culture. None of these writers has considered for a moment the possibility that the horizon of human hope has moved beyond the confines of what Steiner calls "the Mediterranean, north European, Anglo-Saxon racial and geographic matrix."[22] It is of course true that the outlines of Western technological existence are clear and powerful enough to have laid claim to the role of destiny. But the alternative to this does not lie in the erratic counter-culture, in the so-called humanity of Western scientists, or in the enlightenment of young liberals. All such groups exist within the class-ridden barbarism of Western life whether as parasites or helpful agents. Further, all the schemes of these groups continue to treat the oppressed masses of the world as a "problem" to be solved. This only serves to remind us, once again, that by formulating issues in this fashion these groups have an eye to their own prestige and privilege and not to the concerns of the brutalized and suffering. The hope and freedom of the rich, technologically advanced capitalist nations, now racked by their own confusion, disenchantment, and despair, rest not with the intensification of scientific effort nor the exaltation of the youth counter-culture. They rest instead on the Word of God buried in the oppressed peoples of the world. The poor and forsaken carry within them the alternative to the living death that characterizes the West. Whatever the shortcomings of those in the third world (and there are quite a few), their prophetic position remains secure.

The poor and despised do not hope for a future that is merely an extension of the present. They hope instead for a future in which privilege is erased, the rule of elites is replaced with democracy, and individualism is supplanted by solidarity. The present technological order serves only to mask a structure of elite privilege. Any intensification of the present order of things would only ensure bourgeois dominance, and that dominance would at the same time claim for itself the immunity of objective law. It is hardly to be expected that the society and civilization that brought about this situation would or could transfigure itself. If it is to be transformed it must wait upon the apocalypse. It must look to the humiliated and exploited for the visionary and political break with the present. This is the significance of the negative and apocalyptic power of the world's oppressed. This is a sign of the kingdom of God.

Chapter Eight

SOCIALISM

Christianity and capitalism are incompatible.   **Walter Rauschenbusch**

Only Christians who have lost their conscience are capable of defending the rich against the poor. Christianity is a religion of the poor and there is no possibility of turning it into a defense of capitalism and money. Capitalism is a religion of the golden calf. . . . Capitalism is not only an outrage against the "have nots" and the oppression of the "have nots," it is above all an outrage upon, and the persecution of, human personality.

Nicolas Berdyaev

Listen, don't get the idea I'm one of those goddam radicals. Don't get the idea I'm knocking the American system. My rackets are run on strictly American lines and they're going to stay that way. This American system of ours, call it Americanism, call it capitalism, call it what you like, gives to each and every one of us a great opportunity if we only seize it with both hands and make the most of it.   **Al Capone**

1

Most contemporary expressions of Christian ethics are rooted in the personalism of the pre-industrial age. The enthusiasm of many Christians for existentialist systems, or for various forms of small-group psychologies, adds up to an intense concern for the loss of personal identity and authenticity in an increasingly complex world. It also represents a strong bias against the techno-industrial age itself. Thus, efforts are made to commend modes and habits of intimacy, spontaneity, and genuineness which purport to enable people to live more fully in an industrial world that seems to promise little but increased conformity and alienation. But in this alliance with existentialism or small-group psychology, Christianity has not meaningfully come to

175

grips with the depths of modern industrial life. It has simply tried to rescue the beleaguered and confused person who has been inundated by modern pressures of work and social life. In most cases the attempt of various ethical schemes has been to hold up personalism as an alternative to present mechanized existence. Inevitably, however, the vision of that personalism has been drawn from an earlier age when (or so it was believed) life was quieter, simpler, closer to nature, more intimate, and prone to considerations and habits of full, personal existence. Most contemporary Christian ethics would probably agree with the description offered by Charles Reich of the time before industrialization:

> ... Most people were born, lived, worked, and died in the same place, among people they knew and saw every day. There was no separation between work and living. Ties to the community were strong and seldom severed; each man lived within a circle which did not depend upon his own action, began before him, and lasted beyond him. Food and shelter were communal enterprises; no one grew fat or starved alone. The scale of everything was smaller: tools, houses, land, villages. There were no large, impersonal institutions. ... Scale and activity were influenced by nature. ... Laws were administered by visible local people. Most important of all, man's economic activity was rooted in, and subordinate to, his social system. ... Communal traditions ... were the regulators of life. Play, art, ritual, ceremony, and the spiritual were not separated from the other aspects of life. ... This world ... was destroyed in the making of our modern world. ... the forces of industrialism, designed to be beneficent, [had] such devastating, unforeseen effects. ... In pre-industrial societies, change takes place very gradually, subject at all times to a humanistic cultural and social system.[1]

The idyllic content of Reich's presentation of the past is clear and compelling enough; but, alas, it bears little relationship to the reality of the past. The past was as much given to vicious and cruel exploitation as the present. Yet Reich's dazzling remembrance, and the traditional American propensity to allow nostalgia to overwhelm reality, have encouraged us to identify personal fulfillment with existence patterned after an erroneous past vision.

Similarly, even the ethics of much of contemporary Christian activism is based on a pre-industrial vision. The protest against war, racism, poverty, and social injustice, for example, has all too often been narrowed to the issue of conscience. Indeed, fealty to conscience has come very close to being regarded as the mark of true humanity.* Individuals have been exhorted to test in their consciences whether the present state of political or social affairs measures up to justice, and then to confront injustice and inhumanity in acts of conscience. Symbols have been selected which spotlight the clash between conscience and evil. Intense efforts have been made to keep actions free of

---

*Much of Roman Catholic concern for conscience may reflect a need to overcome past constrictions on this notion. In 1830, Gregory XVI had alluded to "The madness that every one is entitled to freedom of conscience."

the inhumanity imbedded in the object of protest. But the acts of conscience, perhaps because there is a great concern about the problem of ethical contamination, tend to be demonstrations of personalism—symbolic acts— rather than major political or social challenges to the present order. Marches or draft card burnings are, of course, political acts in themselves; but when they are separated from any overall conception of the complexity of indus- trial society, and are divorced from any consistent strategy for seizing or effecting political power, they are inherently limited activities. All that can be done tactically, as a follow-up, is to exhort others to engage in similar acts. But this means hope is placed in the power of multiple symbols rather than a few. It has not moved protest beyond the level of moral demonstration or personal statement, that is, beyond calling attention to the contrast between individual conscience and a stricken social order. This has been true because ethical personalism is not a sufficient vehicle for articulating the major issues of industrial society.

It is to the credit of Christian activists that they have brought the matter of social justice into the forefront of Christian ethical concern. However, neither their theory nor their action has moved beyond an implicit definition of personhood in terms drawn from the intimacy of the pre-industrial period. For all their concern with social justice, too many Christians have maintained a naive faith in the appeal to conscience, and in the power of good will, strategies drawn not from scripture but from the morality of a simpler age. Men and women are too often seen apart from the realities of class, property, and power. They are pictured as simple moral agents only tangentially affected by these powerful forces. Hence, by ignoring the full contours of the present techno-industrial order (with some activists going so far as to asso- ciate the order with total evil) the Christian protest movement has failed to make its ethics truly political.

This is very much an industrial age in which one cannot ignore the matter of social or economic form. An ethic that remains concerned with individual feelings of authenticity, or with the symbols of a good conscience, without understanding that these realities are set within an industrial system from which there is no "escape," runs the risk of inadvertently helping to prolong the system itself. The system possesses an almost unlimited ability to absorb or divert campaigns that deal with symbols rather than the structures of the established order. Strategies of conscience which lead toward establishing personalistic beachheads on the land mass of industrialism, however much they claim to be serving the cause of social justice, still remain essentially futile. Only an ethic that takes seriously the present industrial order and the eschatological tendencies for transformation that exist within it, and that wills to grapple with class and capitalism as more than incidental matters, will be able to stand the test of time and contribute to a new future.

Finally, by casting attention back to a so-called golden age, we forget that, according to Paul, the future of mankind corresponds, not with Adamic beginnings, but with the future of Christ (Rom. 5:14-21). Not what we were, but what we shall be, is the hope of the New Testament. Jesus Christ is not the reconstitution of the old Adam; he is the new Adam surpassing the old. Thus, our common future does not involve overlooking the present techno-industrial order which has been given us, but struggling to transform it into an order of love and freedom beyond anything that existed in Eden. Therefore, it behooves the Christian activist to take seriously the promises of God for a new heaven and a new earth.

2

It is the happy task of the Christian to await and serve the signs of the end of the world. In raising Jesus, God confirmed the promises made through Israel to all people. In that Jesus points beyond himself to the consummation of all things, women and men may expect the earth to give form to eschatological hopes. Without any historical confirmation of the promises of God, the Christian message would disintegrate into pious mutterings concerning the sacred nature of the soul or the preciousness of personal relationships. Christians must await the irruption of the signs of the end as they appear in time.

Socialism is such a sign. It is the earthly form of the eschatological hope of freedom for all people. It is a parable of the kingdom of God. Eschatological freedom is found in the hope for economic equality, the eradication of classes, the abolition of the wage system, and the establishment of personal relationships free from commodity fetishism and bourgeois objectification. That socialism has been and will be betrayed by women and men does not count against its transforming power. In the substance of its claim it remains an unmistakable sign of eschatological hope.

Socialist hope arises out of the agony of Western industrial life. It does not deny the reality of the industrial age; it points to its transformation. It calls for a common life of participation in economic, political, and social destiny. Only in socialism does freedom take on the concrete characteristics of service and communality. Only in socialism is freedom defined in terms of neighborly service and the end to privilege and exploitation. This is what the resurrection pointed to in surpassing glory. Unquestionably, the fact that man is a quixotic being, torn by conflicting claims and loyalties (which arise apart from, but are nonetheless influenced by, social and economic systems), limits what one can expect of socialism (or any other ideology). This does not detract, however, from the transforming strength of socialism. The radical reconstruction of society through the socialization of wealth is a possibility imbedded even in the wretchedness of our present capitalist order. Furthermore, it is a necessity if people are to escape this present age of misery. As socialism takes shape in time, it is a dynamic parable of hope, a sign of freedom brought to man's existence by the majesty and loyalty of God.

The economic hopes of socialism are simple enough. Whereas capitalism (whether laissez faire or corporate) determines remunerations on a hierarchical basis and ensures differentials in wages and purchasing power, socialism attempts to alter wage relationships so as to produce egalitarianism. Because private ownership of the means of production institutionalizes inequality, it leads directly to exploitative and dependent relationships between owners and workers, rich and poor. It is true that capitalism can be reformed to produce socially useful services and to permit greater equality, but all social and economic changes are limited by the necessity to safeguard private ownership and the capital-owning class. The result is a class society, and an economy that never balances social need and capital expenditure. As George Lichtheim correctly notes, under capitalism "human needs . . . are still satisfied in relation to the 'effective demand' of paying customers."[2] Socialism, on the other hand, is the "form of society in which men and women are not divided into opposing economic classes, but live together under conditions of approximate social and economic equality, using in common the means that lie to their hands of promoting social welfare."[3] Thus, social ownership of the means of production, the distribution of surplus capital on the basis of need, and the eradication of classes by means of the abolition of wage relationships are the economic substance of socialism. "Socialism," declared Arthur Lewis, "is about equality."[4]

It should be clear that socialism is not the same thing as the welfare state, nor is it equivalent to the state socialism practiced in the Soviet Union and Eastern Europe.

The welfare state is characterized by state intervention into the economy either to stabilize the economy and provide jobs, or to help equalize income, or to control the administrative apparatus to produce social services unattainable in a free market economy. However, the welfare state does not control the market to the point of abolishing the wage relationship, nor does it envisage putting ownership of tools and productive machinery into the hands of society. In this case even the central regulation of key industries through boards or commissions (generally dominated by people from the industries themselves) leaves untouched the main outlines of capitalism. Whereas American conservatives decry state intervention, American socialists have welcomed it. But both err when they confuse such intervention with socialism.[5] The welfare state has always shied away from the questions of the ownership of the means of production and the nature of the wage relationship, and hence betrays its essential capitalist orientation.

Nor is state socialism the same thing as socialism. It is a perversion of socialism (however much it may be an advance over corporate capitalism and a necessary means of accumulating capital in underdeveloped socialist countries) because the inevitable bureaucratic authority or party control turns the goal of democratic ownership into the reality of state property. Social ownership of the means of production is derived from the idea of a society in which the producer owns and controls the tools and machinery of industry. It combines elements of collective ownership *and* collective control. State socialism divorces the two by making democratic control tantamount to ownership by the bureaucracy. In this fashion it is appropriate to speak of expropriation as a mark of state socialism.

In socialist theory social ownership is inextricably wedded to democratic control of the economy: " . . . The material means of production are owned by the whole community and operated by organs representative of and responsible to the community according to a general economic plan. . . ."[6] However difficult this may be in economies of scarcity, the hope is that all people, not just the planners or controllers, are to participate in running the economy. In this fashion the basis is removed for a politics of elitism (whether capitalist or socialist). The most basic form of democracy, economic democracy, is established.

Contrary to the predictions of Marx, socialism has taken root in countries that have not passed through a prolonged period of capitalist development. In every case national economies were at a primitive stage. Thus, socialist forces seized control well before capitalism was to have reached the point where it was choked by its own contradictions, namely by its chronic inability to match advanced productive capacities with human need. For some this fact has been cause enough to dismiss Marxism out of hand. But whether Marxist futurology is absolutely accurate is no more relevant than the fact of the disappearance of the free market from contemporary capitalist economies. On the human level, the advent of socialist power, apart from Marxist projections, has presented enormous economic and theoretical problems. Every demonstration of socialism in the contemporary world comes from countries in which conditions of scarcity exist (or existed when socialism was first installed).* As a result, ruthless measures of control have been enforced in order to accumulate capital and introduce modernization, that is, to accomplish what capitalism was to have accomplished already, prior to giving way to socialism. But Marx had forewarned that if scarcity existed when the

*It is no accident that in socialist countries that reach a stage of industrial advancement (such as Czechoslovakia and Poland) there arises a cry for true democratic socialism.

means of production were socialized, "then want is made general, and with want the need to struggle for necessities must begin again and all the old crap will be reproduced. . . ."[7] Or as Henry Pachter has put it, "A distributive economy is possible only at a fairly advanced stage of development; one cannot distribute poverty, but only wealth."[8] As a consequence, socialist economies have grown in situations in which conditions have too often devolved into authoritarian and bureaucratic rule, in which socialism has come to be associated with oppression and not with democratic egalitarianism.*

It should be noted that the People's Republic of China continues to be something of an exception. There socialism has grown in a country with a long moral tradition in which crude materialism has never been a central component of consciousness as it has been in the West. Further, the Communist Party, prior to seizing national power, had exercised effective control over vast areas of China in which they were able to put into practice the Chinese brand of socialism with its exaltation of egalitarianism and common service above material and technological advance. In China, unlike the West, socialism was able to overcome the problem of scarcity, not with ruthless discipline (though there was that) but by giving precedence to the vision of a classless society.

In the West, the difficult circumstances surrounding the implantation of socialism in various countries have meant that the non-economic hopes of socialism have not been in evidence. They have given place to the economic discipline and control that accompanies the stage of capital accumulation. The attempts, for example, in the early years of the Soviet state to do without money and to organize labor on the basis of moral rather than material incentives, that is, on the basis of a new collective consciousness, only led to confusion and had to be abandoned. According to Wassily Leontief, attempts in Cuba to organize labor along similar lines may not be faring much better.[9]

The appeal of socialism has thus been weakened. On the one hand there is the drab and narrow world of economic socialism—the five-year plans, the quotas—which have produced grey republics dedicated to establishing secure economies without capitalist frills. On the other hand there is the absence of any demonstration of the power of the non-economic aspects of socialism. And in the absence of a new human consciousness, a new and joyous comradeship, a new attitude toward work and play, the bright lights and

*One should not forget that hostility and often aggression by capitalist nations has also figured in the increase of authoritarianism in socialist regimes. The Soviet Union, for example, could hardly forget the intervention of the allied powers in her civil war, nor that she, and not the Western democracies, had to bear the brunt of the fighting against Nazi Germany.

glitter of capitalist life continue to mesmerize Western people. None of this means, however, that the economic accomplishments of socialist economies are unimpressive. For in every case they have marked up notable advances in overcoming poverty, extending medical care, and providing education, social welfare, and public services. Here their record does surpass that of capitalist society.

The socialist vision, however, extends beyond the simple re-allocation of natural and industrial resources and wealth. It points to "the substitution of non-economic goals for the aim of wealth accumulation."[10] It deals with men and women freed from class domination, participants in the affairs of their society, liberated from the fetishism of commodities, given to relationships of racial and sexual equality, linked with one another in a communal comradeship, and open to occupations and leisure that exalt rather than dwarf the human personality. In short there is a spiritual vision to socialism. The economic aspects of socialism provide only the base for the construction of a new human life. Thus Herbert Marcuse writes:

> The concept of the primary, initial institutions of liberation is familiar and concrete enough: collective ownership, collective control and planning of the means of production and distribution. This is the foundation . . . it would make possible the usage of all available resources for the abolition of poverty, which is the prerequisite for the turn from quantity into quality: the creation of a reality in accordance with the new sensitivity and the new consciousness.[11]

Socialism is a full concept embracing man in society, that is, men and women beyond their simple material activity. The socialist notion of the abolition of the wage relationship projects man as a spiritual being. The idea of social control of production builds toward the communal status of all people, and it points to man's destiny as a participant and actor, rather than as a passive creature tossed to and fro by so-called universal economic laws, or mesmerized by consumer opulence. The distribution of wealth on the basis of need rather than in accord with the power, capital, or property of certain individuals or classes leads to human solidarity beyond superficial external differences. The socialization of property focuses attention on public life and its ultimate shape, rather than on the desire for private gain. Thus, personal identity is not measured in economic terms, that is, by wealth or power, but in terms of service to the common good. Socialism is communality taking form, and as such is an invitation to the construction of personality, not in accordance with material ambition, but on the basis of personal concern for and openness toward others who, in fact, are comrades (not, as in capitalist society, higher or lower on the social or economic ladder). Social ownership of the means of production opens up the possibility of overcoming the alienation that manifests itself in capitalism, where the energy of the self is associated not with others but with things. In capitalism the model of human relationships is under the power of objectification; people are treated as things because life is a matter of things. On the other hand, common ownership and democratic control mean that people are not divorced from the things they make or distribute, nor are they under the sovereignty of others. The socialist vision of a corporate commonwealth lays the foundation for building intrinsic relationships. It points to a life of sharing. Socialism is egalitarian and relieves people of the burden of competitive striving. The vision of socialism directs people to a time of freedom and dignity, to the end of alienation and exploitation, to the building of a life beyond material compulsion, a life of true brotherhood and sisterhood.

Contrariwise, capitalism possesses a paucity of vision. Unquestionably it has produced material abundance, but Robert Heilbroner is correct when he writes:

> . . . No capitalist nation or philosopher or economist has any grand designs for the fundamental reshaping of society through capitalism. Certainly capitalism aims at the material well-being of its constituents, but equally certainly it entertains no thought that the pursuit of well-being will alter the basic class character of the system or modify the competitive or acquisitive drives from which the system derives its momentum.[12]

Of course, early capitalism suggested the beneficence of a "hidden hand" bringing eventual harmony out of conflicting self-interests. Later, capitalism claimed correspondence with the so-called evolutionary laws of cultural advance. Still later, Reinhold Niebuhr argued that capitalism concurred with the basic drives of human nature and that, properly regulated, it was superior to utopian forms of socialism because capitalism's essential "realism" concerning man precluded the absolutizing of power and led to situations of balance and restraint. But in none of these instances is there any alternate vision to the misery and exploitation inherent in capitalism.

The doctrine of individualism lies at the heart of capitalist reality. It was Adam Smith's view that the collective good is served by the automatic harmony derived from the exercise of individual efforts. In describing the economy Smith wrote:

> Every individual is continually exerting himself to find out the most advantageous employment for whatever capital he can command. It is his own advantage . . . and not that of society, which he has in view. But the study of his own advantage naturally, or rather necessarily, leads him to prefer that employment which is advantageous to society.[13]

In reality, however, there is no such automatic benefit to society as a whole. Instead, social progress is thwarted precisely because individualism leads to advantage for some at the expense of others. In capitalism the very notion that property is private inevitably leads to a situation in which individuals exercise power over and not with others. It is true that the doctrine of individualism is no longer so dominant in American public and economic life, having been transformed into its opposite (teamwork, deference to authority, conformity to pre-set corporate goals) by the needs and power of the new corporate state. Yet, even as the public sphere is shut off for the exercise of individualism, the arena of private life is still receptive. Here, individualism is closely associated with excessive consumption and competitive status seeking. Indeed, one is hard put to give the phrase "individual freedom" any other meaning. In any event, the practice of individualism limits social progress. The well-being of the individual is inevitably put ahead of everyone else. This is how one sustains economic rewards. As a consequence of individualism, capitalist society is continually plagued with loneliness, isolation, and fear among its people. Suspicious of social goals, unable to carry through consistently on social planning, persistently relating all effort to personal gain, women and men in capitalist society continue to suffer from the insecurity, anxiety, and exhaustion associated with the drive for individual success. And worse, when failure overcomes them, they are left with no other explanation save that of individual responsibility.

In a capitalist society the primary virtues are competitiveness, greed, and ambition. These virtues, it is said, provide the necessary energy which motivates the whole system. Many apologists for capitalism go so far as to suggest that these are the basic components of the human personality. Indeed James Madison argued that the greed of man was such that it necessitated a capitalist form of economy. Reinhold Niebuhr constructed a similar argument which led him to espouse a modified capitalist system. Yet the flaw in this approach is obvious. It might very well be argued that man's finitude—the ultimate awareness of transitoriness—leads to an insecurity which is all too often manifested in aggressiveness and combative striving. But it does not follow from this that a capitalist economy is necessary. That an economic system should be constructed that turns greed and envy into positive virtues is appalling. It carries the so-called tragic view of life and man to an unnecessary and incomprehensible point. That the future of humanity should be set within the context provided by human selfishness is intolerable. It makes more sense to argue that socialism ought to be adopted precisely in order to curb human greed and rapacity. Socialism may not be able to erase greed and ambition, but it surely does not envision encouraging or rewarding them. It attempts to thwart these traits, and instead encourage mutuality and respect for others. Capitalism is burdened with the incredible notion, as F. D.

Maurice once remarked, that universal selfishness will do the work of universal love. Socialism attempts to create contrary conditions of mutuality and respect which, even if they are not fully realized under the conditions of time, are at least a parable of human destiny.

A system of class division characterizes capitalism. In this way capitalism is as conservative as the feudal system it superseded. Apologists for capitalism have been forced to defend as necessary a system of rank and privilege which most of the rhetoric of Western political democracy attempts to obscure. Since the protection of the upper reaches of the capitalist class is one of the highest priorities of the system, an arrangement that fosters elite privilege is inevitable. As a result, capitalism continues to sustain a class system with all its attendant insecurities, hostilities, and instabilities. Surplus wealth continues to go primarily to those with large amounts of capital (2.5 percent of the population owns 45 percent of all the private assets); power is still exercised by the business elite. At the heart of the capitalist system is the assumption that some people have a right to live at the expense of others. The Russian Orthodox theologian Nicolas Berdyaev summed up the morality of the capitalist class system:

> A class society is based upon falsehood and wrong, it is a denial of the dignity of personality. . . . Classes set up distinctions and inequalities among people, which are based not on their personal worth, qualities, and callings, but on privileges which are linked with birth and blood, or with property and money. Such a classification of men is not based on any human principle and is repellent to human nature.[14]

It is quite apparent that the non-economic goals of socialism, that is, the realization of a new socialist woman and man, still remain a distant hope. With the exception of China (and to some extent Cuba) it would appear that no socialist nation will realize the non-economic goals of socialism until it has reached a relatively high stage of material development. Meanwhile in the capitalist countries prospects for economic socialism remain dim. Having found the golden coin of the treasure of technological abundance, Western publics seem unwilling to move toward equality or other non-economic considerations before they have exhausted the contents of the chest. Still, whatever the prospects for success, the socialist hope remains: democratic participation in and social ownership of the means of production, the values of mutuality and intimacy, human relationships that minimize greed and ambition, the end to class privilege. There remains the dream of the transformation of society from one embodying individualism to one manifesting solidarity, where relationships will no longer be dictated by quantity but by quality, where freedom will come to mean freedom for others in a new cooperative commonwealth.

3

In supporting socialism as a sign of the kingdom of God, it should not be supposed I am talking about human perfection or the end of earthly alienation. Unfortunately the rise of socialism has been all too often accompanied by excessive claims about an ideal and irenic future. Such extravagances have been used by the opponents of socialism as an excuse to dismiss the system. Still, an exuberant and utopian metaphysic was bound to accompany the more revolutionary expressions of socialism. The incredible cruelties of capitalism (particularly in the early phase of industrial capitalism), coupled with its puerile view of man and history, literally invited an alternative system of comprehensive, metaphysical deliverance. Indeed, one might speculate that the greater the excesses under capitalism, the more extreme the redemptive promises of socialism. Coupled with this was the fact that, in its zeal, Marxist socialism tended to inform itself about history with a set of optimistic ideals garnered from the Enlightenment. The result was that socialism as a system of human justice took on aspects of metaphysical soteriology.

Marxism was realistic enough to note the tragic dimension of past human existence, but tended to forget it when describing its own future. Whether or not it is fair to ascribe to Marx such a view, Marxism has tended to picture the future classless society in terms derived from the Enlightenment. Future perfection would come because it corresponded to the essential goodness of humankind. Free of the historical factors that oppress them and lead to their alienation, men and women would naturally blossom into free, creative beings. Since, therefore, the socialist or communist future was the result of history and since it was the expression of what man truly is, socialism claimed to be the answer to all things, rather than the amelioration of some. Further, it was often compelled to act in the face of the empirical absence of perfection as though only intensified ruthlessness could make up the deficit. A belief in earthly paradise often provides an excuse for the use of terror in hopes of reaching it.

Any system, much less socialism, that purports to build upon a lost innocence or upon a pristine goodness inherent in humankind is bound for trouble. It leaves out the tragic elements of human existence which dog mankind every step along the temporal way. These tragic elements should not be confused with any doctrine of total sin or evil. To replace a doctrine of essential goodness with one of essential evil leads to fascism and the worst forms of terror and oppression. A totally cynical view of the human condition has always invited the most extravagant totalitarianism. The tragic dimension I refer to is related to the essential ambiguity of women and men in time. It bespeaks the capacity for evil and good inextricably intertwined in every human expression. No future society can erase this reality because it does not derive from society itself; it is rooted in the human condition. It exists because men and women live in time and are forever subject to limitation, insecurity, and ambiguity.

It is therefore fruitless to talk about any past or future goodness of mankind, unless one is prepared to suffer the consequences attendant upon efforts to establish a human utopia. There is no essence to man. Biblically, the claim about the goodness of the earth and of humanity is an eschatological claim whose basic reference is not to some innate human quality, but to God who confers or imputes goodness. In the New Testament the norms and hopes surrounding human life are drawn from the vision of the kingdom of God as it struggles for visibility in the midst of a perishing age. The future possibilities for men and women are related, not to essential goodness, but to the future of Jesus Christ. Even as these possibilities are operative in the present age they are engulfed by the forces of decay and misery. Every present moment finds humankind fragile and vulnerable. Hence, there can be no call to action on the basis of goodness or innocence. The human personality is subject to the control of too many earthly sovereignties to be called good. It awaits the call of another sovereign, namely, God, who in the resurrection of Jesus established, in anticipation, a Lordship of which the political expression is socialism. This precludes talk of a tragedyless future manifesting a time of perfection. Even in a socialist future the ambiguity of personhood will characterize existence. As Reinhold Niebuhr once noted, human problems are never really solved, they only move to different levels. Socialism conforms to the claim of God's eschatological future but not to any essential human goodness. "A socialist society," Berdyaev wisely commented, "is not a society of saints, it is simply a society of sinful and imperfect men, and the manifestation of human perfection is not to be expected of it."[15]

While the ambiguity of human existence provides the limits to socialist expectations and claims, it does not cancel the socialist appeal or its transforming power on earth. Socialism may not be salvation, but it certainly is justice. Socialism promises a freedom capitalism cannot, even though it is helpless to provide true freedom for all men and women. As Berdyaev rightly argued, "The metaphysics of socialism in its prevalent forms are . . . false. . . . But the social and economic side of socialism is right and just, it is elementary justice."[16] The vision of socialism cannot be ignored because it tends to overlook the intractable character of human personality. The socialist vision of a society that goes beyond bourgeois individualism, eliminates the exploitative workings of the so-called free market, erases poverty, eradicates the wage relationship and class distinctions, promotes the goal of human solidarity, and looks toward a day of leisure without the fetish of money, deserves support from any Christian enamored with the miracle of the kingdom of God. As Michael Harrington suggests, "To grant that socialism is not a final redemption should not ... paralyze the imagination. ..."[17] Even flawed with perfectionist pretensions, socialism is superior to the decay of the present capitalist order. Socialism is a new eschatological future, even if it is not perfection. The Marxist vision is still the most humane and just piece of social and economic imagination we possess.

4

The question remains: How can America move from capitalism to socialism? Apart from the fact that the prospects for such a development appear quite remote and are likely to remain so for some time, the need to speculate about future possibilities is as strong as ever. Two strategies, each plagued with limitations, seem to be dominant.

One road to socialism calls for working through the established political process.* The remnants of the old American Socialist party and other moderate socialists adhere to this position. They hope to build popular majorities for legislative policies that would then lead to or embody the socialization of all wealth. The socialization of wealth is distinct from socialism in that the latter proposes collective ownership of the means of production while the former refers to efforts to bring the private sector of the capitalist economy under greater state control in order to meet basic needs and services. This strategy points toward a first stage of "humane capitalism" (Roger Garaudy) that will devolve into socialism. Nationalization, increased regulatory procedures, more central economic planning, redistribution of wealth through more progressive taxation, and more attention to welfare needs constitute a programmatic way station on the road to socialism. It is assumed that it will take time to gather popular majorities for this program, but it is believed that the instabilities of capitalism are such that public support will eventually coalesce around a program involving the socialization

---

*Because American socialism (and much of the American left, in general) has little strength in the labor movement, it has been forced to pursue strategies for change in the political arena. Ideologically, this corresponds to the notion which has been popular for one hundred years that socialism is equivalent to the expanded regulatory power of the state apparatus. Both the left and the right have succumbed to this error. The trouble is that in a capitalist economy there are limits to state activity which are set by the business system. As an alternative, it is best to understand that the central arena of change is the economy and that challenges in this arena most properly arise, not from the regulatory or intervention power of the state (though these may be helpful), but from a strong and militant labor movement. Only labor can wrest from capital those concessions which would transform our political economy into socialism. The European left has understood this better than the American left.[18]

of wealth. From there it would be possible to mount further campaigns leading toward socialism. Ironically, this position has a touch of the old Marxist determinism which suggests that the irreversible developments of economic life will automatically pave the way for socialism.*

What about the various social forces that could conceivably combine to support this scheme? At present it is clear that there is no significant support for socialism. The American public seems securely wedded to the present capitalist order. Having tasted relative prosperity, few Americans seem anxious to experiment with radical social or economic change. But this is not to say there are no trends toward the socialization of wealth. Characteristically, during periods of economic stagnation (such as the present), forces among the working class tend to lose faith in such capitalist staples as upward mobility, beneficent competition, and inevitable material prosperity and begin to shift loyalties to programs that espouse equality, government stabilization, national planning and economic security; that is, programs embodying socialization of wealth are most attractive whenever the more pure forms of capitalist political economy fail to deliver a steady and increasing standard of living. The resurgent populism in the recent campaigns of George Wallace and George McGovern bears testimony to the willingness of the American working class (both white and blue collar) to forego the ideology of individualism, mobility, and free enterprise for the appeal of stability, security, and equality. Yet, apart from such moments of economic decline, indications are that there is still overwhelming loyalty to the capitalist political economy. Indeed the irony of working class commitment to equality and security lies in that programs based on such ideals are not seen to contradict the basic impulses of capitalist endeavor, but rather to strengthen them. Hence, there arises the desire for security *and* competition, equality *and* individualism, stability *and* guaranteed upward mobility. Egalitarian legislation is supported in the hope that it will bolster the capitalist system and provide greater material prosperity. Therefore, even if potential support exists for the extension of the welfare state, there is no evidence that any section of the public is ready to move beyond this to a radical reorientation of class, wage, or property relationships.

Yet, moderate socialists are not without hope. They concede the difference between support for the welfare state (which exists) and support for the full outlines of socialism (which does not exist). They acknowledge that, for the present, practically all sections of the American public wish to promote economic growth rather than social and economic equality, and that most

---

*In Marx's afterword to the second German edition of *Das Kapital* he quotes approvingly a reviewer: "Marx treats the social movement as a process of natural history, governed by laws not only independent of human will, consciousness and intelligence, but rather, on the contrary, determining that will, consciousness and intelligence."[19]

Americans still cling to the hope that increased material prosperity will somehow solve all social problems. Moderate socialists can, however, point to certain tendencies in advanced capitalism which afford significant opportunities for the progress of socialism. Of particular interest is that, as contemporary industrial society provides enough material security for large numbers of people, it seems to invite these same people to demand, not greater prosperity (that is, quantity), but rather a society that fulfills social and cultural needs (quality). Advanced industrial capitalism produces among some of its citizens less allegiance to materialism, hierarchical control, and cultural blandness. This is especially evidenced by some sections of the young, who have become more committed to humane rather than material values. Closely related are those among the new technological elite who find the narrow goals of capitalism contradicting their vision of a planned future utopia of leisure and creativity. The technologists continue to insist that we are moving to a time of universal material abundance and that blind loyalty to restrictive capitalism may hamper a true human vision.

Further, classes within industrial capitalism exhibit a restlessness clearly related to the confining nature of advanced capitalism. For example, elements within the growing professional-technical strata of the working class find themselves without the autonomy they feel should accompany their status. They suffer under a system that requires for stability increased top-down control in every industry. Even as they enjoy the benefits of capitalism they grow restive at the price they pay in lost freedom. Thus, it is not inconceivable that one day they might support the idea of democratic control of industry. In similar fashion, public service workers, and workers in the service industries, while by no means well off financially, may also come to resent the loss of autonomy in their work. Finally, among the (now decreasing) blue-collar workers, resentment at routine, poor pay, and lost status might explode at any time as in the case of workers who struck the General Motors Plant in Lordstown, Ohio,[20] and other more recent such actions.

Because of all this, moderate socialists have some hope for the future. In substance this hope rests on the belief that various classes may eventually become surfeited with economic concerns. At that point they might be ready to accept the socialization of wealth and, even beyond that, a reorganization of society along democratic and egalitarian lines. At present, however, capitalism seems to be able to ensure mass allegiance by guaranteeing an ever increasing material prosperity. So far, efforts to attack capitalism on the basis either of its erratic economic performance or on the basis of the inequality it engenders have failed. If, in a time of abundance, issues of quantity evolve into questions about quality, it may very well be that socialism could become a live option in America.

The obvious difficulty with this position is that it does not seriously account for the ability—so often demonstrated in the past—of American capitalism to absorb reform movements. There is good reason to believe that future structural reforms (even those arising out of a society of vast abundance) will leave the substance of bourgeois society basically untouched. A more or less socialized economy is not the same thing as a socialist society, nor will one necessarily lead to the other. Economic and social reforms of the kind envisioned by moderate socialists do not, in fact, change the basic class structure of society, nor do they mean the end to private ownership of the means of production, or the construction of an egalitarian republic.

It is for this reason that we must consider a more radical strategy, one that holds little hope for the gradual change of society. It assumes that capitalist society possesses an unlimited ability to reproduce itself. It is highly skeptical of notions pointing to the end of material drives within capitalism. Consequently, radical socialists ignore general economic trends and so-called signs of the emergence of new, frustrated classes. Instead they concentrate on agitation and confrontation and they work among the most oppressed people of society: minorities and blue-collar workers. They posit a series of crises (often self-generated) leading to a breakdown of society which in turn could create opportunities for a bold seizure of power. This scheme assumes a voluntarism in which change occurs less because of the fortuitous concurrence of human action and historical opportunity than because of sheer stubbornness and expediency of will; "Man makes his own history," said Marx. For this reason the Cuban, Chinese, and Vietnamese revolutions serve as models. In those revolutions the ascetic discipline, revolutionary élan, anti-materialism, and collective energy make quite a contrast to the bloated and disheartened West. In each of these revolutions a prolonged period of struggle preceded the seizure of power, and exemplified the triumph of heroic activity in the face of overwhelming adversity, rather than conformity to classical Marxist schemes for revolution.

Still it remains unclear how any of these models have relevance to the American experience. American society is highly integrated, her economy is industrial and technological, her institutions are securely controlled, and her police and military forces are disciplined and loyal. Revolutionary schemes that plan for direct confrontations designed to create confusion and havoc, which are in turn supposed to create possibilities for the seizure of state power, have little chance of success. Indeed, if direct assaults were to undermine public confidence, create great disorder, and seriously destabilize the economy, chances are they would provoke not a revolutionary opportunity but a fascist reaction. We do not live in a feudal society, nor in a confused pre-industrial time, but in a highly developed, successfully managed, and culturally unified state. The chances for a general societal collapse are almost non-existent.

The radical socialists do, however, point to something that cannot be ignored, namely that there is no inevitability to the triumph of socialism. Without a crisis of some sort it is most unlikely that any mass demand for structural change will arise. Clearly, the strategy of moderate socialists, which posits the gradual emergence of popular demand for a non-materialistic culture, will not provide that shock. This country is too enamored with capitalist materialism simply to surrender it, or risk its demise because some affluent members of the disenchanted upper-middle class, along with radical intellectuals and resident moralists, have suggested it. As George Lichtheim has wryly noted, "This kind of talk is common among people who do not have to work for a living." Materialist desires are likely to be with us for a long while, and only events that provoke mistrust in the ability of capitalism to provide an abundance of goods and services could unsettle the status quo. Traditionally, depressions, recessions, and severe mass hardship have unhinged confidence in capitalism. The modern corporate state, however, has saved capitalism by reducing economic instabilities and hardships to an acceptable level. Overseas expansion and the creation of a large defense industry have been key factors in stabilizing consumer demand and employment. But this, in turn, has meant that American capitalism is seriously exposed. The public demands steady employment and an increasing array of goods and services with minimal dislocation. In order to secure this, American business has forged a world-wide commercial empire which the American government is sworn to protect. Were the growth of this empire to be stunted in any significant way, the repercussions at home would be very serious. "We have to face up to the realities of the competitive world market. If we want to keep open markets and create jobs and growth, the government has to foster . . . industries . . . that hold . . . promise . . . in international competition," [21] notes Mr. Peter Peterson, formerly of the President's Council on International Economic Policy. Without a certain rate of growth there would be severe unemployment and mass discontent. At present there is a high rate of growth, but prosperity is sustained by the systematic exploitation of the rest of the world. We are, it is worth repeating again and again, only six percent of the world's people, yet we control close to sixty percent of the world's goods and services. This is but another way of saying that the American commercial empire, so dependent upon exploiting the rest of the world, is at the same time quite vulnerable.

Foreign competition (particularly from Japan and Western Europe) severely limits our growth. American businesses must continue to compete favorably on the world market. To fall behind either in terms of an unfavorable balance of trade* or in terms of a smaller proportional share of the overall world market would risk the prospect of a reduced standard of living at home and potential domestic discord. As *The Wall Street Journal* noted in an interview with then Treasury Secretary John Connally, there persists

> ... the fear that the U.S. has lost its competitive edge to nations such as Japan and Germany. Unless the U.S. recoups rapidly, the consequences will be inability to meet military and diplomatic obligations abroad and a deteriorating standard of living at home that could lead to outright "revolution" in this country, Mr. Connally says.[22]

The present American trade deficit (primarily in low-technology manufactured items) bodes ill for the future, because even in areas where we have a trading surplus (high-technology items) overseas competition is growing stronger. For example, trade in automotive products showed a $2 billion deficit in 1970. In addition, there is the possibility that national revolutions will succeed and severely restrict American economic opportunities. Each year, for example, the United States consumes $100 million worth of twenty-six types of raw materials of which she has an inadequate domestic supply. The oil situation is particularly crucial. By 1985 the United States will be dependent upon foreign oil resources to the tune of fifteen million barrels a day (currently it is four million) and will have a balance of payments deficit of $30-35 billion per year in oil alone (the total now is about $3 billion).[23] To lose access to these resources or to be forced to buy them on other countries' terms would cause serious dislocations.† Similarly, to lose markets or to face reduced profits would further contribute to instability. It is not the complete loss of markets that is at issue here. No such possibility exists. What is at stake is significantly reduced opportunities for expansion. This would automatically have serious repercussions in domestic prices, unemployment, and economic stability. In that event the American domestic scene would be seriously confused. Indeed, this prospect accounts, in some measure, for the recently successful American effort to force other nations to adjust their currencies in our favor and for the new attempts on the part of the Nixon administration to give the multinational corporations more politi-

---

*It should be noted that with an extensive multinational corporate set-up it would be possible for the nation to run periodic trade deficits, provided they were offset by increased capital income derived from the financial success of the corporations, i.e. dividends.

†Because the industrialized capitalist West provides the largest and most consistent market for raw materials, it is unlikely that this flow will be interrupted at any time soon or with any great effect. Underdeveloped countries have little choice at this time but to sell to the West.

cal protection and greater financial freedom in their efforts to expand abroad. On the success of these corporations depends the future of the American economy and the American society.

But even if one granted the possibility of future economic crises, such a state of confusion and doubt would not necessarily lead to socialism; the confusion and doubt would merely make socialism in America a possibility. There must exist a socialist reality that transcends crude materialism and holds out hope for a new society which could be built upon the old. Material factors cannot be ignored; but the outline of a truly human society must be clear even before the advent of socialism. Basically this means that some anticipatory sign of a new future must occur.

Hope for radical change must find expression in activities and struggles embodying the crux of the socialist vision: that human beings can collectively take charge of their lives. Since, however, no present possibility exists for the imminent democratization of all the aspects of human life, the starting point for "the long march through the existing institutions" (Rudi Dutschke) is at the local level where organizing sets the stage for the future.

The guiding principle involved in any strategy for the transition to socialism is that people should assume, however gradually, the prerogatives and options heretofore exercised solely on the basis of capital or property ownership. Thus the demand for higher wages in a plant is not, in principle, as significant as striving for the right to control production or to have extended privileges in hiring and firing. In a neighborhood, the right of people to join with an incoming business in planning parking and traffic control is not as important as securing the right to decide if that business should be in the area at all. The transition to socialism, therefore, is marked by that kind of radical reform which does not aim for material concessions but for the exercise of power on the basis of popular need and will.

Radical democratization of control is not the same thing as the formal exercise of power through consumer choices or representational democracy through the institutions of the state. In the first instance, the so-called freedom of the market means popular will is mediated through capital structures, and inevitably transformed into the needs of capital. In the second instance, while state control is often a progressive and necessary step, it differs from popular control because public machinery depends so heavily on private interests for economic progress. The state's legislative, regulatory, or confiscatory functions are limited precisely to the degree that they do not threaten the health of the economic market.* This brings us back to the

---

*When the state does interfere it is to bail some enterprise out. An example of this is its increasing tendency to take over companies, such as railroads, which are unable to succeed on the private market.

difference between Marx and Hegel: politics at the level of society, not politics at the level of the state, determines human dignity.

In classical socialism the industrial working class provided the motor power for the expected transformation of human society. Hence, organizing workers on the job was central to all socialist strategy. However, the general integration of the industrial working class into the need-reward system of modern capitalism, coupled with the decline of militant trade unionism, would seem to suggest that nothing of great import can be expected from the industrial workers, and that only those not completely integrated into the system—the young, the poor, minorities—offer any hope for radical change. Further, since cultural myths now tend to assign meaning and dignity to the period of time off the job, work exists without any ennobling ideology; it is regarded as a painful necessity providing the material wherewithal to enjoy the "good life."* Thus the older radical ideology, which focused on work as the crucial arena within which human dignity was determined, and consequently made democratic control of the means of production a necessity, appears either quaint or exotic nowadays.

In addition, there is the elaboration of the American work force. The relative numbers and overall influence of the industrial workers have declined steadily over the last two decades† as a white-collar work force of engineers, technicians, clerks, teachers, salespeople, and service workers have come to exercise greater power in society.‡ Their growing influence challenges the traditional socialist view of a two-class society locked in a life-and-death struggle.** Further, since this new class of workers no longer suffers under the same constraints as the industrial worker, nor shares the same expectations, radical organizing is rendered even more difficult.

This pessimistic view is open to criticism, however. First, whatever the decline in relative numbers and prestige, the industrial workers still remain the most militant of all workers. Second, it is by no means inevitable that these workers should remain forever tied to the prevailing capitalist system.

*" 'The time you have to spend at work is all out of proportion with the time you have left for your family and yourself,' says Frank Runnels, president of local 22 . . . 'In the old days the concept was that a man's whole life was built around his job. Now he's not willing to sell himself into industrial prostitution.' "[24]

†This decline was evidenced in the inability of organized labor to play a key role in the Democratic Presidential nomination in 1972.

‡Housewives, it should be added, as a part of the labor force remain a constant and exploited labor group.

**In addition, some European leftists define class simply in terms of those who identify with or oppose the struggle for socialism, further transforming traditional notions of class.

Stanley Aronowitz has argued compellingly that a new generation of workers (influenced by, among other things, the youth movement of the 1960's) is arising, and promises to be far more militant than those of the last twenty-five years. Aronowitz points out that the new workers do not suffer from the frightening remembrance of the Depression, are no longer affected by the divisiveness of ethnicity, and do not relate to the capitalist system simply in terms of material needs.[25] As a result the boredom and routinization of industrial work is met with increased on-the-job rebellion, absenteeism, wild-cat strikes, and mounting industrial sabotage. Moreover, the United Auto Workers' strikes in Norwood and Lordstown, Ohio, fought over issues of plant discipline, workers' grievances, and the firing of fellow workers, clearly demonstrated that young workers have needs far beyond those of wages or pensions and that they will fight to secure them.* Whether such industrial discontent, rooted as it is in the alienation and anomie associated with industrial life, can be converted into a sustained movement for workers' control is not clear.† However, the potential is there, and organizing with traditional trade unions or among informal networks in the shop or factory could very well produce a breakthrough in American industry.

As for the prevalent notion that prestige associated with non-manual work, lesser disciplinary control, higher pay, and greater mobility on the job precludes labor militancy among white-collar workers, it should be added that for great numbers of these people such freedom and prestige is mainly short-lived or illusory. They can still be laid off, as the engineers learned in 1970-71. Their pay is not always so high as is often supposed. Further, white-collar work is becoming as routinized as factory work, as the large holders of capital attempt to increase productivity in the 1970's. This new stratum of the working class, therefore, is equally amenable to organizing around issues that are not merely economic. In large measure, though, success will depend on their ability to overcome captivity to certain myths. For instance, teachers and professors will have to drop the myth of professionalism and come to see that they are merely part of a capitalist labor force, and that their present economic predicament as well as their decreasing

*Behind Richard Nixon's post-election effort to reinstate the "work ethic" in American life lies the remembrance of the decline of industrial productivity in the 1960's. Absenteeism, sabotage, theft, and turnover (at Chrysler, for example, the rate was forty-seven percent in 1969) rose alarmingly in the 1960's, undercutting the competitive advantage of the industrial economy. In 1971 an enormous effort (nicely aided by fear of unemployment) to increase productivity was launched. Thus, spurred by the fear of joblessness and cornered by the wage-price freeze which worked unfairly against the workers, worker productivity and docility have increased. However, it does not seem likely that the lid can be kept on this situation very long.

†Aronowitz argues that increased mobility coupled with boredom may mean workers will turn into peripatetics instead of radicals.[26]

autonomy is due, not to the "decline of professional standards," but to the fact that as workers in a capitalist economy they will be ordered about and subject to labor discipline like any other worker. White-collar technicians and salespeople will have to understand the distinction between administrative or operational authority, and decisional authority, for while they enjoy the former they are without the latter. Finally, white-collar workers will have to understand that the occupational euphemisms of "lower management," "public employee," "educator" and the like, serve only to mask their basic status as workers. Only the cultural denigration of workers, i.e. blue-collar workers, prevents unity among all workers; white-collar workers are continually told that their non-manual status bears a great measure of prestige. But such invidious distinctions hide the basic fact that, despite the existence of different strata of workers and different needs, workers are united in their exclusion from democratic control over their work life.

The working class, therefore, remains crucial to any hope for radical change. As old needs (wages and benefits) are translated into new wants (autonomy and control), creative possibilities are bound to emerge. Thus in the office, shop, or factory, the drive for workers' control over capital's prerogatives is the first step toward socialism.

But organizing to advance workers' options on the job is by no means the only way of furthering the cause of socialism. Community organizing also presents radicals with unique opportunities.

The traditional socialist objection to organizing around community, i.e. geographic or non-work issues, is that these matters are only tangential to the central issues of capitalist power and are therefore an inadequate substitute for the struggle over ownership of the means of production. In a sense this criticism is still valid; but, given the reality of contemporary life, community issues may reveal the contradictions and injustices of capitalist society in a clearer fashion than those matters associated with the job.

After all, as I have tried to suggest, popular ideology still holds work to be the realm of necessity, devoid of meaning and dignity. The private realm, that is, the time off the job, is seen as the realm of freedom. But if this is so, then it is not clear to vast numbers of Americans why deteriorating health care, collapsing schools, poor traffic, high rents and interest, and arbitrary neighborhood realignments should characterize the very realm of liberation where the great American dream is supposedly coming true. Consequently, community organizing can indicate how private production and social need clash in a capitalist economy, and that the difficulties experienced in the private realm are not mere accidents but a result of the inadequacies of capitalist society. Tenants do not have extended rights to balance the privileges of landlords; rising hospital and doctors' fees do not consider working class wages; school needs suffer because of limited public financing; neighborhood sanctity or safety is not recognized by the corporations who wish to expand. Any one of these (or similar) community issues could develop into a crucial struggle for democratic control; any one could be the occasion to seize the prerogatives of capital.*

Community organizing is but another way to organize the working class. It concentrates on issues facing workers off the job, and hopes that successful, collective effort there will provide the breakthrough that could spur comparable activity on the job. For contrary to popular mythology, which tends to view events as isolated or unrelated to other events, there is an underlying unity in the way American society works. The oppression apparent in one event or in one realm is very much related to others. If, in the private sphere, people break out of individual isolation and privatism, that is, if they come to understand that the promises of the "good life" and the exercise of selfish freedoms are not advances in democratic practice, but instead diversions and illusions designed to ensure a de-politicized and mesmerized public, then indeed there will be new hope.

Organizing, whether on the job or in the community, must begin with the principle that people must recover control of their destiny. Often this is exhibited in simple fashion with a struggle for minimal rights in a school, a new contract in the plant, an electoral victory in a university town. However, insofar as each of these victories manifests democratic control and equal sharing, they are, in principle, acting contrary to the prevailing system, and pointing toward socialism at a fundamental level. Successful organizing during a time of economic stability, or during a time of crisis, must move beyond the level of vague utopian hopes of communal love and primitive democracy: true socialism means a planned economy and discipline, during the time of the end of a class society. Yet, preliminary and realizable strategies that embody the future of socialism are necessary in the present. These strategies must deal with the too often buried hopes of women and men for the end to oppression and the reassertion of collective power to determine lives. Herbert Marcuse writes:

Socialist solidarity is autonomy: self-determination begins at home—that is with every I, and the We whom the I chooses. And this end must indeed appear in the means to attain it, that is to say, in the strategy of those who, within the existing society, work for the new one. If the socialist relationships of production are to be a new way of life, a new Form of life, then their existential quality must show forth, anticipated and demonstrated, in the fight for their realization.

*Provided, of course, people do not rely too heavily on the law—which serves primarily the needs of property and capital—or expect too much from public officials—whose advocacy is tempered by political considerations. People must be prepared, from time to time, to pursue extra-legal means, as did the great union organizers in the 1930's.

Exploitation in all its forms must have disappeared from this fight: from the work relationships among the fighters as well as from their individual relationships. Understanding, tenderness towards each other, the instinctual consciousness of that which is evil, false, the heritage of oppression, would then testify to the authenticity of the rebellion. In short, the economic, political and cultural features of a classless society must have become the basic needs of those who fight for it. This ingression of the future into the present, this depth dimension of the rebellion accounts, in the last analysis, for the incompatibility with the traditional forms of the political struggle .... the joy of freedom and the need to be free must precede liberation.[27]

The road to socialism is clearly a rocky one. At present, capitalism provides a degree of affluence that is apparently satisfactory to the bulk of the populace. Meanwhile, bourgeois cultural hegemony successfully precludes the appearance of political and social alternatives at the cultural level. In addition, the American left remains plagued with sectarianism and a general lack of direction. Unable to fashion stable institutions, seemingly cut off from any sensible left tradition, and without any national cohesion, American socialism does not face a rosy future. But these factors are not so much the result of past failures as they are part of the predictable troubles associated with new beginnings. It is not that the left tried and failed in the 1960's, it is simply experiencing the troubles that accompany any new promise. Hope resides in the activities and dedication of many militants throughout America. It will take many generations for their work to come to fruition; the long march through the existing institutions is just that: long and arduous; but as the old French Huguenot motto put it: there is no need of success in order to persevere.

If the earthly expression of the kingdom of God is not to be a mockery, then all effort must be made to present a humane alternative to the oppression of capitalism. This cannot be done out of ideological rigor, or by the simple exercise of the will; rather it arises from the sure confidence that the destiny of all people is to live in a sharing community, and that solidarity and consideration will one day rule the hearts of those who openly, or by the greater mystery of God's providence, seek the will of God.

BIBLIOGRAPHY

CHRISTIANITY

Biblical Thought

Bornkamm, Günther. *Jesus of Nazareth*. London, 1963.
_____. *Paul*. New York, 1971.
Jeremias, Joachim. *Rediscovering the Parables*. New York, 1966.
Käsemann, Ernst. *Jesus Means Freedom*. London, 1969.
_____. *New Testament Questions Today*. London, 1969.
_____. *Perspectives on Paul*. London, 1971.
Koch, Klaus. *The Growth of the Biblical Tradition*. New York, 1969.
Rad, Gerhard von. *Old Testament Theology*. 2 vols., New York, 1962-65.
Rendtorff, Rolf. *God's History*. Philadelphia, 1969.
Ringgren, Helmer. *Israelite Religion*. Philadelphia, 1966.
Wilckens, Ulrich. *God's Revelation*. Philadelphia, 1967.

Theology

Barth, Karl. *Church Dogmatics: A Selection*. New York, 1962.
_____. *Community, State and Church*. Gloucester, 1968.
_____. *Dogmatics in Outline*. New York, 1959.
Berdyaev, Nicolas. *The Destiny of Man*. New York, 1960.
_____. *Slavery and Freedom*. New York, 1944.
Ellul, Jacques. *The Meaning of the City*. Grand Rapids, 1970.
_____. *The Politics of God and the Politics of Man*. Grand Rapids, 1972.
_____. *Violence: Reflections from a Christian Perspective,* New York, 1969.
Gollwitzer, Helmut. *The Demands of Freedom*. New York, 1965.
_____. *The Rich Christians and Poor Lazarus*. New York, 1970.
Lampert, E. *The Apocalypse of History*. London, 1948.
Moltmann, Jürgen. *Hope and Planning*. London, 1971.
_____. *Religion, Revolution, and the Future*. New York, 1969.
_____. *Theology of Hope*. London, 1965.
Niebuhr, Reinhold. *The Children of Light and the Children of Darkness*. New York, 1944.
_____. *Love and Justice. Selections from the Shorter Writings of Reinhold Niebuhr,* ed. D. B. Robertson. Philadelphia, 1957.
_____. *Moral Man and Immoral Society*. New York, 1932.
_____. *The Nature and Destiny of Man*. New York, 1949.
_____. *The Self and the Dramas of History*. New York, 1955.
Pannenberg. Wolfhart. *Jesus: God and Man*. Philadelphia, 1968.

_____. *Theology and the Kingdom of God.* Philadelphia, 1969.

_____. *What is Man?* Philadelphia, 1970.

_____, ed. *Revelation as History.* New York, 1969.

Robinson, James M. and John B. Cobb, Jr., eds. *Theology as History.* New York, 1967.

Stringfellow, William. *Dissenter in a Great Society.* New York, 1966.

_____. *Free in Obedience.* New York, 1964.

Stringfellow, William, and Anthony Towne. *Suspect Tenderness,* New York, 1971.

Christianity and Marxism

Garaudy, Roger. *The Christian-Communist Dialogue.* Garden City, 1968.

Metz, Johannes B., Karl Rahner, and Milan Machovec. *Can a Christian be a Marxist?* Chicago, 1969.

Ogletree, Thomas. *Opening for Marxist-Christian Dialogue.* Nashville, 1969.

Oestreicher, Paul, ed. *The Christian-Marxist Dialogue.* New York, 1969.

West, Charles C. *Communism and the Theologians.* New York, 1962.

POLITICS AND SOCIETY

American History

Ambrose, Stephen E. *Rise to Globalism.* Baltimore, 1971.

Barnet, Richard J. *Intervention and Revolution; The United States in the Third World.* New York, 1968.

_____. *The Roots of War.* New York, 1972.

Bernstein, Barton J., ed. *Towards a New Past: Essays in American History.* New York, 1968.

Fischer, George, ed. *The Revival of American Socialism.* New York, 1971.

Fitzgerald, Frances. *Fire in the Lake: The Vietnamese and the Americans in Vietnam.* Boston, 1972.

Gabriel, Ralph. *The Course of American Democratic Thought.* New York, 1956.

Genovese, Eugene. *The Political Economy of Slavery.* New York, 1965.

_____. *The World the Slaveholders Made.* New York, 1969.

Klare, Michael T. *War without End: American Planning for the Next Vietnams.* New York, 1972.

Kolko, Gabriel. *The Politics of War.* New York, 1968.

_____. *Roots of American Foreign Policy.* Boston, 1969.

LaFeber, Walter. *America, Russia, and the Cold War, 1945-1966.* New York, 1967.

_____. *The New Empire.* Ithaca, 1963.

Laslett, John H. M. *Labor and the Left.* New York, 1970.

Magdoff, Harry. *The Age of Imperialism.* New York, 1969.

Meyers, Marvin. *The Jacksonian Persuasion.* Stanford, 1966.

Potter, David M. *People of Plenty.* Chicago, 1966.

Smith, Henry Nash. *Virgin Land.* New York, 1950.

Williams, William Appleman. *The Contours of American History.* Chicago, 1966.

Weinstein, James, and David W. Eakins, eds. *For a New America.* New York, 1970.

Contemporary Class Analysis

Bottomore, T. B. *Classes in Modern Society.* New York, 1966.

Garaudy, Roger. *The Turning-Point of Socialism.* London, 1970.

Gintis, Herb, "Activism and Counter-Culture," *Telos,* Summer, 1972, pp. 42-62.

Gorz, Andre. *Strategy for Labor.* Boston, 1967.

Ossowski, Stanislaw. *Class Structure in the Social Consciousness.* New York, 1963.

Development of Contemporary Society

Arendt, Hannah. *The Origins of Totalitarianism.* New York, 1951.
Gay, Peter. *The Enlightenment: An Interpretation,* Vol. I, *Rise of Modern Paganism.* New York, 1966.
Hill, Christopher. *The Century of Revolution 1603-1714.* New York, 1961.
Hobsbawm, Eric J. *The Age of Revolution 1789-1848.* London, 1962.
_____. *Laboring Men.* Garden City, 1967.
Lichtheim, George. *Europe in the Twentieth Century.* New York, 1972.
Marx, Karl, and Frederick Engels. *The German Ideology.* New York, 1969.
Moore, Barrington, Jr. *Social Origins of Dictatorship and Democracy.* Boston, 1967.

Economics

Baran, Paul, and Paul M. Sweezy. *Monopoly Capital.* New York, 1966.
Galbraith, John Kenneth. *The New Industrial State.* Boston, 1967.
Heilbroner, Robert. *Between Capitalism and Socialism.* New York, 1970.
_____. *The Limits of American Capitalism.* New York, 1966.
Lange, Oskar, and Fred M. Taylor. *On the Economic Theory of Socialism.* New York, 1965.
Mandel, Ernest. *An Introduction to Marxist Economic Theory.* New York, 1970.
_____. *Marxist Economic Theory.* 2 vols., New York, 1968.
Marx, Karl. *Das Kapital.* Abridged edition, New York, 1967.
Robinson, Joan. *An Essay on Marxian Economics.* New York, 1966.
_____. *Freedom and Necessity.* New York, 1970.
Weisskopf, Walter A. *Alienation and Economics.* New York, 1971.

International Business

Barber, Richard J. *The American Corporation.* New York, 1970.
Kindleberger, Charles P. *American Business Abroad.* New Haven, 1969.
Vernon, Raymond. *Sovereignty at Bay.* New York, 1971.
Wilkins, Mira. *The Emergence of Multinational Enterprise.* Cambridge, 1970.

Political and Social Thought

Arendt, Hannah. *The Human Condition.* Garden City, 1958.
_____. *On Violence.* New York, 1970.
Birnbaum, Norman. *The Crisis of Industrial Society.* New York, 1970.
Bloch, Ernst. *Man on His Own.* New York, 1971.
_____. *A Philosophy of the Future.* New York, 1970.
Garaudy, Roger. *Marxism in the Twentieth Century.* London, 1970.
_____. *The Whole Truth.* London, 1971.
Habermas, Jürgen. *Knowledge and Human Interests.* Boston, 1971.
_____. *Toward a Rational Society.* Boston, 1970.
Harrington, Michael. *Socialism.* New York, 1972.
_____. *Toward a Democratic Left.* Baltimore, 1969.
Lane, Robert. *Political Ideology.* New York, 1962.
Lichtheim, George. *The Concept of Ideology and Other Essays.* New York, 1967.
_____. *Imperialism.* New York, 1971.
_____. *Marxism: an Historical and Critical Study.* New York, 1961.
Lowi, Theodore J. *The End of Liberalism.* New York, 1969.
Lukacs, Gyorgy. *History and Class Consciousness.* Cambridge, 1971.
Marcuse, Herbert. *Counterrevolution and Revolt.* Boston, 1972.
_____. *An Essay on Liberation.* Boston, 1969.
_____. *One-Dimensional Man.* Boston, 1964.
Marx, Karl. *Economic and Philosophical Manuscripts of 1844,* ed. Dirk J. Struik. New York, 1964.

McClelland, David. *The Achieving Society*. Princeton, 1961.
MacPherson, C. B. *The Political Theory of Possessive Individualism: Hobbes to Locke*. Oxford, 1962.
_____. *The Real World of Democracy*. Oxford, 1966.
Wellmer, Albrecht. *Critical Theory of Society*. New York, 1971.

Youth and Counter-Culture

Cockburn, Alexander, and Robin Blackburn, eds. *Student Power*. Middlesex, 1969.
Miles, Michael. *The Radical Probe*. New York, 1971.
Nobile, Philip, ed. *The Con III Controversy: The Critics Look at the Greening of America*. New York, 1971.
Reich, Charles A. *The Greening of America*. New York, 1971.
Roszak, Theodore. *The Making of a Counter Culture*. Garden City, 1969.
_____. *Where the Wasteland Ends: Politics and Transcendence in Postindustrial Society*. Garden City, 1972.
Slater, Philip. *The Pursuit of Loneliness*. Boston, 1970.

NEWSPAPERS AND PERIODICALS

New York Review of Books
Radical America
Socialist Revolution
Telos
The Wall Street Journal

NOTES

INTRODUCTION

[1] For a complete delineation of the private and public spheres throughout history, see Hannah Arendt, *The Human Condition* (New York, 1959).

[2] "We pray also for the Caesars, for their ministers, and for all who are in high positions . . . ," noted Tertullian. Quoted in Jaroslav Pelikan, *The Emergence of the Catholic Tradition (100-600)* (Chicago, 1971), p. 129.

[3] Tertullian, quoted in Arendt, *op. cit.,* p. 65.

[4] Cf. F. C. Copleston, *Aquinas* (Baltimore, 1961), pp. 228-234. It was the medieval conception of Natural Law that provided the framework for the political dimension.

[5] Karl Marx, quoted in Albrecht Wellmer, *Critical Theory of Society* (New York, 1971), p. 79.

[6] G. W. F. Hegel, quoted in Wellmer, *op. cit.,* p. 77.

[7] *Ibid.,* p. 78.

[8] "*Communism* as the *positive* transcendence of *private property,* as *human self-estrangement,* and therefore as the real *appropriation of the human* essence by and for man; communism therefore as the complete return of man to himself as a *social* (i.e. human) being—a return become conscious, and accomplished within the entire wealth of previous development. This communism, as fully developed naturalism, equals humanism, and as fully developed humanism equals naturalism; it is the *genuine* resolution of the conflict between man and nature and between man and man—the true resolution of the strife between existence and essence, between objectification and self-confirmation, between freedom and necessity, between the individual and the species. Communism is the riddle of history solved. . . ." Karl Marx, *The Economic and Philosophic Manuscripts of 1844,* translated by Martin Milligan (New York, 1964), p. 135.

[9] Mark Hopkins, quoted in Ralph Gabriel, *The Course of American Democratic Thought* (New York, 1958), p. 157.

[10] Billy Graham, *Peace With God* (Garden City, 1955), p. 190.

[11] Gabriel, *op. cit.,* p. 225.

[12] Reinhold Niebuhr, *Love and Justice. Selections from the Shorter Writings of Reinhold Niebuhr,* ed. D. B. Robertson (Philadelphia, 1957), p. 65.

[13] For Stringfellow's key works consult *Free in Obedience* (New York, 1964), *Dissenter in a Great Society* (New York, 1966) and, with co-author Anthony Towne, *Suspect Tenderness* (New York, 1971). Two of Berrigan's most explicit statements are *Prison Journals of a Priest Revolutionary* (New York, 1970) and *The Dark Night of Resistance* (Garden City, 1971).

[14] Daniel Berrigan, *The Dark Night of Resistance* (Garden City, 1971), p. 2.

15Thomas Merton, quoted in *Delivered into Resistance* (Cantonsville Nine—Milwaukee Fourteen Defense Committee, New Haven, 1969), p. IV.

16Berrigan, *op. cit.*, p. 3.

17*Ibid.*, p. 181.

18*Ibid.*, pp. 174, 178.

19Particularly Stringfellow and Towne, *Suspect Tenderness*, pp. 59-68, 85-93.

20In Will Herberg, ed., *Community, Church and State* (Gloucester, 1968).

21Cf. *The Politics of God and the Politics of Man* (Grand Rapids, 1972), p. 14.

22Milan Machovec, Helmut Gollwitzer and Hans Joachim Giroch, "Tasks for the Dialogue," in Paul Oestreicher, ed., *The Christian Marxist Dialogue* (New York, 1969), p. 127.

23Stanislaw Ossowski, *Class Structure in the Social Consciousness* (New York, 1963), p. 189.

24Cf. Jürgen Moltmann, *Hope and Planning* (New York, 1971), pp. 155-177.

25C. B. Macpherson, *The Real World of Democracy* (Oxford, 1966), pp. 47-48.

26Helmut Gollwitzer in Paul Oestreicher, ed., *The Christian Marxist Dialogue* (New York, 1969), pp. 123f. See also Michael Walzer, *The Revolution of the Saints: A Study in the Origins of Radical Politics* (Cambridge, 1965).

27Cf. Ernst Bloch, *Man on His Own* (New York, 1971).

CHAPTER ONE

1For much of what follows I am indebted to E. Lampert, *The Apocalypse of History* (London, 1948).

2Gilbert Murray, *Greek Literature* (New York, 1927), p. 249.

3"The first city and the first state were founded by a man who slew his brother; fratricide also stains the origins of Rome—stains them so one may call it a general rule that blood must have been spilled wherever a state shall rise." Cf. Saint Augustine, *City of God*, ed. Vernon J. Bourke (Garden City, 1958), p. 328 (xv. 5).

4Rubem Alves, *Theology of Human Hope* (Washington, 1970), p. 108.

5"Apocalyptic remains . . . the intellectual context . . . of the proleptic occurrence of God's rule through Jesus." Wolfhart Pannenberg, *Jesus: God and Man* (Philadelphia, 1968), p. 61.

6*Ibid.*, pp. 192-193.

7Lampert, *op. cit.*, p. 56.

8Lampert, *op. cit.*, p. 59.

9*Ibid.*, p. 51.

10Ernst Käsemann, *New Testament Questions of Today* (London, 1969), p. 181.

11Rudolph Bultmann, *Theology of the New Testament*, 2 vols. (New York, 1951, 1955), Vol. II, pp. 229-230.

12Quoted in Anne Fremantle, ed., *A Treasury of Early Christianity* (New York, 1953), p. 241.

13Quoted in Robert M. Grant, *Augustus to Constantine* (London, 1971), p. 108.

14Günther Bornkamm, *Paul* (New York, 1971), pp. 40-41.

CHAPTER TWO

1Robert Heilbroner, *Between Capitalism and Socialism* (New York, 1971), p. 94.

2W. A. Lewis, *The Principles of Economic Planning* (London, 1949), p. 12.

3Alexis de Tocqueville, quoted in Michael McGiffert, ed., *The Character of Americans* (Homewood, Ill., 1964), p. 41.

4Alexis de Tocqueville, *Democracy in America*, ed. J. P. Mayer and Max Lerner (New York, 1966), p. 47.

5James Bryce, quoted in Robert Lane, *Political Ideology* (New York, 1962), p. 58.

6David M. Potter, "Individual and Conformity," in Michael McGiffert, ed., *The Character of Americans,* p. 241.

7Perry Miller, *The New England Mind: The Seventeenth Century* (Boston, 1965), p. 429.

8*Federalist Papers* #10.

9Arthur Twining Hadley, "The Constitutional Position of Property in America," in Alpheus T. Mason, ed., *Free Governments in the Making* (New York, 1965), p. 711.

10For a brilliant anthropological discussion of the relation of land, labor, and expropriation see Ernest Mandel, *Marxist Economic Theory* (New York, 1970), Vol. I, pp. 23-68.

11Jackson Main, *Social Structure of Revolutionary America* (Princeton, 1965).

12Henry Nash Smith, *Virgin Land* (New York, 1950), p. 220.

13Harold U. Faulkner, *Politics, Reform and Expansion: 1890-1900* (New York, 1959), p. 91.

14Karl Marx, quoted in Michael Harrington, *Why We Need Socialism in America* (New York, 1970), p. 35.

15Heilbroner, *op. cit.,* p. 82.

16*Milwaukee Sentinel,* August 1, 1971.

17*Ibid.*

18*Ibid.*

19*Ibid.;* William O. Douglas, *Points of Rebellion* (1970), p. 70.

20*Milwaukee Sentinel,* August 1, 1971.

21*Ibid.*

22Ralph Nader, "How to Think About the American Economy," *New York Review of Books,* September 2, 1971, p. 16.

23*Time,* June 29, 1970, p. 72.

24Interview with Dr. Gar Alperowitz, *American Report,* May 7, 1971, p. 11.

25Hans Morgenthau, "Reflections on the End of the Republic," *New York Review of Books,* September 24, 1970, p. 40.

26*American Report,* May 7, 1971, p. 11.

27Mandel, *op. cit.,* Vol. II, p. 533.

28Harrington, *op. cit.,* p. 4; *Milwaukee Sentinel,* February 17, 1971.

29Harrington, *op. cit.,* p. 6.

30*Ibid.*

31Douglas, *op. cit.,* p. 72.

32Michael G. Michaelson, "The Coming Medical War," *New York Review of Books,* July 1, 1971, pp. 32-38; *Milwaukee Journal,* August 4, 1971.

33Quoted in Harrington, *op. cit.,* p. 9.

34Mandel, *op. cit.,* p. 171.

35Quoted in Mandel, *op. cit.,* Vol. II, p. 399.

36See Noam Chomsky, *American Power and the New Mandarins* (New York, 1969), pp. 159-220.

37"Connally Suggests New Monetary Rules Discipline Nations with Chronic Surpluses," *Wall Street Journal,* March 20, 1972.

38Harry Magdoff, *The Age of Imperialism: The Economics of U. S. Foreign Policy* (New York, 1969), p. 178.

39*Los Angeles Times,* June 21, 1970.

40George Ball, quoted in *Tempo,* October 1, 1969.

41Courtney C. Brown, "A New World Symphony," *Saturday Review,* November 22, 1969, p. 56.

42Magdoff, *op. cit.,* p. 20.

43*Los Angeles Times,* August 26, 1969.

44Joan Robinson, *Freedom and Necessity* (New York, 1970), pp. 108-109.

45Philip H. Trezise, quoted in "The Multinational Corporations," *American Report,* November 19, 1971, p. 8.

[46]*Ibid.*

[47]Joan Robinson, *op. cit.*, p. 109.

[48]Cf. Michael Klare, *War Without End* (New York, 1972).

[49]George Lichtheim, *Imperialism* (New York, 1971), p. 12.

CHAPTER THREE

[1]Francis Grund, quoted in Marvin Meyers, *The Jacksonian Persuasion* (Stanford, 1966), p. 123.

[2]Quoted in William A. Williams, *The Contours of American History* (Chicago, 1966), p. 240.

[3]Cf. E. P. Thompson's graphic and incomparable, *The Making of the English Working Class* (New York, 1963).

[4]C. B. Macpherson, *The Political Theory of Possessive Individualism* (Oxford, 1972), p. 3.

[5]Cf. Christopher Hill, *The Century of Revolution, 1603-1714* (New York, 1961). Also, Louis Hacker's somewhat extreme judgment is still instructive: "The struggle [The American Revolution] was not over high-sounding political and constitutional concepts: over the power of taxation or even, in the final analysis, over natural rights. It was over colonial manufacturing, wild lands and furs, sugar, wine, tea, and currency. . . ." "Economic and Social Origins of the American Revolution," in John Wahlke, ed., *The Causes of the American Revolution* (Boston, 1966), p. 11. Like other vulgar economic determinists Hacker fails to recognize the way in which ideology and culture are inextricably entwined with economic factors.

[6]Williams, *op. cit.*, p. 246.

[7]Joseph A. Schumpeter, quoted in George Halm, *Economic Systems* (New York, 1955), p. 54.

[8]Alfred D. Marshall, Jr., "The Beginnings of 'Big Business' in American Industry," *Business History Review,* 33 (Spring, 1959), pp. 1-31.

[9]The Preliminary Report of the Industrial Commission of 1902, The Pule Committee findings of 1913, and Richard Barber's *The American Corporation* (New York, 1970) combine to show very well the consistent pattern of corporate growth and monopolistic control which has contributed to the destruction of the traditional values of free enterprise and competition.

[10]Ernest Mandel, *Marxist Economic Theory* (New York, 1970), Vol. I, p. 164.

[11]Karl Marx, *Das Kapital* (Chicago, 1967), Gateway abridged edition, p. 309.

[12]Marx, quoted in André Gorz, *Strategy For Labor* (Boston, 1967), pp. 77-78.

[13]David Potter, *People of Plenty* (Chicago, 1954), p. 173. Again it is to be noted that consumption elaborates but does not replace production. The gist of Potter's quote is accurate but not its precise formulation. The American ruling class does not live off consumption, but from production.

[14]*Ibid.*, pp. 173-174.

[15]Herbert Marcuse, *Essay on Liberation* (Boston, 1969), p. 11.

[16]Potter, *op. cit.*, p. 188.

[17]*The New Industrial State* (New York, 1967), p. 316. And again, "It is the genius of the industrial system that it makes the goals that reflect its needs—efficient production of goods, a steady expansion in their output, a steady expansion in their consumption, a powerful preference for goods over leisure, an unqualified commitment to technological change . . . an adequate supply of trained and educated manpower—coordinate with social virtue and enlightenment. These goals are not thought to be derived from our environment. They are assumed to be original with human personality." P. 350.

[18]*Ibid.*, pp. 103-105. Galbraith also recounts the story of John D. Rockefeller's reaction to a recalcitrant company committee in 1882: "There is some clashing of opinion and

a great deal of individuality in the committee . . . that may be detrimental to correct conclusions. . . ." P. 100.

19 Jürgen Habermas, *Toward a Rational Society* (Boston, 1970), p. 105.

20 Herbert Marcuse, quoted in Alexander Cockburn and Robin Blackburn, eds., *Student Power* (Middlesex, 1969), p. 181.

CHAPTER FOUR

1 As I use the phrase, "confidence in the world" implies trust in the created order and in the course of human history. Further it implies the existence of comprehensive meaning in the totality of human affairs—political, social, and cultural.

2 Cf. Peter Gay, *The Enlightenment: An Interpretation* (New York, 1966).

3 Karl Marx, quoted in Robert Freedman, ed., *Marxist Social Thought* (New York, 1968), p. 178.

4 Karl Marx, *The Economic & Philosophic Manuscripts of 1844,* ed. Dirk J. Struik (New York, 1964), p. 167.

5 Lord Macaulay, quoted in George Steiner, *In Bluebeard's Castle* (New York, 1971), p. 8.

6 Robert Heilbroner, *Between Capitalism and Socialism* (New York, 1970), p. 122.

7 Martin Heidegger, quoted in Jürgen Moltmann, *Hope and Planning* (New York, 1971), p. 54.

8 Tito Perlini, quoted in Steiner, *op. cit.,* p. 134.

9 Michael Polanyi's *Personal Knowledge* (New York, 1964) and *The Tacit Dimension* (New York, 1966) convincingly demonstrate the presence and role of implicit factors in all knowledge.

10 Margaret Mead, quoted in Stanley Diamond, "Tape's Last Krapp," *New York Review of Books,* Dec. 2, 1971, p. 31.

11 Jürgen Habermas, *Toward a Rational Society* (Boston, 1970), p. 56.

12 Cf. Richard Kostelanatz, ed., *Beyond Left and Right* (New York, 1967).

13 Cited in Hannah Arendt, *On Violence* (New York, 1970), p. 29.

14 Kostelanatz, *op. cit.,* p. 321.

15 Arendt, *op. cit.,* pp. 6-8.

16 Hannah Arendt, *The Human Condition* (New York, 1959), pp. 292-293.

17 Ruel W. Tyson, Jr., "Confusions of Culture," in Harold L. Hodgkinson and Myron Bloy, eds., *Identity Crisis in Higher Education* (San Francisco, 1971), p. 45.

18 George Steiner, *Extraterritorial* (New York, 1971), p. 96.

19 Habermas, *op. cit.,* p. 58.

20 Ernst Käsemann, *Perspectives on Paul* (London, 1971), p. 9.

21 Ernst Bloch, *Man on His Own* (New York, 1971), pp. 235-236.

CHAPTER FIVE

1 Cf. Ulrich Wilckens, *God's Revelation* (Philadelphia, 1967), pp. 24-52.

2 Oscar Cullmann, *Jesus and the Revolutionaries* (New York, 1970).

3 Ernst Käsemann, *Perspectives on Paul* (London, 1971), pp. 1-78.

4 *Ibid.*

5 Christopher Hill, *Society and Puritanism in Revolutionary England* (New York, 1964), pp. 124-144, 253-297.

6 Edmund Burke, quoted in E. H. Carr, *What is History?* (New York, 1963), p. 73.

7 Michael Harrington, *Towards a Democratic Left* (London, 1968), p. 58.

8 *Ibid.*

9 Cf. Howard Zinn, *The Politics of History* (Boston, 1970), pp. 57-70.

10 Jürgen Habermas, *Toward a Rational Society* (Boston, 1970), pp. 109-110.

11Studs Terkel, *Hard Times* (New York, 1970), p. 19.
12Nicolas Berdyaev, *Slavery and Freedom* (New York, 1944), p. 212.

CHAPTER SIX

1Cf. Daniel Bell, *The End of Ideology* (New York, 1960), and Seymour Martin Lipset, *Political Man* (New York, 1960). Both depict America as a land of stability.
2Cf. Michael W. Miles, *The Radical Probe* (New York, 1971), pp. 77-86.
3Jürgen Habermas, *Toward a Rational Society* (Boston, 1970), pp. 120-122. Habermas correctly notes that the young successfully moved beyond the need-reward system of advanced capitalism. As a result there was no way that the usual enticements of society could be used on them. Material advance was no longer of interest. Instead they turned to questions involving the quality of life.
4Cf. Tom Hayden, "The Politics of 'The Movement'," in Irving Howe, ed., *The Radical Papers* (New York, 1966).
5What follows draws heavily on the brilliant insights offered by Hannah Arendt in *On Violence* (New York, 1970).
6Harvey Swados, "The UAW—Over the Top or Over the Hill?" in *The Radical Papers*, p. 239.
7Mary McCarthy, "The American Revolution of Jean-Francois Revel," *New York Review of Books*, September 2, 1971, p. 5.
8Jerry Rubin, *Do It!* (New York, 1970), p. 116.
9Miles, *op. cit.*, p. 264.
10Cf. Robert Jay Lifton, *Boundaries* (New York, 1970).
11Charles Reich, *The Greening of America* (New York, 1970).
12*Ibid.*, p. 241.
13Peter Berger, *The Sacred Canopy* (New York, 1969), pp. 8-9.
14Donald Michael, *The Next Generation* (New York, 1963), p. 39.
15Michael Novak, "No New Spring in America," in Philip Nobile, ed., *The Con III Controversy* (New York, 1971), p. 123.
16Reinhold Niebuhr's *The Self and the Dramas of History* (New York, 1955) remains the best single volume on the Christian understanding of the role of the self in the historical process.

CHAPTER SEVEN

1C. D. Darlington's *The Evolution of Man and Society* (New York, 1970) carries us one step further. He grounds the predominance of the West in genetics.
2Hannah Arendt, *Imperialism* (New York, 1968), p. 6.
3Mira Wilkins, *The Emergence of Multinational Enterprise* (Cambridge, 1970), p. 70.
4*Ibid.*, p. 72.
5Quoted in *ibid.*, p. 166.
6Cf. William A. Williams, *The Contours of American History* (New York, 1966), pp. 371-372.
7Cf. Walter LaFeber, *America, Russia, and the Cold War, 1945-1966* (New York, 1967), pp. 47-49.
8Quoted in Stephen E. Ambrose, *Rise to Globalism* (Baltimore, 1971), p. 116.
9*Ibid.*, pp. 148, 151.
10Joseph Jones, quoted in J. William Fulbright, "In Thrall to Fear," *The New Yorker*, January 8, 1972, p. 42.
11*Milwaukee Journal*, February 13, 1972.
12Cf. Ambrose, *op. cit.*, pp. 240-271.
13*Public Papers of the Presidents. . . , Eisenhower, 1954* (Washington, 1960), pp. 382-383.

14Cf. Leslie H. Gelb, "On Schlesinger and Ellsberg: A Reply," *New York Review of Books,* December 2, 1971, pp. 31-34.

15For specifics consult any issue of *American Report* for 1971 and 1972.

16Tom Wicker, *American Report,* March 5, 1971.

17Quoted in Michael Klare, *War Without End* (New York, 1972), p. 208.

18Quoted in Noam Chomsky, *Problems of Knowledge and Freedom* (New York, 1971), p. 97.

19Cf. Robert Tucker, *The Radical Left and American Foreign Policy* (Baltimore, 1971). Arthur Schlesinger notes "the fallacy that ideology is more important in international affairs than national interest" (editorial in *The Wall Street Journal,* November 30, 1972). The irony here, of course, is that Schlesinger was at first a strong supporter of American intervention in Vietnam.

20Cf. Richard Barnet, "Nixon's Plan to Save the World," *New York Review of Books,* November 16, 1972, pp. 14-18.

21Herbert Marcuse, *Reason and Revolution* (New York, 1940), p. 26.

22George Steiner, *In Bluebeard's Castle* (New York, 1971), p. 65.

CHAPTER EIGHT

1Charles Reich, *The Greening of America* (New York, 1970), pp. 27-30.

2George Lichtheim, "What Socialism Is and Is Not," *New York Review of Books,* April 9, 1970, p. 43.

3G. D. H. Cole, quoted in R. H. S. Crossman, ed., *New Fabian Essays* (London, 1952), p. 61.

4*Ibid.*

5Cf. Gabriel Kolko's brilliant essay, "The Decline of American Radicalism in the Twentieth Century," in James Weinstein and David W. Eakins, eds., *For a New America* (New York, 1970), pp. 202-203.

6H. D. Dickinson, quoted in Lichtheim, *op. cit.,* p. 42.

7Karl Marx, quoted in Michael Harrington, *Why We Need Socialism in America* (New York, 1970), p. 27.

8Henry Pachter, "Three Economic Models," in Irving Howe, ed., *The Radical Papers* (New York, 1966), p. 54.

9Wassily Leontief, "The Trouble with Cuban Socialism," *New York Review of Books,* January 7, 1971, pp. 19-23. However, in China (and to some degree in the Democratic Republic of Vietnam) moral incentives have replaced material incentives to a large extent in economic activity.

10George Lichtheim, "The Future of Socialism," in Irving Howe, ed., *The Radical Papers* (New York, 1966), p. 65.

11Herbert Marcuse, *Essay on Liberation* (Boston, 1969), p. 87.

12Robert Heilbroner, *Between Capitalism and Socialism* (New York, 1970), p. 81.

13Adam Smith, quoted in Harold Faulkner, *American Economic History* (New York, 1949), p. 431.

14Nicolas Berdyaev, *Slavery and Freedom* (New York, 1944), p. 215.

15*Ibid.,* p. 208.

16*Ibid.,* p. 209.

17Harrington, *op. cit.,* p. 42.

18Cf. André Gorz, *Strategy For Labor* (Boston, 1967).

19Cf. Svetozar Stojanovic, "Marxism and Socialism Now," *New York Review of Books,* July 1, 1971, p. 16.

20Cf. Emma Rothschild, "GM in Trouble," *New York Review of Books,* March 23, 1972, pp. 18-25.

21*The Wall Street Journal,* January 13, 1972.

22*The Wall Street Journal,* April 24, 1972.

23*The Wall Street Journal,* June 6, 1972 and July 14, 1972.

[24]Quoted in *The Wall Street Journal,* December 8, 1972.

[25]Stanley Aronowitz, "The Working Class: a Break with the Past," *Liberation,* August, 1972, pp. 20-31. Aronowitz makes the interesting observation that Post-World War Two trade union activity has been directly related to the fears and hopes of the generation of workers traumatized by the Depression. In the 1940's and 1950's the unions concentrated on wages, job security, and benefits; in the 1960's they focused on pensions and retirement schemes.

[26]*Ibid.*

[27]Marcuse, *op. cit.,* pp. 88-89.

INDEX